Union Public Library
1980 Morris Avenue
Union, N.J. 07083

P9-CFW-005

the **Tra Vigne Cookbook**

the Tra Vigne Cookbook
Seasons *in the*
California Wine Country

Union Public Library
1980 Morris Avenue
Union, N.J. 07083

Michael Chiarello
with Penelope Wisner
Photographs by Karl Petzke

CHRONICLE BOOKS
SAN FRANCISCO

First Chronicle Books LLC paperback
edition, published in 2008

Text copyright © 1999 by Michael Chiarello
Photographs copyright © 1999 by Karl Petzke
Design: Michael Mabry, Kristen Malan
    Michael Mabry Design
Food Styling: Sandra Cook
Prop Styling: Diane McGauley

All rights reserved.
No part of this book may be
reproduced in any form
without written permission
from the publisher.

978-0-8118-6379-7
The Library of Congress has cataloged
the previous edition as follows:
Chiarello, Michael.
    The Tra Vigne Cookbook: seasons
in the California wine country/by
Michael Chiarello with Penelope Wisner;
photographs by Karl Petzke.
        p. cm.
    Includes index.
    0-8118-1986-2
    1. Cookery, American—California
style. 2. Wineries—California, Northern
3. Cookery—California, Northern
I. Wisner, Penelope II. Title
    TX715.2.C34 C47 1999
    641.59794—dc21
98-32289
CIP

Manufactured in China.

10 9 8 7 6 5 4 3 2 1

Chronicle Books LLC
680 Second Street
San Francisco, California 94107

www.chroniclebooks.com

Dedication

To my family. Especially my mother, Antoinette, who continues to be my guiding light and inspiration. And to Ines, my friend, for her love, encouragement, support, and sacrifices. To my Margaux, Felicia, and Giana, my sun, moon, and stars. To my brothers Ron and Kevin whom I love very much. And to my father, Fortunato, thanks Pop for being there.

Acknowledgments

Tra Vigne is far more than a beautiful wine country restaurant. To me it is a family composed of every cook, waiter, busboy, and customer who has ever been with us. After more than ten years and hundreds of thousands of meals, Tra Vigne's family is very large indeed. Each member has contributed to our success.

I am grateful to all those who have loved and shared in the dream that became Tra Vigne. And especially thankful to all those who had the courage to stick when things were less than perfect and work even harder so that the restaurant would grow and improve until it met the lofty goals we set.

From the beginning there were my partners, Bill Higgins, Cindy Pawlcyn, and Bill Upson. They saw me through my sometimes fumbling beginnings and gave me the advice and stalwart support on which I depend.

To Kevin Cronin, General Manager and partner, who created Tra Vigne from the ground up with me. It is as much his restaurant as mine. I will be forever grateful for his patience while I grew into my kitchen clogs. ❧ To Michael Gyetvan, my partner and friend, who knows me so well he can finish every sentence I start. I am very proud of who you are. ❧ To Carmen Quagliata, who can't find a place high enough from which to scream his love for cooking. Your heart is food. ❧ To Michael Laukert, who lives the dream of Tra Vigne and Cantinetta and puts their hearts in bottles. ❧ To Burgess Smith. "Monsieur Lapin, Monsieur Lapin . . . Pauvre lapin!" ❧ To Paul Leary, what a pleasure to watch you work truly as if the dream were your own. ❧ To Tony Prince, who has been with us so long he can pick whatever he wants to do and will embrace whatever it is. ❧ To Mariano Orlando, the grandfather of ethnicity whom we all adore. ❧ To Rogelio Jacinto, from the river to the winner's circle, I am most proud of you. ❧ To Gerry Moss, whose gift is not only the quality of pastry that Tra Vigne dreamed of but also giving friendship.

To Jim Humberd. I always knew you could do it. To Frank Whitacker, one of the very best cooks I know. There's no one I would want to cook beside me more when the going is fast and hard. To Nick Morfogen, whose cooking lives on in the heart of Tra Vigne. To Peter Hall. Are you ready to make another forty prosciutto? So many local vintners, through their generosity and loyalty, have made substantial contributions to our success and become personal friends along the way. When I was new in the valley, I was asked to teach at Trefethen's cooking school and through those classes was introduced to nearly everyone in the valley. To Bart and Daphne Araujo for all their wonderfully encouraging voicemails the morning after they've eaten at the restaurant. To Gary Andrus at Pine Ridge for understanding that fly fishing is as important as great wine. To Francis Ford Coppola for his friendship and support. To Ray Corison, who would gladly trade a bottle of Zinfandel for a quart of rabbit stock. To Jamie Davies of Schramsberg and her late husband Jack for believing that we could cook for four hundred in their redwood grove without electricity or running water. To Dan and Margaret Duckhorn, who feel so at home at Tra Vigne that Dan will arrive in his muddy hunting boots with a duck in full plumage and ask us to cook for him. How can I ever thank Susan and Tor Kenward, Michael Moone, Madeleine Kamman, and Jerry Comfort of Beringer for all they have given? To Rich and Connie Frank, from Disney to delivery, you have shared it all. To the Harrison clan, including Michael, Jill, and Lindsey, for investing in the vision, great friendship, and amazing olive oil. To Bob Long, you will be Italian in your next life. To Peter Mondavi, who ate lunch with us every Friday even when we didn't have the sense to put his wines on our list. To Robert Mondavi, whose faith in us allowed him to walk into the kitchen and give us direct feedback, good and bad, and then come back for lunch again the next week. To Joan and Koerner Rombauer for their love of life and his passion for anchovies. To Doug Schafer, whose humor keeps all our heads out of the clouds. To Larry Turley, who has shown me that yes, Zinfandel does go with everything, including dessert. To Belle and Barney Rhodes, who have acted as mother and father to me, my family, and the restaurant. They have introduced our food to the world, love our children like their own, make sure Ines sits next to her best friend Barney at every event, and always make sure to have a bowl of warm pistachios on hand. To Darrell Corti, who has been a mentor and much, much more.

To Barbara Eisley and Martha May, who represent the best of what has made Napa Valley. To Dorothy Tchelicheff and her late husband, Andre, who taught me that taste has a memory and memories have a taste. To Ashley and Joe Criscione. How many days a year could you eat food from the Cantinetta? To Ferdinand Metz and the Culinary Institute of America for their support, recognition, and participation in our growth and goals. *Mille grazie* to the farmers, cheesemakers, fishmongers, and purveyors who have provided us with the stellar products that have contributed so much to the taste of Tra Vigne. To Ana Pineda. From sauté cook to pastry chef, Cantinetta manager to software designer, and then to Tomatina director. After all that success, perhaps her greatest challenge was working with me through the hundreds of recipes tested for this book. You will always be my dear friend. To Karl Petzke for capturing the flavor of Tra Vigne in his photographs. To Penni Wisner, my book partner, dear friend, and Nurse Cratchet of the writing world. You bring vision to my thoughts, taste to my words, and flavor to my recipes. Without you many seasons would have passed by *The Tra Vigne Cookbook* without it going to print. You have helped make a dream come true and for that and for all the rest, you have a life's worth of appreciation and gratitude.

Note from Penelope Wisner:
From cookies to callbacks, the staff at Tra Vigne generously gave me everything I needed as soon as I needed it. I deeply appreciate all the help I received—including the recipe testing of Carol Mason and Sue Verna. Tra Vigne has played an important role in my life for years, and I am grateful to have participated in the telling of its, and Michael's, stories.

Note from Diane McGauley, stylist:
Special thanks to: Fillamento, San Francisco, CA; Sue Fisher King, San Francisco, CA; Nest, San Francisco, CA; The Gardener, Berkeley, CA; and Coquelicot, Larkspur, CA.

TABLE *of* CONTENTS

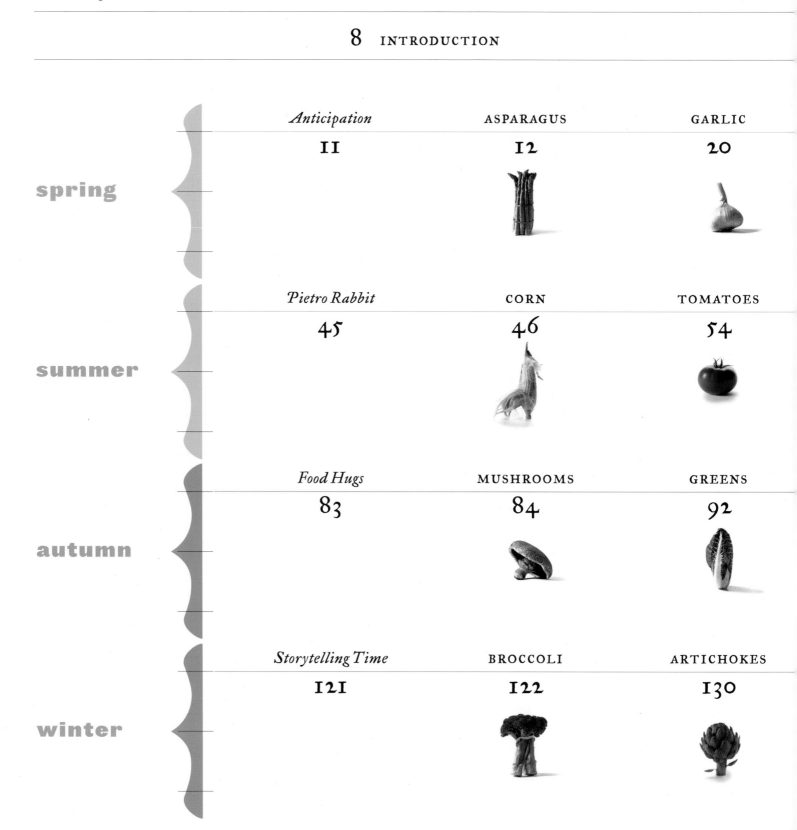

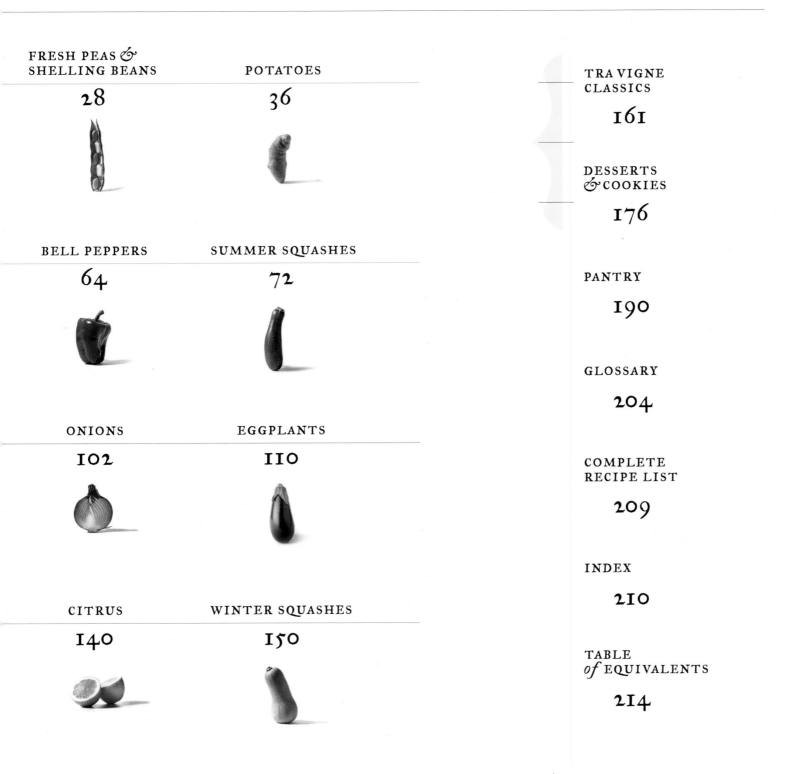

introduction

TraVigne, Italian for "among the vines," re-creates the feeling of the Italian countryside in California's Napa Valley. Grapevines grow to within a few feet of high walls that enclose the restaurant in its own private world, ruled by food and wine. The mingled scents of flowers and cooking greet guests as they step through iron gates swung wide onto the spacious brick courtyard shaded by mulberry trees. A white wooden signpost directs newcomers to the restaurant and to our take-out shop, the Cantinetta. Guests can laze away the afternoon in the dappled shade of the courtyard, under the striped awnings of the restaurant's raised wraparound terraces, or inside the high sweeping space of the restaurant itself. Fourteen-foot-high glass doors and windows open the restaurant to the sky and the weather. As the seasons color, strip, and then re-clothe the courtyard's trees, the restaurant's atmosphere changes. In winter, the bare, reaching tree limbs draw patterns against the sky, while inside, the wood-fired oven with its hammered copper front creates a cheering warmth. In spring, as green leaves emerge, the restaurant hums with renewed energy. Guests order espressos and biscotti at the Cantinetta's bar, then carry them outdoors to granite-topped tables to soak up the newly warm sunshine. By summer, the arms of the fully clothed trees interlace to create a tranquil shade. The kitchen shifts into high gear, and we make a batch of mozzarella as often as every twenty minutes, shaping the fresh, warm cheese around the season's first bloodred tomatoes. As the leaves begin to color and fall, the sky turns a crisp blue, and the shade becomes a little too cool for lingering. We harvest the grapes from our vines, cook with them, make wine, and prepare for our annual prosciutti-making and olive harvest. ❦ In 1997 Tra Vigne celebrated its tenth birthday while I celebrated my thirty-fifth. In many ways, the restaurant and I have grown up together. I have wanted to be a chef for as long as I can remember. My mother saved one of my fourth-grade essays, entitled "This Is My Life." I described how a neighbor ate five poisonous crickets and the consequences, and I ended with the bold declaration: "I want to be a chef and own a restaurant." In 1986, I became a partner and the founding chef of Tra Vigne and drew on my family's culinary heritage to develop the menu. For generations my family on both sides worked the land in Calabria, in Southern Italy. My grandparents continued that tradition when they migrated to the lumber towns of Northern California. By the time I was born, my father had moved our family to Turlock, in California's rich agricultural Central Valley. Food—its cultivation, preparation, and preservation—centered our family life. When I was very young, I would stand on a chair next to my mother so I could reach the kitchen countertop and help her cook. Throughout my youth, my mother and I hiked the hills looking for mushrooms and wild greens, worked in her huge garden, and canned her harvest. By her side, I learned that food is more than a combination of tastes, more than just fuel or nutrition. Our shared activities taught me about the cycle of seasons, about life itself, and put food on the table, too. When I married, my mother taught my wife, Ines, the family specialties that she had learned from her mother and mother-in-law. When I returned to Calabria in 1997, the dishes on my relatives' tables tasted just like the ones I had eaten as a child. ❦ This book has developed into an extended meditation on the origins of my cooking style. I often describe my cooking style as three-fold, combining spectacular ingredients, professional technique, and imaginative presentations. But as I tested these recipes, translating the style of cooking I have evolved at Tra Vigne into dishes for the home cook, I was surprised how frequently I remembered my mother and the taste of her tomato sauce, or how she fed us bits of toasted Parmesan from her electric skillet. The heart of this book belongs to her. She taught me that the closer your cooking stays to the seasons, the simpler —and better—your cooking will be. Therefore, I have organized this book by the seasons. Each is represented by four of my favorite vegetables that are normally at their peak at that time of year. These, in turn, are represented by recipes. In this way, if you are hungry for, say, peas, you can look them up and decide what you might like to cook. Although produce drives the structure, this is neither a vegetarian nor a high-fiber book. It seems to me that many people spend too much time learning recipes and not enough learning the underlying techniques. Each technique is like a tool in your tool kit. The benefit of a good tool kit is that when you stroll around a market, the produce, meats, or seafood you see will suggest preparations to you. If a bunch of spinach catches your eye, you will know what you need to make a dish out of it. To support more confident cooking, I've included several "master" recipes that incorporate techniques to add to your "tool kit." You only need to learn one recipe in order to add several new dishes to your repertoire. For instance, Lemon-Braised Artichokes (page 132) can be served on their own, as a bruschetta topping, as a pasta sauce, or as a puree with white beans to form a tasty bed for a lamb loin. Soft Polenta with Pancetta and Broccoli Rabe (page 128) is a good example of a cooking technique that can be applied to several ingredients. The same method can be employed for just about any other vegetable. Make a master recipe several times in quick succession. You will then get a feel for the recipe and be able to cook it without the book in front of you. ❧ Every recipe in this book represents a dish you are likely to have at Tra Vigne, perhaps modified slightly by using more commonly available ingredients and simpler presentations. I have included some customer favorites such as our Fritto Misto (page 174) and Forever Roasted Pork (page 172) in a separate chapter called Tra Vigne Classics. Our most popular desserts, such as our Chocolate Tiramisù (page 187), fruit crostata (page 182), and biscotti, are grouped in a chapter of their own. You will find a chapter of pantry recipes, because I believe the secret to imprinting cooking with individuality and spontaneity lies in a well-stocked pantry. Our home-cured prosciutti, olives, spice rubs, and olive oil are the ingredients that distinguish a dish made at Tra Vigne from that of any other restaurant. My cooks and I continue to spend more than half our creative time on ingredients, adding items to our pantry stores. In this way, a sauce made in December can take on a summer-fresh taste with the addition of a spoonful of our house-dried tomatoes. A cooking style is not defined by a dish or even by a collection of ingredients. Style results from a series of actions whose final statement is a dish. Practiced often enough, these actions turn into a way of life. Where you choose to shop—a supermarket, a discount store, a farmers' market—and how often you shop affects your cooking style. Whenever you take a moment during a hike to collect some wild herbs, you are building a personal cooking style. My hope is that the recipes in this book will inspire you to cook, and that your increasing confidence and excitement in the kitchen will in turn inspire your family and friends, making the circle around your table grow wider and deeper. I cannot imagine a better way to touch people than through the pleasure of food.

SPRING | anticipation

One spring evening as I was testing recipes for this book, I opened the kitchen window. All winter I had cooked with the doors and windows closed. I suddenly remembered how, as a child, I was always late for dinner in the winter. But in spring, when my mother opened the window as she cooked, the delicious smells of supper wafted over the yard and called me to the table. ❧ Spring in Napa Valley arrives independently of the calendar. The sound of running water and the sight of lush green hillsides are winter phenomena. In late February, long before the equinox, the valley blazes with bright yellow mustard and pink almond blossoms. Then, seemingly overnight, the naked, sculptural vines burst into delicate feathers—budbreak in March. ❧ Spring is the season of my greatest anticipation and greatest frustration. Those twin feelings sharpen the appetite for the first delicate tastes of spring. Imagine a day at the end of February when the midday temperature hits nearly eighty degrees. Such days are not uncommon. Grilled asparagus or tiny new potatoes are what I want to eat, but the menu seems stuck in winter. Nothing tastes right, though I know the food is as well cooked as it was yesterday when the temperature was less than sixty degrees. By now I have prepared parsnips every way I know how, and I want to cook asparagus. But just because the sun is hot and bright today does not mean the asparagus came to full maturation, went to market, and was delivered to my restaurant all within a few hours. I feel as if I am running in a dream and I can't quite reach spring. ❧ While waiting for spring produce to reach the market, I go outdoors and forage. I know a couple of morel mushroom patches. Or I may pick fiddlehead ferns, ramps, or the first of the wild cresses. Miner's lettuce, an abundant weed that delivered a healthy dose of vitamin C to the diets of early California miners, is at its sweetest now. Later in the spring, it bolts and tastes sour. ❧ Spring doesn't last long. Our rule at the restaurant is never to buy an item until the second week of its season, then as the harvest travels northward, we buy continually until the harvest passes into the Pacific Northwest, and we stop. My advice to home cooks is to wait one or two weeks into a vegetable's season, eat it twice a week during the height of the season, then give it up. Stopping may be hard, but freshly arriving seasonal tastes will distract you soon enough. ❧ Spring is when we cut into our first prosciutto, curing since last November in the cool darkness provided by the thick stone walls of the Cantinetta's second story. The meat is so good, we eat it off the knife without embellishments. It is also the time I go mushroom hunting for spring-runoff porcini. The aromatic Meyer lemons are abundant, and green garlic arrives at farmers' markets. One of my best childhood memories of spring is of the trout fingerlings we fished from the river just as it thawed. We cooked the little fish right on the riverbank, then ate them, bones and all. A few weeks later, the trout would be good sized. ❧ But spring is about more than food. It is also a time when chores turn into opportunities to be outdoors spending time with your family. When I say to my daughter, "Come on, Felicia, get your boots on. We're going to the vineyard to pick up rocks out of the road," I am thinking of past springs when our family would visit my grandfather's ranch. He and I would get up before anyone else. He'd tie a bandanna around my neck, and we'd go clear rocks out of his ranch roads. We drank water from an old whiskey bottle that he kept behind the seat of his truck. He always had Black Jack gum in the ashtray. We'd eat a little something and work really hard. ❧ What keeps me motivated is not the food itself, but all the bonds and memories the food represents.

asparagus

Asparagus in the market signals the return of spring. Celebrate the season with platters of vividly green spears drizzled with your best extra-virgin olive oil or melted sweet butter. If the evening is warm, grill them and serve them with a tangy tangerine mayonnaise (page 15). Add a loaf of crusty bread and a bottle of crisp white wine and you've got supper. ❦ Some people claim the sweetest asparagus spears are pencil slim, while others prefer the fat ones. I like thin and thick asparagus, but if I had to choose, I'd want spears as big as my thumb. ❦ What does indicate quality in asparagus is freshness. Stalks should be firm, straight, and not at all wilted. The cut base should look moist, while the small leaves that form the tips should be tightly closed. If they are open and seedy, the asparagus is beyond its prime and will be tough.

TRIMMING ASPARAGUS Trimming asparagus may seem unnecessary, but it insures that all the spears in a bundle, from their tips to their bases, will cook in the same amount of time. When presentation matters, the spears should be of the same length. Snap the tough end off one spear, then cut the remaining spears to match. Now look carefully at the spears. Some will be evenly green down to the base, while others will take on a lavender color. These are the ones that need to be peeled, as the purple color indicates woodiness. Use a swivel-bladed vegetable peeler, and note that the skin at the base is thicker than the skin toward the tip. If presentation does not matter, simply snap off the tough ends from the whole bunch.

COOKING ASPARAGUS If you're cooking a lot of asparagus, use a big stockpot or pasta cooking pot. If you're cooking just a single bunch, you can use a large sauté pan. Cook the asparagus in rapidly boiling, well-salted water. The timing will vary from 3 to 5 minutes, depending on how the dish is to be served. Will it be eaten without further cooking or reheating? If the asparagus are to be grilled or roasted, cook the spears only until they barely bend when held by one end, about 3 minutes. If the spears will not be cooked again, boil them until they are bright green and flexible, but still al dente, about 5 minutes. If the spears will need reheating, cook for about 4 minutes. Do not overcook or cover the pan or the asparagus will turn army green and odiferous. ❦ If you are cooking asparagus a day ahead of serving, it is a good idea to immerse them in an ice-water bath immediately after removing them from the boiling water in order to halt the cooking. If you plan on serving asparagus within a few hours of the preliminary cooking, you can omit the ice-water bath. Instead, scatter the spears on a baking sheet lined with a tea towel.

asparagi

Grilled Asparagus
with Tangerine Mayonnaise

Grilling adds a wonderful flavor to asparagus and makes this dish a popular addition to our spring menu. Unless you serve platter after platter of asparagus (not a bad idea at all), however, you will have more mayonnaise than you need. But that is good news, as it tastes great on all sorts of vegetables and on poached fish, and can be used to bind a chicken salad or as a sandwich spread. I prefer to parboil asparagus spears before grilling them. Unless very thin, the spears become acrid and dehydrate if grilled raw. Cook them over an ebbing fire. You want a delicate grilled flavor to add complexity, rather than overwhelm the taste of the asparagus.

Serves 4 to 6

2 cups freshly squeezed tangerine juice

2 tangerines

1 tablespoon coarsely chopped fresh tarragon

1 egg yolk

Salt and freshly ground pepper

1 cup pure olive oil, plus more for tossing
    with and brushing on asparagus

2 large bunches asparagus, about 2 pounds total,
    trimmed and cooked for 3 minutes according
    to instructions on page 12

Long curls of tangerine zest, fresh or candied

Coarsely chopped toasted hazelnuts
    or pine nuts (optional)

Put the juice in a small nonreactive saucepan and bring to a boil. Cook until reduced to $1/2$ cup. Let cool to room temperature. Peel the tangerines, removing all the white pith, and segment over a bowl to catch both the segments and the juices. Cover and refrigerate until very cold.

Combine the reduced juice, tarragon, egg yolk, and salt and pepper to taste in a blender and blend until well mixed. With the machine running, add the 1 cup olive oil, at first by drops and then, as mixture emulsifies, in a thin, steady stream until all the oil is incorporated. Taste for seasoning. Scrape into a jar, cover, and refrigerate until needed. You should have about $1\,2/3$ cups mayonnaise. (Keeps 2 to 3 days, refrigerated.)

Prepare the grill and let burn down to medium coals. Toss the cooled asparagus with about 1 tablespoon olive oil and season with salt and pepper. Grill over medium to low coals, turning the spears as needed, until they take on a little color and are just tender, about 6 minutes. Cover the grill if necessary to maintain the heat.

Arrange the asparagus on a platter with the reserved tangerine segments. Dot with the mayonnaise, and drizzle with any tangerine juice left in the bowl. Garnish with fresh or candied zest and the nuts, if using. Serve at once.

CHEF'S NOTES: *Every cook has insecurities. One of mine is mayonnaise. I always get a little anxious until I see it coming together in the blender. If the mayonnaise is too thick, thin it, with the machine running, by pulsing in a little cool water.*

If you are concerned about raw eggs, use a pasteurized egg product or an egg substitute such as Egg Beaters.

Asparagus Risotto *with* Shiitake Mushrooms

Risotto is a regular entry on our menu, but its flavor and presentation can change on a daily basis depending on what is in season. You could serve this dish with fish, chicken, or beef, but I'm not sure it's necessary. Serve it alone as a light spring supper and everyone will be happy. Spring is also a time to be aware that ingredients are changing. The flavor of thyme is more delicate now, as the plant pushes out new growth. Therefore, I add it late in this recipe. Give the risotto an extra hit of flavor by adding the tough asparagus stems to the simmering stock for several minutes only.

Serves 3 or 4

About 4 cups chicken stock (page 204)
　　or canned low-salt chicken broth
1 large bunch asparagus, about 1 pound
¼ cup extra-virgin olive oil
2 cups sliced shiitake mushrooms (¼ inch thick)
Salt and freshly ground pepper
1 cup finely chopped onion
1 tablespoon minced garlic
1 cup Arborio rice
½ cup dry white wine (optional)
1½ teaspoons finely chopped fresh thyme
1 tablespoon unsalted butter
¼ cup coarsely grated Fontina cheese
¾ cup freshly grated Parmesan cheese
1½ tablespoons finely chopped fresh
　　flat-leaf parsley (optional)
1½ teaspoons freshly grated lemon zest (optional)

Pour the stock into a saucepan, place over high heat, and bring to a boil. Meanwhile, snap off the ends from the asparagus and peel any tough skin from the stalks (page 12). Add the asparagus ends to the stock, reduce the heat to low, and simmer gently until the stems are tender, about 7 minutes. Dip out and discard the stems. Slice the spears ¼ inch thick on the diagonal. Set aside.

Heat the olive oil in a heavy medium saucepan over medium-high heat until hot. Scatter in the mushrooms and do not move them until they begin to brown, about 1 minute. Then season with salt and pepper and sauté until brown, about 5 minutes. Remove to a plate.

Lower the heat to medium, add the onion, season lightly with salt, and cook until soft but not brown, about 2 minutes. Add the garlic and cook briefly. Add the rice and stir until the grains look pearly white, about 2 minutes.

Add the wine, if using, and cook until the pan is nearly dry. Adjust the heat so the rice cooks at a slow simmer. Add ½ cup of the stock, stir, and cook until the pan is nearly dry again. Season lightly with salt and pepper now so the flavor permeates the rice. Add another ½ cup of the stock and continue to stir and cook, adding stock as necessary, until the rice is three-fourths cooked, about 15 minutes. Stir in the thyme, mushrooms, and sliced asparagus tips. Continue to cook until the rice is al dente and the asparagus is bright green and just tender, about 4 minutes longer.

Remove from the heat and stir in the butter, Fontina cheese, ½ cup of the Parmesan cheese, the parsley and the lemon zest, if using. Taste for seasoning. Dust with Parmesan before serving. Pass more cheese at the table.

Asparagus Pesto *with* Tiny Potatoes *and* Pasta

At Tra Vigne, we often borrow classic dishes, treat them as techniques, then reinvent them with unexpected ingredients. And so you might find asparagus pesto on a spring menu or tomato carpaccio on a summer menu. Pasta and potatoes may seem like starch on starch to Americans, but it would make a typical Friday night meal for Italian families. Look for the tiny potatoes in farmers' markets, or cut larger ones into ½-inch dice. You will have twice as much of the pesto as you need. You can cut the pesto amounts in half, but I encourage you to make the full recipe. It will disappear quickly on bread, toast, or baked potatoes. If you are sensitive to raw garlic, blanch the peeled, whole cloves in several changes of salted water (page 19).

Serves 4

For the pesto

1 large bunch asparagus, about 1 pound, trimmed and cooked for 5 minutes according to instructions on page 12

½ cup packed coarsely chopped fresh basil

2 tablespoons pine nuts, toasted

1 tablespoon minced garlic

Salt and freshly ground pepper

About 1 cup pure olive oil

½ cup freshly grated Parmesan cheese

¾ pound marble-size potatoes

2 tablespoons extra-virgin olive oil

Salt and freshly ground pepper

¾ pound dried orecchiette or other pasta the same size as potatoes

About ½ cup freshly grated Parmesan cheese

Cut the asparagus spears into thirds. Put in a food processor with the basil, pine nuts, garlic, and salt and pepper to taste. Keep in mind you will add Parmesan as well, so be careful not to oversalt. With the machine running, slowly add the cup of olive oil. When the sauce is about the consistency of mayonnaise, it has enough oil. Pulse in the Parmesan. Thin with water if necessary to achieve a slick, saucy pesto. Scrape into a bowl or jar, cover, and refrigerate until needed. You should have about 3 cups. (Keeps about 2 days, refrigerated.)

Put the potatoes in a pan of salted cold water to cover and bring to a boil. Cook until tender, about 10 minutes. Drain and let cool for a few minutes. If the potatoes are larger than about ½ inch in diameter, cut in half.

Heat the olive oil in a medium sauté pan over medium-high heat until hot. Add the potatoes and cook until browned and crispy all over, about 5 minutes. Season to taste with salt and pepper. Keep warm.

While the potatoes are browning, return the water used for cooking the asparagus, if reserved, to a boil. Add more salt and the pasta and cook until al dente, about 12 minutes. Drain, reserving about ½ cup of the pasta cooking water. Pour the pasta into a warm serving bowl, add the potatoes, about 1 cup of the asparagus pesto, several twists of pepper, and ¼ cup of the Parmesan. Toss well, thinning with the pasta cooking water as necessary. Dust with a light grating of Parmesan before serving and pass the remaining cheese and a bowl of pesto at the table.

Roasted Asparagus Bundles

This is a quick, attractive dish, terrific with softly fried eggs for a spring weekend breakfast, as an appetizer for lunch or dinner, or as a side vegetable with roast chicken.

Serves 4

For the seasoned bread crumbs
1½ teaspoons extra-virgin olive oil
1 teaspoon minced garlic
¼ cup fine dried bread crumbs
Pinch salt
Freshly ground pepper
1 tablespoon finely chopped fresh parsley
1 teaspoon freshly grated lemon zest
1 tablespoon freshly grated Parmesan cheese

Unsalted butter for baking dish
1 large bunch asparagus, about 1 pound, trimmed to even lengths and cooked for 4 minutes according to instructions on page 12
2 tablespoons extra-virgin olive oil
Salt and freshly ground pepper
8 thin slices prosciutto

To make the seasoned bread crumbs, heat the olive oil in a small skillet over medium-high heat until hot. Add the garlic and sauté briefly until pale gold. Add the bread crumbs, season with salt and pepper, and lower the heat to medium. Cook, stirring occasionally, until the bread crumbs are toasted, about 3 minutes. Pour into a small bowl and add the parsley, lemon zest, and Parmesan. Toss well. (The crumbs keep, tightly sealed and refrigerated, for several days.)

Preheat the oven to 400°F. Butter a shallow baking dish that is long enough to hold the asparagus. Toss the cooled asparagus with the olive oil and season with salt and pepper.

Divide the asparagus into 4 equal bundles. Arrange 2 slices of the prosciutto on a work surface so they slightly overlap each other. Place an asparagus bundle on top and roll up carefully in the prosciutto. Arrange in the prepared baking dish. Flatten the top of each bundle slightly and sprinkle with one-fourth of the seasoned bread crumbs.

Roast in the oven until heated through and crisp, about 10 minutes. Serve at once.

Whole Roasted Fish *with* Asparagus *and* Extra-Virgin Olive Oil

Here, the presentation does all the work for you. Serve a whole 1 ½-pound fish per person. With the fresh fish, great olive oil, and the fat asparagus, you don't have to do any embellishing. My favorite North American fish is the genuine American red snapper from Florida that has a yellow tail, a definite pink color, and a gold stripe running the length of its body. But look out, it bears a close resemblance to the mangrove snapper, which lacks the gold stripe. Its flesh has a slight gray cast and muddy flavor compared to the white, sweet flesh of red snapper. You can also make this recipe with whole Pacific or gulf snapper, or trout, or with thick fillets instead of whole fish. This dish is a great showcase for a late-harvest extra-virgin olive oil, if you have one. Such oils are made from very ripe olives and have a soft, rich, round flavor perfectly suited to fish. The sharp, snappy, deep green early harvest oils are more appropriate with vegetables.

Serves 4

25 garlic cloves, peeled and left whole

¼ cup extra-virgin olive oil, plus more
   for oiling roasting pan(s)

4 fish, 1½ pounds each, heads on,
   cleaned, and scaled

Salt and freshly ground pepper

1 bunch fresh thyme

1 bunch large thick asparagus, about 1 pound,
   trimmed and cooked for 4 minutes according to
   instructions on page 12

¼ cup late-harvest extra-virgin olive oil
   or extra-virgin olive oil

2 lemons, halved

Put the garlic in a small pot of salted water and bring to a boil. Drain and repeat twice. Reserve the garlic.

Preheat the oven to 450°F. Oil 1 or 2 roasting pans or baking sheets. Make 3 diagonal slashes, ½ inch deep, on both sides of each fish so they will cook evenly. Season on both sides with salt and pepper, and rub each fish all over with about 1 tablespoon of the extra-virgin olive oil.

Arrange the fish in the prepared pans. Scatter the thyme sprigs inside the fish and over them. Roast until almost done, about 15 minutes. Remove from the oven, scatter the asparagus and garlic over the fish, return to the oven, and continue to cook until done, about 10 minutes longer.

Arrange the fish, asparagus, and garlic on warmed individual oval plates. Drizzle with the late-harvest extra-virgin olive oil. Squeeze the lemon halves over all and serve immediately.

garlic

In our home garden in Napa Valley, garlic begins to form bulbs in May and is ready to use in June. Fresh garlic is a joy to cook with, and my measurements are always generous. The first bulb garlic, from Mexico, comes to market in spring, as does green garlic. ❧ Green garlic, usually only available in farmers' markets and some natural-foods groceries, is immature bulb garlic. It looks like a large scallion or a slim leek. The whole stalk can be used in cooking to give a wonderful, delicate garlic flavor without sharpness or heat. It can also be eaten raw, of course. Taste the greener part of the stalk to make sure it is tender, then clean the stalk by cutting off the root and peeling off an outer layer of skin. ❧ If left in the ground for a short while longer, green garlic begins to form a bulb, although no individual wrappers yet separate the tightly packed cloves. Some growers bring this stage of garlic to market as well and call it spring garlic. The flavor is slightly more intense than the younger garlic, but still without sharpness. You can substitute green or spring garlic for bulb garlic unless you want to roast garlic. For that you need fully formed bulbs. Because green and spring garlic are so rarely found and their season is so short, my recipes call for bulb garlic. ❧ Like most storage crops, recently harvested garlic tastes best. Look for heavy, firm bulbs without cuts or bruises. Whenever I have to peel several bulbs, it never fails that they are made up of many tiny cloves. Save yourself time and select bulbs with large cloves. I am not referring to elephant garlic, a different, although related, vegetable. Elephant garlic can be delicious, but it is not something I cook very often. ❧ Although raw garlic might be traditional in a recipe, for instance, in pesto, I will often cook it first to avoid the harshness it can sometimes add. I like to sauté it briefly in a little olive oil until light brown. The browned garlic adds both a garlic and a sweet toasted flavor that can be intriguing and unexpected in the pesto or other recipes such as Caesar salad dressing. Try it if cooking for someone who is sensitive to raw garlic.

PEELING GARLIC The easiest way to peel garlic is still the old-fashioned way. Tuck a clove under the flat side of a chef's knife and slap the blade sharply. The skin will split and is then easily pulled away from the clove. To peel a whole head of garlic, put it in a plastic bag and pound with a rubber mallet until the head breaks apart and the skin around the individual cloves has split. Please never, ever use a garlic press. Pressed garlic is very strong because the action of the press crushes and bruises the cellular structure of the cloves.

aglio

Poached Garlic Soup

One of our tests for a new cook at Tra Vigne is to prepare a seasonally appropriate soup. It is the test most often failed. To be good, a soup does not need exotic or expensive ingredients. My mother's spring meals were built around dishes like this soup, with only some focaccia and a simple grilled flank steak to round out the menu. Believe it or not, the garlic is a delicate flavor and you don't want to overwhelm it. To vary the flavor, however, you can add a cup of a broccoli or asparagus puree. Just enough potatoes are included to give the soup body, but not enough to make it a potato soup. Serve it hot on a cool spring evening or cold for a summer lunch.

Makes about 7 cups, serves 4 to 6

2 cups garlic cloves

Salt and freshly ground pepper

2 tablespoons extra-virgin olive oil

1 cup diced onion (¼-inch dice)

1 cup finely chopped leek, white part only

½ cup diced celery (¼-inch dice)

1 bay leaf

4 cups chicken stock (page 204)
    or canned low-salt chicken broth

1 cup diced, peeled russet potatoes (½-inch dice)

1 tablespoon coarsely chopped fresh oregano

4 cups loosely packed spinach leaves

1 cup heavy cream, half-and-half, or buttermilk

Peel the garlic cloves, cut in half lengthwise, and remove the central greenish core. Put in a small pan of salted water and bring to a boil. Drain and repeat twice to remove the garlic's heat and leave only sweetness behind.

Heat the olive oil in a large, heavy pot over medium heat until hot. Add the onion, leek, celery, bay leaf, and a little salt to draw the water out of the onion. Cover and cook until the vegetables are soft but not brown, about 5 minutes. Add the blanched garlic, stock, and potatoes. Season with salt and pepper. Bring to a boil over high heat, reduce the heat to a simmer, cover, and cook until the vegetables are very tender, about 15 minutes. Add the oregano and spinach and simmer for another minute, just until the spinach wilts into the soup. (If you are making the soup ahead of time, cool it now in an ice bath to maintain the color.)

Puree the soup in a blender or use an immersion blender. (The blender will result in a smoother, evenly green soup. The immersion blender will leave some unevenness, which is also nice. Which is best depends on how refined you want the soup to be or what equipment comes easily to hand.) Taste for seasoning. (The soup can be made ahead to this point, covered, and refrigerated for several days or frozen.)

Reheat the soup in a large pan over low heat. Whisk in the cream, heat through, and taste for seasoning. Ladle into warm bowls and serve.

Piadine *with* Blue Cheese Caesar Salad

Cold greens and dressing on a warm, crunchy crust. Who could resist? I adopted the idea of a blue cheese Caesar from Jacques Pépin. You can make the dish more substantial with the addition of grilled chicken or shrimp.

Serves 6

For the Caesar mayonnaise dressing

1 tablespoon champagne vinegar

2 tablespoons freshly squeezed lemon juice

1 ½ teaspoons minced garlic

1 egg yolk

1 tablespoon Dijon mustard

Dash Worcestershire sauce

6 anchovy fillets (if watching salt intake, rinse and pat dry with paper towels)

Pinch freshly ground pepper

1 cup pure olive oil

About ¼ cup crumbled Gorgonzola or other blue cheese

2 tablespoons freshly grated Parmesan cheese

12 cups loosely packed torn romaine lettuce (about 2 heads)

¾ pound cooked, shredded chicken or cooked, peeled shrimp (optional)

1 recipe Piadine Dough (page 194)

All-purpose flour for dusting work surface

½ cup Roasted Garlic Paste (page 197)

1 tablespoon finely chopped fresh thyme

6 tablespoons freshly grated Parmesan cheese, plus extra for garnish (optional)

Coarse cornmeal for sprinkling on baking sheets

Crumbled Gorgonzola cheese or other blue cheese for garnish (optional)

CHEF'S NOTE: *If you are concerned about raw eggs, use a pasteurized egg product or an egg substitute such as Egg Beaters.*

To make the mayonnaise dressing, put the vinegar, lemon juice, garlic, egg yolk, mustard, Worcestershire sauce, anchovies, and pepper in a blender and blend until well mixed. With the machine running, add the olive oil, at first by drops and then, as the mixture emulsifies, in a thin, steady stream until all the oil is incorporated. Pulse in the Gorgonzola to taste (the riper the cheese, the less you will need) and the Parmesan. Scrape into a bowl, cover, and refrigerate until needed. You should have about 1⅓ cups. (The dressing keeps, refrigerated, for 2 to 3 days.)

Place 2 large baking sheets in the oven and preheat to 500°F. Put the lettuce in a bowl with the chicken or shrimp, if using. Pour the dressing over and toss well.

Divide the dough into 6 equal balls. Working on a surface free of flour, roll each ball under your palm. As it rolls, it will stick slightly to the surface, creating tension that helps form a tight, round ball. Dust the work surface lightly with the flour, pat each ball down lightly, dust the tops with flour, cover with a tea towel, and let rise again for about 15 minutes.

With a rolling pin, roll each ball into a circle 8 or 9 inches in diameter and about ⅛ inch thick. Brush each round with a generous tablespoon of the garlic paste and sprinkle with ½ teaspoon of the thyme and 1 tablespoon of the Parmesan.

Remove the baking sheets from the oven, sprinkle evenly with cornmeal, and transfer the rounds to the sheets. Bake until slightly underdone (they should be lightly browned around the edges, but still pliable), 8 to 12 minutes. Let the crusts cool very briefly before filling.

Transfer the crusts to plates, top with a large handful of salad, and sprinkle with a small amount of blue cheese, Parmesan, or a mixture of both, if desired. Serve "open face." Diners fold their piadine in half.

Variation for Caesar Mayonnaise Dressing: Omit the blue cheese. Increase the amount of Parmesan to 3 to 4 tablespoons, or to taste.

Spaghettini Squared:
Pasta *with* Olive Oil, Garlic,
and Zucchini

³/₄ pound dried spaghettini

³/₄ pound zucchini (for the spiral slicer,
   the fatter the zucchini the better)

Salt and freshly ground pepper

¹/₂ cup extra-virgin olive oil

2 tablespoons minced garlic

¹/₂ teaspoon red pepper flakes

3 tablespoons coarsely chopped fresh basil

2 tablespoons finely chopped fresh
   flat-leaf parsley

¹/₂ cup plus 2 tablespoons freshly grated
   Parmesan cheese

So simple, yet this dish, paired with a glass of jet-cold Vernaccia, is the stuff of suppertime dreams. While far from essential, a turning slicer such as the kind made by Benriner (see Glossary, page 207), adds so much whimsy and fun to the preparation that it seems more like magic than cooking. The slicer cuts long, long spirals of vegetables. It is precisely this unexpected touch that characterizes the way we like to rethink and re-create dishes at Tra Vigne. The slicer is great fun for making cucumber and zucchini salads and for turning out potato spirals to deep-fry or wrap around shrimp bound for the grill.

Serves 4

Bring a large pot of water to a boil and add salt. Add the pasta and cook until al dente, about 10 minutes.

While the water comes to a boil and the pasta cooks, cut the zucchini on the medium blade of a Benriner Turning Slicer or Cook's Help or with the fine French-fry cutter on a mandoline. If you do not have these, cut by hand into the longest, finest julienne you can manage. Season with salt and pepper. If your zucchini is very finely cut (as it will be with one of the slicers), it does not need to be cooked. Otherwise, place in a colander, suspend over the pasta pot, cover the pot, and steam the zucchini until still slightly crunchy, about 2 minutes.

Heat $^{1}/_{4}$ cup of the olive oil in a small skillet over medium-high heat until hot. Add the garlic and sauté briefly until light brown. Turn on the exhaust fan and add the red pepper flakes. Quickly add the basil and parsley, mix well, and remove from the heat.

When the pasta is al dente, drain, reserving about $^{1}/_{2}$ cup of the pasta cooking water. Pour the pasta into a warm serving bowl, add the zucchini, the remaining $^{1}/_{4}$ cup oil, the garlic mixture, and $^{1}/_{2}$ cup of the cheese. Toss well, adding cooking water as needed to make a smooth sauce. Taste for seasoning and add salt and pepper as needed. Sprinkle with the remaining 2 tablespoons Parmesan and serve at once.

CHEF'S NOTE: *The reason to save half the olive oil to toss with the pasta at the end is so the oil will have a fresh, uncooked taste.*

Famous Roast Garlic Crab

6 tablespoons unsalted butter

6 tablespoons extra-virgin olive oil

2 tablespoons minced garlic

4 Dungeness crabs, about 1¼ pounds each,
    cooked, cleaned, and cracked

Salt and freshly ground pepper

3 tablespoons freshly squeezed lemon juice

¼ cup finely chopped fresh flat-leaf parsley

I don't think I have ever made a simpler or more successful dish in my life. As long as we can get fresh Dungeness crabs, it's on the menu. If you buy the cooked crabs, make sure to ask what day they were cooked, so you know how fresh they are. Also be aware that the saline content may be high, as salt increases shelf life. To cook and clean the live crabs at home, see the sidebar that follows. Stone crabs, spider crabs, blue crabs, or lobsters can all be given this garlic treatment.

Serves 4

Preheat the oven to 500°F. Heat the butter, olive oil, and garlic in a very large ovenproof sauté pan over medium-high heat until hot. (You may need 2 pans.) Add the crab, season to taste with salt and pepper, and toss well. Transfer to the oven and roast until the garlic turns light brown and the crab is heated through, about 12 minutes. Toss once halfway through.

Pour the contents of the pan into a large warm serving bowl, add the lemon juice and the parsley, and toss well. Serve pronto with plenty of napkins!

To cook and clean Dungeness crabs: Bring 1 recipe Court Bouillon (page 204) to a simmer. Pick up a live crab by its last 2 hind legs. Hold them together tightly and stroke the top of the head just behind the mouth until the crab goes to sleep. Lower into the pot slowly so you don't splash and scald yourself. Simmer the crabs until they turn pink and are done, about 10 minutes. Remove from the pot and let cool on a plate on their backs. Let rest until cool enough to handle. On the underside of the carapace you will see a triangular piece. If it is large, the crab is a female. If small, it is a male.

To clean and crack the crab, grasp the legs and twist them off the body. Crack them lightly in several places with a nutcracker. Hold the body backside up, and put your right thumb in the joint between the upper and lower shell on the side opposite the mouth. Your palm will then be stretched across the top of the shell. Hold the bottom of the crab in your opposite hand. Force your thumb in and pull up and back to your right. The shell will snap off.

Scrape the contents of the shell into a bowl. Snap the rest of the face off the upper shell, and rinse out the shell. If you intend to use it for presentation in some dishes, pull off the spongy lungs clinging to both sides of the upper body and discard. Turn the body over and snap off and discard the hard, V-shaped sex. Clean out the center of the body—the liver and green tomalley—into a separate bowl with the juices from the shell and reserve.

Snap off the rest of the face by inserting your thumb deeply into the hole behind the face and pulling back and up. Cut the body into quarters and put in a bowl with the legs.

To make a sauce with the reserved liquids, push them through a sieve into a saucepan and cook with a pinch of saffron and some dry white wine. Simmer until very reduced. Stir this essence into homemade or purchased mayonnaise and season with red pepper flakes, raw garlic, freshly squeezed lemon juice, and finely chopped fresh parsley. Serve as a dip for your crab.

fresh peas and shelling beans

One of the things that I like best about fresh peas and shelling beans is that their short seasons force a hurried celebration. My favorite shelling beans are tender, green fava beans, perhaps because one week the beans are tiny and tender, the next they are an inch long, and the next they are fit only for drying. When dried, shelling beans are our familiar pantry staples. When eaten fresh, they have a delicate, earthy, sweet flavor and a smooth, satiny texture. ❧ Fava beans, like green peas, begin their season in late spring when the weather is warm but not yet hot. Other fresh shelling beans, such as white beans, limas, and cranberry beans, reach the market later in the summer. You may have to pay close attention to farmers' markets throughout spring and summer to catch whatever shelling bean farmers decide to harvest fresh and bring to market. ❧ You may not equate dried beans with a springlike flavor, but I use them throughout the year, often as a puree mixed with other vegetables and served as a side dish or as a topping for bruschetta. Fresh or dried, shelling beans are low in fat, high in protein and fiber, and lend themselves to many easy dishes. One of the best ways to serve them fresh is quickly boiled until tender and dressed with good extra-virgin olive oil, salt, and pepper. Or toss them in pasta and salads. ❧ Buy fresh peas and shelling beans where the turnover is good and open displays permit you to sample. Peas should be full, sweet, and tender, even when raw. Bean pods should be firm and full. The pods should be neither too slim, meaning the peas or beans are immature, nor too fat, indicating that the peas or beans may have overmatured and become starchy. ❧ Just-picked English peas, like corn, are all sugar and sweetness. Sometimes they are so sweet, it seems a shame to cook them at all. If so, you may want just to dip them in boiling water to bring out their color. Don't get distracted when cooking fresh peas. It takes only an extra twenty seconds for them to turn army green. ❧ While beans found in Egyptian pyramids have been sprouted, they are best within a year of harvest. The older they are, the longer they take to cook to tenderness. Do not add acid ingredients such as vinegar or tomatoes to beans until they are at least three-fourths cooked. Acid, as well as salt, toughens their skins.

COOKING AND PEELING FAVA BEANS Favas come packed by nature in amply padded shells. Consequently, you need to buy a large amount of beans to have any volume left when you finish shelling and skinning them. For instance, 5 pounds of beans will yield about 2 pounds shelled beans, and just 3 cups peeled, cooked beans. ❧ With luck, children and friends will help you shell the beans. Don't release your helpers once the beans are shelled. That is only the first half of the job. ❧ Favas cook to tenderness very quickly, so be careful. This initial cooking is all the beans will need unless they are large. Bring a large pot of water to a boil, add salt, and then the beans, and cook until tender and bright green, 3 to 5 minutes, depending on the size and freshness of the beans. Drain and scatter on a baking sheet to cool. Notice the translucent skin around each bean has loosened. If you are blanching or cooking a series of ingredients along with the favas, always do the beans last. The skins release a compound that turns the water the color of tea. ❧ Very young beans may not need to be peeled. To peel off the white skin, pinch through the skin opposite the growing tip. Then press the growing end of the bean between two fingers and the bean will slip out of the skin. Put the peeled beans in a nonreactive bowl. Cooked beans will keep several days in the refrigerator.

piselli e fagioli

Pan Stew *of* Scallops, Peas, *and* Pearl Onions

½ pound dried pasta shells the same size
    as the scallops
2 tablespoons extra-virgin olive oil
1 generous cup pearl onions, peeled
1 pound scallops
1½ teaspoons minced garlic
1 cup dry white wine
1 cup chicken stock (page 204)
    or canned low-salt chicken broth

Salt and freshly ground pepper
1½ cups shelled English peas
    (about 1¼ pounds unshelled)
3 tablespoons coarsely chopped fresh basil
1 teaspoon freshly grated lemon zest
1½ tablespoons finely chopped fresh
    flat-leaf parsley
1 tablespoon unsalted butter (optional)

Quick, light, delicious—a spring supper in thirty minutes, including chopping and peeling. I added a little pasta to the pan stew to give it substance. You want the scallop and pea flavors to dominate, so make sure the pasta shells are thin not thick. (Names, sizes, and thickness vary from brand to brand.) And you want shells, because they will catch the juices. You can, of course, omit the pasta if you prefer.

Serves 4

Bring a large pot of water to a boil and add salt. Add the pasta and cook until al dente, about 12 minutes.

While the pasta water comes to a boil, begin cooking the pan stew. Heat the olive oil in a large sauté pan over medium-high heat until hot. Add the onions, reduce the heat to medium, and cook until light brown, about 3 minutes. Remove to a plate and reserve. Add the scallops, and cook without moving them until they brown on one side, about 1 minute. Turn and cook just until cooked through, about 1½ minutes longer. (The timing will vary according to the size of the scallops. Bay scallops require only seconds.) Remove the scallops to a plate.

Add the garlic to the pan and sauté briefly until light brown. Add the wine and bring to a boil, while stirring and scraping all over the bottom of the pan to loosen any browned bits. Add the stock, return to a boil, season with salt and pepper, and add the reserved onions. Simmer gently until the onions are tender, about 10 minutes. Add the peas and continue to cook until just tender, about 3 minutes.

Return the scallops to the pan with the basil, lemon zest, parsley, and the butter, if using. Cook just until the scallops are warm.

When the pasta is cooked, drain well and add to the sauté pan with the pea mixture. Taste for seasoning and serve immediately.

CHEF'S NOTES:

If you prefer less wine flavor, reduce the amount to ½ cup or leave it out altogether, replacing the liquid with 1 cup water and 1 tablespoon freshly squeezed lemon juice.

Scallops may be the most abused seafood on the market. Scallop fishermen tend to go way out to sea to find their catch. Once that far out, they are not inclined to return until their holds are full. In order to keep the scallops fresh, they may add preserving agents, including bleach.

There has been a growing demand, spearheaded by American chefs, for untainted product. We call these "day boat scallops," which means the fishermen go out for a single day, returning to market with untreated fresh shellfish. You can identify a day boat scallop by its ivory and coral color. Bleached scallops are very white. Also, ask your fishmonger to remove the side muscle of the scallop; this will save you valuable minutes in the kitchen.

Pastina Risotto
with English Peas, Prosciutto Bits, *and* Carrot Broth

Pastina, delicious little pellets of pasta, is a year-round favorite at Tra Vigne, and it seems we never get tired of creating new dishes for it. Risotto made with rice can seem too heavy in hotter weather, so we adapted the technique and applied it to pastina for a lighter-tasting dish. We are using vegetable juices as sauces more and more at the restaurant. They add bright, jewel-like colors and natural sweetness, giving dishes an extra dimension of whimsy and flavor.

Serves 4

4 cups chicken stock (page 204)
    or canned low-salt chicken broth
2 tablespoons extra-virgin olive oil
1 tablespoon minced garlic
¾ cup finely chopped onion
Salt
¾ pound dried pastina, orzo, riso, or stelline
Freshly ground pepper
1½ cups shelled English peas
    (about 1¼ pounds unshelled)
2 tablespoons unsalted butter
1½ teaspoons finely chopped fresh oregano
1½ teaspoons finely chopped fresh thyme
¾ cup freshly grated Parmesan cheese
¼ cup Prosciutto Bits (page 192), or about 4 slices
    bacon, cooked until very crisp, well drained,
    and minced
½ cup fresh carrot juice

Bring the stock to a low simmer in a saucepan. Heat the olive oil in a large saucepan over medium-high heat until hot. Add the garlic and cook briefly until light brown. Add the onion and a pinch of salt, lower the heat to medium, and cook until the onion is soft but not brown, about 2 to 3 minutes. Add 2 cups of the stock and bring to a boil. Add the pastina, stir well, and reduce the heat to maintain a slow simmer. Season with salt and pepper.

Simmer, adding the stock ½ cup at a time as the previous addition is absorbed and stirring occasionally to prevent the pastina from sticking to the bottom of the pan, until the pasta is about three-fourths done, about 10 minutes. Add the peas and the remaining stock and cook until the peas are tender and the pasta is al dente, about 3 minutes. Remove from the heat and add 1 tablespoon of the butter, the oregano, thyme, Parmesan, and 3 tablespoons of the prosciutto bits. Stir well. The consistency should be quite loose, like a thick soup.

During the last few minutes of cooking, warm the carrot juice in a small pan over medium heat. Do not allow it to get too hot or solids will form. Whisk in the remaining 1 tablespoon butter until just melted.

To serve, pour about 2 tablespoons carrot juice onto each of 4 warmed dinner plates. Spoon the pastina into the center of the plates, garnish with a light sprinkling of the remaining prosciutto bits, and serve immediately.

CHEF'S NOTE: *Plates are better than soup bowls or rimmed soup plates here, because they allow the carrot juice to spread out around the pastina.*

Pasta *with* Fresh Fava Bean Sauce

This is a version of a sauce I learned while visiting my mother's hometown in Calabria. When I asked what was in it, the reply was a shrug. No one could understand why I was curious about a sauce of fresh fava beans, pasta water, and salt. Yet it has a delicious, delicate flavor, and I put it on the menu as soon as I returned home. We like to serve it with a thick, hand-cut noodle. It is also a terrific sauce for fish.

Serves 4

2 tablespoons extra-virgin olive oil

1½ teaspoons minced garlic

1 tablespoon finely chopped fresh oregano

1½ cups chicken stock (page 204)
 or canned low-salt chicken broth

Salt and freshly ground pepper

2 cups cooked, peeled fava beans (page 28)

¾ pound dried fettuccine

½ cup freshly grated pecorino cheese
 or Parmesan cheese

Heat the olive oil in a medium saucepan over medium-high heat until hot. Add the garlic and sauté briefly until light brown. Stir in the oregano, then add 1 cup of the stock. Bring to a boil, season with salt and pepper, and add 1½ cups of the fava beans. Simmer to blend the flavors, about 3 minutes.

Scrape into a blender container and puree with the remaining ½ cup stock until smooth. Return the sauce to the pan and add the remaining ½ cup favas. Simmer gently and taste for seasoning. Add salt and especially pepper.

Meanwhile, bring a large pot of water to a boil and add salt. Add the pasta and cook until al dente, about 12 minutes. Drain, reserving about ½ cup of the pasta cooking water. Pour the pasta into a warm serving bowl and add the sauce. Toss well and thin with the pasta water, if necessary, until the sauce is glossy and not sticky. Serve immediately and pass the cheese at the table.

Barely Smoked Salmon *with* Pea *and* Potato Salad

1 to 1¼ pounds thick salmon fillet, skin intact,
    cut into 4 equal pieces (4 to 5 ounces
    per serving)
Salt
Extra-virgin olive oil for brushing on grill
    and salmon, plus ½ cup (see Chef's Notes)
Soaked wood chips for smoking
2 cups diced potatoes, peeled if desired
    (½-inch dice)

2 cups shelled English peas
    (about 1¾ pounds unshelled)
1 tablespoon Dijon mustard
2 tablespoons tarragon vinegar
    or champagne vinegar
1½ teaspoons coarsely chopped fresh tarragon
    (if using champagne vinegar)
Freshly ground pepper
2 tablespoons finely chopped fresh chives
4 large handfuls salad greens

We smoke all sorts of things at Tra Vigne—salmon, lobster, prawns, and even cooked beans. It is definitely not difficult to smoke at home. All you need is a covered grill and some wet wood chips. Maintaining a low, even temperature, about 300°F, retains moisture. At the restaurant, we have developed techniques that allow us to serve dishes efficiently without compromising quality. This salmon dish is a good example, making it a great candidate for a summer party. The individual elements—salmon, vinaigrette, and pea and potato salad—can all be made ahead, leaving only the assembly to do at serving time.

Serves 4

Prepare the grill and let it burn down to medium coals. Leave the coals piled in the center of the grate. Sprinkle the salmon all over with salt and let rest for about 25 minutes. Rinse and pat dry with paper towels. Brush with olive oil.

Add a handful of soaked chips to the coals, oil the grill rack, if necessary, and place the salmon, skin side down, on the grill toward the outside of the coals. Cover the grill and cook, without turning, until the salmon is opaque through, about 20 minutes (for 1 1/2-inch-thick fillets).

Meanwhile, put the potatoes in a pot of cold salted water and bring to a boil. Cook until tender, about 5 minutes. Lift out with a slotted spoon and spread on a baking sheet to cool. Return the water to a boil, add the peas, and cook just until bright green and tender, about 3 minutes. Drain well and scatter on the baking sheet with the potatoes to cool.

In a small bowl, whisk together the mustard, vinegar, the tarragon, if using, and salt and pepper to taste. Pour in the 1/2 cup olive oil while whisking to form an emulsion.

Put the peas and potatoes in a large bowl and add about 1/4 cup of the vinaigrette. Toss and taste for seasoning. Add more of the vinaigrette, if needed. Toss well with 1 tablespoon of the chives and divide among 4 plates. Pull the skin off each piece of salmon (reserve, if desired), then place on top of the salads. Dress the greens with another tablespoon of the vinaigrette and arrange around the salmon. Stand the salmon skin against the side of the salmon as a garnish, if desired. Sprinkle the salads with the remaining 1 tablespoon chives.

CHEF'S NOTES: *A lightly flavored olive oil, such as a Spanish or French one, is better here than a Tuscan or other strongly flavored olive oil. I do not mean the so-called light olive oils in supermarkets, especially blended to have little or no flavor at all.*

Find out your preferred balance for vinaigrettes. I like to use a ratio of about ten parts oil to one part vinegar for a dinner when the wine is a star, and four parts oil to one part vinegar for "all-purpose" vinaigrettes, such as this one. If you like a more pronounced acidity, do not be afraid to decrease the ratio to equal amounts oil and vinegar.

You could also serve this dish as a mixed salad by shredding the salmon into the pea salad and then tossing with the greens.

potatoes

Potatoes, the soul of comfort food, in spring? I might be rushing the season a bit, but I like very fresh potatoes. In storage, their natural sugars turn to starch. They also lose moisture and flavor. If you take a laid-back attitude to the potato season, you may miss it; when testing recipes for this book, the vegetable I was most worried about missing at its best was the potato. ❧ I divide the year into eight seasons, with four short "bridge" seasons spanning the widely recognized ones. For instance, chives flourish in the bridge season between winter and spring, while potatoes, for me, exemplify the season between spring and summer. New potatoes—freshly dug potatoes of any variety—begin to arrive in early June. Pounce on them, no matter whether it is late spring or early summer. To get your hands on them, you must either grow them, haunt farmers' markets, or find a very good produce market. In European markets, you often see shoppers sorting through bins of potatoes for the smallest ones they can find. These are addictive when roasted whole with salt and pepper, generous splashes of extra-virgin olive oil (and goose or duck fat, if you happen to have it on hand), and rosemary sprigs. ❧ I'm crazy about potatoes. They are almost nutritionally complete, can be dressed up or down, change their character from spring to fall, and come in many colors, shapes, and sizes. Try all the varieties you find in your market. Thankfully, your choices are expanding beyond the familiar russets and red potatoes. You will also find Yukon Golds, Yellow Finns, and maybe even a Purple Peruvian. Don't worry too much about whether a variety is better suited for boiling or roasting. With a good potato, you can't make bad food.

patate

Potato Soup
with Warm Clam Salad

For the soup

3 tablespoons extra-virgin olive oil

$1/2$ cup diced onion ($1/4$-inch dice)

$1/2$ cup diced leek ($1/4$-inch dice)

$1/4$ cup diced celery ($1/4$-inch dice)

1 teaspoon minced garlic

1 bay leaf

Salt and freshly ground pepper

3 cups chicken stock (page 204)
   or canned low-salt chicken broth

1 pound russet potatoes, peeled
   and cut into large chunks

$1 1/2$ teaspoons finely chopped fresh oregano

Dash Tabasco sauce

$1/2$ cup diced new or fingerling potatoes
   ($1/4$-inch dice)

$1/2$ cup heavy cream

For the warm clam salad

1 tablespoon extra-virgin olive oil

1 tablespoon slivered garlic

$1/2$ cup dry white wine

1 pound Manila or other small clams
   in shells, scrubbed

Salt and freshly ground pepper

2 tablespoons finely chopped fresh
   flat-leaf parsley

1 cup packed coarsely chopped arugula
   or watercress

Potato Focaccia

Focaccia is a daily item on our Cantinetta menu. Serve this potato focaccia with
Potato Soup with Warm Clam Salad (page 38). The focaccia looks pretty
with sliced potatoes on top, but the slices slip and fall off and I hate chasing
my food around. The recipe may be doubled.

Makes about 1 1/4 pounds dough, serves 6

For the dough

1 envelope active dry yeast

1 1/2 teaspoons sugar

1 cup lukewarm whole milk

About 2 1/4 cups all-purpose flour,
    plus more for dusting work surface

2 tablespoons extra-virgin olive oil,
    plus more for oiling bowl and baking sheet

3/4 teaspoon gray salt or kosher salt

For the topping

3/4 cup diced pancetta or bacon
    (1/2-inch dice; about 1/4 pound)

1 tablespoon extra-virgin olive oil

1 1/2 cups diced new or russet potatoes
    (1/2-inch dice; about 1/2 pound)

2 teaspoons finely chopped fresh rosemary

Gray salt or kosher salt and freshly ground pepper

1 teaspoon freshly grated lemon zest

Combine the yeast, sugar, and milk in the bowl of a stand mixer. Add 1/2 cup of the flour. Stir well, cover with a tea towel, and let rest in a warm place for about 25 minutes.

With the dough hook, mix in 1 tablespoon of the olive oil, the salt, and 1 cup of the flour. Knead until well incorporated. Add the remaining flour, 1/4 cup at a time, until the dough adheres to the hook. It should remain soft and slightly sticky. Knead until the dough is smooth and elastic, about 6 minutes.

Shape the dough into a ball, flatten slightly, and put into an oiled bowl. Turn to coat. Cover the bowl with a tea towel and put in a warm place to let the dough rise until doubled in bulk, about 1 hour.

Heat the pancetta and olive oil in a skillet over medium heat. Cook slowly until crisp. Tilt the pan to collect the fat against the side and scrape the pancetta into the fat. Cook for another minute to make sure the pancetta is very crisp. Remove to paper towels to drain. Reserve the pancetta and fat separately.

Put the potatoes in cold salted water to cover and bring to a boil over high heat. Cook until tender, about 8 minutes. Drain well and put in a bowl. Pour the pancetta fat over the warm potatoes, add the crisped pancetta, 1 teaspoon of the rosemary, salt and pepper to taste, and the lemon zest. Toss well and set aside.

Preheat the oven to 375°F. Oil a baking sheet with olive oil.

Lightly flour the dough and punch it down. Turn it out onto a lightly floured surface and knead lightly until smooth. (The dough may be wrapped well at this point, and frozen for up to 1 month.)

Roll out the dough into a rectangle about 12 by 10 inches. Brush off any excess flour and transfer to the prepared baking pan. Brush the dough with 1 tablespoon olive oil and leave to rise for 30 minutes.

Sprinkle the potato mixture onto the dough and press it in with the flat of your hand. Press your stiff fingers into the dough to make evenly spaced indentations all over the surface, being careful not to puncture or tear the dough. Scatter the remaining teaspoon rosemary over the dough.

Bake until the potatoes are golden brown and the bread is crisp on the bottom, about 25 minutes. Let cool in the pan to room temperature. Cut into squares, "fingers," or triangles to serve.

Polpette *of* Potato *with* Avocado, Red Onion, *and* Cucumber Salad

1 ½ pounds russet potatoes, peeled
   and cut into large chunks

½ red onion

½ cup cider vinegar

½ teaspoon dried oregano

Salt and freshly ground pepper

2 ounces fresh mozzarella cheese,
   cut into 4 equal pieces

2 tablespoons plus ½ cup olive oil

1 large cucumber, peeled, halved,
   seeded, and cut on the diagonal into
   ¼-inch-thick crescents

2 avocados, pitted, peeled,
   and cut into ½-inch dice

1 large, ripe tomato, cut into bite-sized chunks

½ small head iceberg lettuce, shredded

This dish is the creation of my wife, Ines. The mingling tastes and textures of cold, crisp, fresh salad and warm, soft, rich polpette—patties—are not be to beaten, nor forgotten either. In spring, we like polpette for supper on their own with salad and when summer rolls around, we make an all-tomato salad to accompany them. In winter, we serve them alongside pork chops, roasts, and chicken, and any time of year we like them at breakfast with an egg on top. Children love them, too; they like to cut them open and discover the warm, melting cheese inside.

Serves 4

Preheat the oven to 325°F. Put the potatoes in a large saucepan with cold salted water to cover and bring to a boil over high heat. Cook until tender, about 10 minutes. Drain well, scatter on a baking sheet, and let cool for several minutes. Place in the oven to dry out, about 5 minutes. Let cool, then press through a ricer, the large holes of a box grater, or a colander.

While the potatoes are in the oven, cut the onion half into quarters and slice thinly to yield slim pieces about 1 inch long. Put in a nonreactive bowl with the vinegar and oregano and let rest for 15 minutes.

Season the potatoes with salt and pepper, then divide into 8 equal balls. Place a ball in the palm of your hand, top with a piece of cheese, and then a second potato ball. Shape the potato around the cheese to form a 4-inch patty. Repeat with the remaining potato balls and cheese. (The recipe may be prepared to this point, covered, and refrigerated up to 1 day before cooking.)

Heat the 2 tablespoons olive oil in a nonstick skillet over medium heat or in an electric frying skillet set at 350°F. Add the polpette and cook, turning once, until brown and crispy on both sides, about 20 minutes total.

While the polpette are cooking, finish making the salad. Whisk the remaining ½ cup olive oil and salt and pepper to taste into the onion-vinegar mixture. Add the cucumber, avocados, and tomato and toss well.

Arrange a nest of lettuce on each of 4 plates. Spoon the salad over each nest. Top with a polpette and spoon more dressing over all. Serve at once.

CHEF'S NOTE: *You can flavor the potato mixture with a tablespoon of Fennel Spice (page 193), herbes de Provence, or red pepper flakes. Be careful when adding other flavorings, however; too much moisture or too large an amount of dried seasonings will make the polpette fall apart during cooking. If you have an electric skillet, use it for this recipe. Its even heat is terrific for cooking polpette. My mom had one and loved it, which is how I learned to use it.*

SUMMER

pietro rabbit

Mother Nature is in charge of when summer begins, not the calendar. From the first day of summer until early September, I have a tomato *panino* at ten o'clock every morning for my *colazione*, a traditional midmorning snack meant to carry me through until lunch at two. The sandwich is simply great bread, fragrant tomato, gray sea salt, and freshly ground black pepper. No oil. *Niente più*. The tomato isn't one of those miracles of scientific engineering but an old-fashioned tomato that grows on a vine in the good dirt of someone's garden or small field. This tomato has had a chance to soak up the sun and give it back in its aroma and flavor. ❧ Unfortunately, summer for many of us becomes more and more a phenomenon of the calendar and less and less the boisterous freedom of no school and days that last a lifetime. Eating seasonally can be a way to hang onto summer as a living event. ❧ Summer is not my favorite cooking season primarily because the challenge now is to stay simple. Anyone can cook with truffle oil and foie gras and create a dish that tastes good. For me, the best cook is the one who can make zucchini taste great, the one who will be true to its flavor and not overwhelm it. This is hard to do. The temptation is always to fuss too much, if only to show that, yes indeed, you can in fact cook. ❧ Wait for fall and winter to cook. Summer should not be about rushing around. As I look over the summer recipes, many of them are supper dishes meant to be eaten at ambient temperature with perhaps a glass of Sauvignon Blanc. This is casual food that can be cooked at four o'clock and eaten at eight o'clock. It will wait until the children who, like I did, disappear from the house early in the morning to return only at dusk. ❧ While there must have been traditional dishes we always ate in summer, I barely remember them. Instead I remember pure flavors, like Nonno Chiarello's cherries. He grafted his own fruit trees and had three or four cherry varieties on a single tree. Sitting in it, I could sample a cherry buffet. When out playing in the fields, my friends and I would turn watermelons over to expose their cool sides. Then we'd give them a good kick and grab big hunks of the heart. We ate green almonds before the nuts solidified, when they tasted like an almond Jell-O. ❧ The food and spirit at Tra Vigne takes on that same spontaneity. We throw open the French doors onto the dining patios. Our guests love to eat grilled figs wrapped in prosciutto on the brick patio cooled by the dappled shade of the mulberry trees and the light splashing off the central fountain. At this time of year more than any other, it is the job of the cook to let the ingredients speak for themselves. I had to cook complicated dishes for years before I had the courage to serve Simply Tomatoes, a salad of thinly sliced tomatoes with little adornment. ❧ Whenever I eat corn, I remember how, as the corn ripened, my boyhood friends and I would keep our eyes out for city slickers who stopped their cars by the side of a cornfield and helped themselves to a bagful. Only that evening when they cooked it would they learn it was silage, cow corn. We knew, of course having learned the hard way, that the farmers hid the sweet corn deep within the cow corn, and we made it our job to find those few rows. We ate it right there in the field. It was our own version of Peter Rabbit and Farmer MacGregor.

corn

Summer begins for me when the corn and tomatoes ripen in the garden. I prefer old-fashioned yellow corn for its real corn flavor to the new hybrid corn that I find overly sweet. I like corn that tastes sweetest eaten in the field, the kind with sugars that start turning to starch the minute it is picked, corn that needs to be cooked the day, if not the hour, it is harvested. The new hybrids are convenient; the corn stays sweet and tender for several days after bringing it home. Unfortunately, they have enjoyed such success—they make farmers' jobs much easier since the corn does not deteriorate as quickly—that they are squeezing yellow varieties such as Golden Bantam out of the marketplace. If you, like me, prefer corn-tasting corn, tell growers at farmers' markets and produce buyers at your supermarket. ❧ When choosing corn, feel the cobs to make sure the rows are plump and full. The husks should be green and moist and the corn silk tassel a light brown. The only reason to worry about worms is whether they have eaten more of the ear than you are willing to share. If you find any, just flick them off and trim the ear. ❧ Some grocery stores install big garbage cans next to their displays of corn on the cob. If you plan to cook the corn that day, husk your corn there and forgo the mess at home. If your store does not do this, suggest it and the can might be there the next time you shop. To store corn for succeeding days, refrigerate it, unhusked, in a plastic bag. ❧ If corn is freshly harvested and at its peak, there is no need to cook it. I love to make dishes with raw corn such as the Raw Corn, Arugula, and Pecorino Salad on page 49. Take a small bite from a raw ear, and if the corn is a little chewy, blanch it for a few minutes in boiling salted water before using it in a recipe. ❧ Since summer is barbecue season, you might want to get in the habit of grilling corn. I simply husk it, season it, and put it on the grill, to the edge of the fire where it is not too hot. Grilling gives the corn a wonderful flavor for eating off the cob or for making salsas (page 50), salads, or for adding to polenta, pasta, and risotto.

CUTTING KERNELS FROM COBS To cut corn kernels off the cob, set the butt end of the cob in a large, deep bowl. Using a sharp knife, cut downward close to the surface of the cob, traveling its length. Rotate the cob after each pass with the knife. Kernels and corn juice tend to fly and squirt. The bowl will keep things somewhat contained. I find it helpful to set the bowl in the sink. The lower height makes it easier to cut down to the bottom of the cob. One full ten-inch ear yields about ¾ cup kernels.

granturco

Raw Corn, Arugula, *and* Pecorino Salad *with* Grilled Chicken Breast

Tra Vigne opened in the summer of 1987. This salad was on that opening menu. It makes a perfect summer supper—simple, cool, and fullflavored. Undeniably delicious.

Serves 4

2 bone-in whole chicken breasts, halved
Extra-virgin olive oil
Salt and freshly ground pepper
2 cups absolutely fresh corn kernels (about 3 ears)
3 cups packed arugula
1 1/2 teaspoons coarsely chopped fresh oregano
About 1/2 cup Whole Citrus Vinaigrette (page 143)
1 1/2 ounces pecorino cheese

Prepare the grill and let it burn down to medium-hot coals. Brush the chicken breasts on both sides with olive oil and season well with salt and pepper. Grill over the coals, skin side down, until well browned, about 2 minutes. Move to the edge of the grill, away from direct heat, cover the grill loosely, and cook, turning once or twice, until opaque throughout, about 20 minutes.

While the chicken is cooking, make the salad. Combine the corn kernels, arugula, and oregano in a bowl. Add the vinaigrette, toss, and season with salt and pepper. With a vegetable peeler, shave the cheese onto the salad. Toss lightly.

To serve, arrange the chicken breasts on plates and pile the salad alongside.

Variation for Roasted Chicken Breast: If you don't want to light the grill, season the chicken well with salt and pepper and brown in olive oil over medium-high heat. Finish cooking in a hot oven.

Grilled Corn Salsa

We like to do this kind of cooking at Tra Vigne, using a technique such as grilling to intensify and add surprising new dimensions to flavors. Once the coals have burned down, most of the work for this dish has been done. It's so simple, it can easily be assembled amid the tumult of family gatherings. Grill some crusty bread as well and serve the salsa on it as a first course. Or use the salsa as a bed for fish, squab, grilled lamb chops, or chicken. It also makes a great pasta salad tossed with small pasta shapes such as shells or riso. To make ahead, grill and dice ingredients, then mix together just before serving.

Serves 4

½ cup diced red onion (¼-inch dice)
2 tablespoons red wine vinegar, or more to taste
5 large ears corn, husked
Extra-virgin olive oil
Salt and freshly ground pepper
4 large vine-ripened tomatoes, about 1 pound total
¼ cup julienned fresh basil

Prepare the grill and let it burn down to medium coals.

Put the onions in a nonreactive medium bowl and toss with the 2 tablespoons of vinegar. Let marinate until the color changes, about 10 minutes.

Brush the corn liberally with olive oil and season well with salt and pepper. Grill, turning every few minutes, until light gold all over and cooked, about 12 minutes. Let cool and cut off the kernels. Discard the cobs. Add the corn to the onions.

Core the tomatoes and cut a small X on the bottom of each. Brush with olive oil, season with salt and pepper, and place on the grill, X side down, away from direct heat. Cover the grill and cook until the tomatoes begin to soften but are not cooked all the way through (or they will melt through the grate!), about 15 minutes. Set aside until cool enough to handle, then peel. Cut the tomatoes in half crosswise and squeeze out the juice and the seeds through a sieve into a bowl. Reserve the juices and chop the flesh.

Add the chopped tomatoes, reserved tomato juice, and basil to the corn. Toss well. Taste for seasoning and adjust with salt, pepper, and more vinegar, if necessary. The salsa is best eaten the same day but will keep, covered and refrigerated, a day or so.

Corn Pasta *with* Dried Tomatoes

Fresh corn and pasta make a great combination. When you add dried tomatoes and toasted garlic, you get an intensity of flavors that belies the simplicity of the cooking.

Serves 4

⅓ cup dried tomatoes, not packed in oil
(see Chef's Note)
3 tablespoons boiling water
1½ teaspoons sugar
1½ tablespoons balsamic vinegar
1 teaspoon plus 1 tablespoon finely chopped
fresh marjoram
¾ pound dried capellini
3 tablespoons extra-virgin olive oil
2 tablespoons minced garlic
2 cups corn kernels (about 3 ears)
Salt and freshly ground pepper
½ cup freshly grated Parmesan cheese
1½ tablespoons finely chopped fresh
flat-leaf parsley

CHEF'S NOTE: *You can substitute ½ cup drained, oil-packed dried tomatoes or Oven-Dried Tomatoes (page 199) and omit the rehydration step.*

Mix the dried tomatoes in a small bowl with the boiling water, sugar, vinegar, and the 1 teaspoon marjoram. Let rehydrate until soft, about 20 minutes. Drain well, squeezing out excess liquid. Cut the tomatoes into fine julienne and set aside. Discard marinade.

Bring a large pot of water to a boil and add salt. Add the pasta and cook until al dente, about 8 minutes.

While the pasta is cooking, make the sauce: Heat the olive oil in a large sauté pan over medium-high heat until hot. Add the garlic and sauté briefly until light brown. Add the remaining 1 tablespoon marjoram, the corn, and about 1 cup of the pasta cooking water. Cook, uncovered, until the corn is just tender, about 2 minutes. Season with salt and pepper.

When the pasta is cooked, drain, reserving about ½ cup of the pasta cooking water. Add the pasta to the sauté pan with the corn. Add the tomatoes, half of the Parmesan, and 1 tablespoon of the parsley and toss well. Toss with some of the reserved cooking water, if necessary, to moisten.

Pour the pasta into a warmed serving bowl, dust with a little Parmesan, and scatter the remaining parsley on top. Pass the remaining Parmesan at the table.

Halibut *and* Corn Salad
with "Broken" Tomato Vinaigrette

3 large vine-ripened tomatoes

²/₃ cup extra-virgin olive oil

1 teaspoon minced garlic

1 tablespoon freshly squeezed lemon juice

Salt and freshly ground pepper

2 large ears corn, shucked

1 cup shelled lima beans, fava beans,
 or other fresh shelling beans

2 tablespoons champagne vinegar

1 tablespoon finely chopped fresh tarragon

¼ cup Prosciutto Bits, recrisped (page 192)
 or about 4 slices bacon, cooked until very crisp,
 well drained, and minced

4 halibut fillets, about 5 ounces each, or other
 firm-fleshed, meaty fish such as swordfish

This is another of those dishes built of parts that can be enjoyed separately or together: grilled fish, a vegetable salad, and the big accent flavor of a vinaigrette made from reduced fresh tomato juice and olive oil. In about 1992, we began experimenting to create the intensely flavored dressings we call "broken" vinaigrettes, which take their name from the fact that they are purposely not emulsified. Instead, we lightly shake reduced fruit or vegetable juices with a complementary flavored oil. The colored drops of juice glisten within the olive oil. When they are shaken onto a salad or a plate, they create a striking pattern of contrasting colors and set up the same vibrant contrast in your mouth. Try this tomato vinaigrette on meat or sliced tomatoes. You can make broken vinaigrettes with beets and carrots by following the same process outlined here for tomatoes.

Serves 4

Core the tomatoes, cut into pieces, and place in a blender. Blend until pureed. Strain through a sieve into a bowl. You should have about 1 1/2 cups puree.

Heat 1 tablespoon of the olive oil in a nonreactive medium saucepan until hot. Add the garlic and sauté briefly until light brown. Add the tomato puree and bring to a boil. Simmer gently about 5 minutes. Strain through a fine-mesh sieve into a bowl. Discard the solids. Rinse out the saucepan, return the tomato juice to the pan, and bring to a boil. Simmer and strain twice more until the tomato juice is as thick as heavy cream, about 15 minutes' total cooking time. Be sure to lower the heat as the mixture thickens to prevent scorching. You should have about 1/4 cup of very smooth tomato juice. Add 1 tablespoon lemon juice and taste for salt and pepper.

Pour 1 tablespoon of the olive oil into a small, clean glass bottle with a stopper and swirl to coat the inside. Strain the tomato juice into the bottle. Let it cool to room temperature. Add 2 tablespoons of the olive oil. Do not shake or mix!

Bring a large pot of water to a boil and add salt. Add the corn and cook just until tender, about 3 minutes. Remove and set aside. Cook the beans in the same water just until tender, about 3 minutes. Drain. If using favas, peel them. When the corn is cool enough to handle, cut the kernels from the cobs. Toss together in a bowl.

In a clean jar with a lid, shake together the vinegar, tarragon, 3 tablespoons of the prosciutto bits, and 6 tablespoons of the olive oil. Pour enough of the dressing onto the corn and beans to coat, toss well, and taste for seasoning.

Adjust with salt, pepper, and more dressing as necessary. Set aside to marinate for about 15 minutes.

Season the fish on both sides with salt and pepper. Heat the remaining 2 tablespoons olive oil in a large sauté pan over medium-high heat until hot. Add the fish and cook until brown on the first side, about 3 minutes. Turn and continue to cook until opaque throughout, about 3 minutes longer. Remove from the pan and keep warm.

When ready to serve, pile the corn mixture on a platter or divide among 4 large plates. Arrange the fish on top of the salads. Shake the tomato vinaigrette bottle gently. You do not want the mixture to emulsify, but to have separate droplets suspended within the oil. Spoon or shake about 1 tablespoon of the "broken" tomato vinaigrette on each piece of halibut and then drizzle or shake more tomato vinaigrette around the edges of the platter or plates. Garnish with the remaining prosciutto bits.

CHEF'S NOTE: *You may vary the flavor of your tomato vinaigrette by using flavored oils (see Glossary), especially a spicy one such as Five Pepper Oil.*

tomatoes

My eldest daughter, Margaux, has loved tomatoes since she was small. One day when she was about six, she came inside, tomato juice and seeds on her chin, and announced, "Wow, Pop, you can taste the smell!" That is why I believe it is so important never to refrigerate or even wash a garden-ripe tomato. If you do, you will no longer be able to "taste the smell." ❧ Summer tomato recipes should be simple. Since the first frosts of last fall, you have avoided tasteless, anemic off-season tomatoes and waited for the return of bursting-ripe fruits to your garden and to farmers' markets. These tomatoes need no adornment. ❧ Employ the many colors, shapes, and varieties available to add drama to your presentations and a complex flavor to your dishes. For instance, make a tomato salad by combining the sugary sweetness of striped green tomatoes, the sweet-acid tang of Sweet 100 cherry tomatoes, and the low-acid round flavors of yellow tomatoes. ❧ Ripe tomatoes should feel firm and juicy at the same time, have smooth and unblemished skins, and smell of ripe fruit. I have noticed some "vine-ripened" tomatoes with a terrific aroma but surprisingly little flavor. Their aroma had the green snappiness of the tomato vine, not the juicy sweetness of the fruit. Don't be seduced! ❧ I prefer to cook with regular round tomatoes of a high-acid variety. The acid gives the tomato flavor its zip. When I cook with canned tomatoes (yes, I do, off-season), I use an organic brand, Muir Glen or S&W's Ready-Cut tomatoes. I also like canned plum (Roma) tomatoes because they have such a high proportion of flesh to juice.

CORING TOMATOES Many cooks take a small knife and saw around the core. Instead, hold the tomato in your left hand (if right-handed) and insert the point of a small, sharp paring knife into the tomato next to the core. Then twist the tomato with your left hand while holding the right hand steady. It's a small thing, but if you are coring a lot of tomatoes you will save yourself time and energy.

PEELING, SEEDING, AND CHOPPING TOMATOES Core the tomatoes. If very ripe and from the garden, sometimes the skin will just peel off when pulled with a sharp knife. Otherwise, cut a shallow cross in the bottom and blanch briefly, about 15 seconds, in boiling water. Drain and let stand until cool enough to handle. Working from the cross, pull off the skin with a sharp knife. Cut the tomatoes in half horizontally. Then, working over a sieve suspended over a bowl, squeeze the tomato halves to rid them of juice and seeds, easing out the seed sacs with the tip of your finger. Lay the seeded tomatoes on a chopping board and roughly chop with a large, sharp nonreactive knife. Pour the juices from the chopping block into the bowl with the rest of the juice. Reserve the juices, if you like, to use in tomato sauce or the "broken" tomato vinaigrette on page 52, or to add to soups and sauces. They can be used as is or reduced until thick. One 6-ounce tomato yields about $\frac{1}{3}$ cup peeled, seeded, and chopped tomato.

pomodori

Simply Tomatoes

This recipe is embarrassingly simple and sublimely good. To make it you want seasonal tomatoes ripened on the plant, grown in dirt outdoors in the sun. This is also the time to use that forty-dollar bottle of olive oil you could not resist buying after you tasted it. In my opinion, the best salt is gray salt from Brittany with its clean marine flavor. Go all out and use two drops of the fabulously expensive and worth-every-penny *aceto balsamico traditionale*. You could also use flavored olive oils for the sake of variety. What herb you use depends on what is readily available and what else is being served. I like to use the wild fennel that grows in the Napa Valley all summer. Choose tomatoes of various colors, or use all red but vary the size, and then cut them into different shapes—slices, wedges, halves. Make sure to serve the salad with crusty bread to soak up the juices.

Serves 4

2 large vine-ripened tomatoes
4 small vine-ripened tomatoes
1 pint cherry tomatoes
Gray salt and freshly ground pepper
About 2 tablespoons extra-virgin olive oil
Aceto balsamico traditionale
    or other high-quality vinegar
Several small sprigs of fresh basil, oregano,
    flat-leaf parsley, and/or chervil (optional)

Cut large round tomatoes horizontally into $1/2$-inch-thick "steaks." Cut medium and small round tomatoes into wedges and cut cherry tomatoes, unless very small, in half. Arrange on a platter or 4 plates and season with gray salt and pepper to taste. Drizzle with the olive oil and sprinkle with a little vinegar to taste. Do not refrigerate. The tomatoes taste best at room temperature. Garnish with small herb sprigs, if using.

Grilled Avocado *and* Tomato Salad *with* Basil Pesto

Grilled avocado is one of my favorite flavors. Try a grilled-avocado guacamole—you can add even more flavor by putting a handful of soaked chips in the fire, covering the grill, and lightly smoking the avocados. Add some arugula and this salad makes a great sandwich or piadina filling.

Serves 4

Juice of 2 lemons

2 large, firm, ripe avocados

½ medium red onion, thinly sliced

Salt and freshly ground pepper

1 pound vine-ripened tomatoes, preferably several
   varieties of different shapes and colors

About 3 tablespoons extra-virgin olive oil

4 teaspoons Basil Pesto (page 200),
   made without pine nuts

Parmesan cheese

1 tablespoon pine nuts, toasted (optional)

Prepare the grill and let it burn down to medium-hot coals. Squeeze the lemon juice into a nonreactive bowl large enough to hold the avocados in a single layer. Halve the avocados, discard the pits, and scoop out the flesh in one piece with a rounded spoon. Immediately toss the avocados with the lemon juice to prevent discoloration.

Separate the onion into rings and place in another bowl. Pour some of the lemon juice from the avocados over the onions and season with salt and pepper. Toss well and set aside. Cut the tomatoes lengthwise into thin wedges, season with salt and pepper, and reserve.

Remove the avocados from the lemon juice and set the bowl aside. Season the avocados on all sides with salt and pepper and drizzle very lightly with about 1 tablespoon of the olive oil. Too much and the oil might cause flare-ups.

Grill the avocados, cut side down, until the outside edge looks a little dry and browned, about 2 minutes. Turn onto the rounded side and cook for another 2 minutes. Since so little area is exposed to the heat, this is just to soften, not cook, the avocados. If the avocados were very firm, leave on another minute. Do not turn too often or they may disintegrate. Return the grilled avocados to the bowl with the lemon juice. Spoon the lemon juice over them and set aside until cool enough to handle, then cut into thin wedges.

Place several onion rings in the center of each salad plate. Arrange the avocados on opposite sides and the tomatoes on the remaining two sides. Drizzle each salad with about 1½ teaspoons olive oil and 1 teaspoon pesto. Season again with salt and pepper to taste and give each salad a coarse grating of cheese. Scatter the pine nuts on top, if using, and serve immediately.

CHEF'S NOTE: *These directions are for a plated salad. These same ingredients can be used to make a layered salad in a bowl. Cut the avocados and tomatoes into large, equal-size pieces and layer in a bowl with the onion rings, seasoning and drizzling with olive oil and pesto as you layer.*

Spiedini *of* Fresh Mozzarella *and* Tomatoes

About ¹/₂ pound fresh mozzarella cheese

4 vine-ripened tomatoes, preferably different colors
  such as red and yellow

Salt and freshly ground pepper

¹/₄ cup loosely packed fresh basil leaves

1 cup Tomato Confit or Oven-Dried Tomatoes (page 199)

We have served variations on this dish at Tra Vigne for many years. We make fresh mozzarella several times a day, so it is still warm and moist when it goes to the table. We have served the spiedini with a "broken" vinaigrette of basil oil and balsamic vinegar reduced to a syrupy consistency. Recently, we started forming small mozzarella balls around ripe, deeply colored small tomatoes. When we cut the balls in half, they look like eggs but with red yolks. In the fall, we serve this dish with roasted red and yellow peppers instead of fresh tomatoes. For presentation, we often grill the skewers to give them grill marks, but you can omit this step or try toasting them in a toaster oven.

Serves 4

Cut the mozzarella balls in half and then into half-moon slices. Choose tomatoes the same size as the mozzarella balls and slice in the same manner. Season the cheese and tomatoes on both sides with salt and pepper. Divide the cheese and tomatoes into 4 equal portions, and set them on edge, rounded sides up, alternating wedges of tomato and cheese. Tuck the basil leaves between the slices. Fasten each portion with two skewers, running them straight from front to back or crossing them to form an X.

To serve, arrange the skewers on a platter or 4 plates. Spoon the confit around the skewers.

Tomato Carpaccio *with* Panzanella

At home, there is usually not a written menu. At the restaurant, our menu must create a picture—and hopefully, a delicious expectation in the diner. Abracadabra, and thinly sliced tomatoes turn into tomato carpaccio. It makes a great base for just about any dish, especially fish, or you can pile the slices into a mold, seasoning as you go. Use tomatoes of different colors and layer them with thin orange slices and you have the new tomato tart from Tra Vigne's Cantinetta. The panzanella of croutons and tomato sauce can be enjoyed as a cold soup, as it is traditionally served in Italy, or as a salad, its more common role in the United States.

Serves 4

About ½ loaf good, crusty bread

2 tablespoons unsalted butter

1 tablespoon minced garlic

1 tablespoon finely chopped fresh sage

Salt and freshly ground pepper

2 large vine-ripened tomatoes, preferably
     of different varieties and/or colors

1½ cups Summer Tomato Sauce (page 199),
     made without jalapeños, cold

1 tablespoon freshly grated Parmesan cheese

2 cups arugula

About 1 tablespoon Whole Citrus Vinaigrette
     (page 143) or vinaigrette of choice

About 1 ounce ricotta salata cheese

Preheat the oven to 375°F. Remove the crusts from the bread, but it is not important to be perfect about it. Slice the bread, then cut into ¼-inch cubes until you have about 3 cups. In a medium skillet, heat the butter over medium heat until melted and lightly browned. Add the garlic and sauté briefly until light brown. Add the sage, bread cubes, and salt and pepper to taste and toss well. Scatter on a baking sheet. They should be in a fairly tight single layer. If they are too loose, they will cook too rapidly and dry out. Bake, stirring several times, until crisp on the outside but still chewy inside, about 10 minutes. (The croutons can be made a day or so ahead of time and stored in an airtight container at room temperature.)

Slice the tomatoes as thinly as possible and arrange in overlapping circles on each of 4 plates. Season with salt and pepper. Just before serving, in a nonreactive bowl, mix the croutons with the tomato sauce and Parmesan. Do not mix ahead of time or the bread will get soggy. Pack about one-fourth of the tomato mixture into an individual 3-inch mold, such as a tea cup or tart pan, and unmold onto one of the prepared plates. Repeat with the remaining mixture.

Place the arugula in a bowl, add the vinaigrette and salt and pepper to taste, and toss to coat evenly. Arrange the arugula on top of each portion of the tomato mixture.

With a vegetable peeler, shave the ricotta salata evenly over the tops of the salads. Serve immediately.

Rigatoni *with* Spicy Grilled Tomato Sauce

This sauce has a wonderful smoky, spicy flavor and an unexpected richness. Flavoring tomato sauce with cheese takes me back to my childhood. Mom would warm a piece of provolone in her tomato sauce. She fished it out as it became softened, diced it, then tossed it with the cooked pasta and sauce. I like to do the same with fresh mozzarella, and I particularly love to contrast the pungent tang of Gorgonzola with the juicy, sunny flavor of garden tomatoes. A sauce like this needs no Parmesan.

Serves 4

3 pounds vine-ripened tomatoes

1 large red bell pepper

2 jalapeño chilies

3 to 4 tablespoons extra-virgin olive oil

Salt and freshly ground pepper

1 cup minced onion

1 tablespoon minced garlic

1 tablespoon finely chopped fresh oregano

2 tablespoons red wine vinegar

2 tablespoons Gorgonzola cheese

¾ pound dried rigatoni

2 tablespoons finely chopped fresh flat-leaf parsley

Prepare the grill and let it burn down to medium coals. Core the tomatoes and cut an X through the skin on the bottom of each. In a bowl, toss the tomatoes, bell pepper, and chilies with 1 to 2 tablespoons of the olive oil; season with salt and pepper. Secure the jalapeños with metal or soaked wooden skewers so they won't fall through the grill grate. Place the tomatoes on the grill, X side down and away from direct heat, with the other vegetables. Cover the grill and cook, turning the bell pepper and chilies to char evenly all over, until the tomatoes have softened but are still firm enough to stand on their own and the bell pepper and chilies are blistered, about 15 minutes. Put the pepper and chilies in a bowl and cover to steam and loosen the skins. Let the tomatoes cool to room temperature.

Peel the grilled vegetables. Cut the tomatoes in half horizontally and squeeze out the seeds into a sieve suspended over a bowl to catch the juices. Finely chop the tomatoes. Return the tomato pulp and any juices from the chopping board to the bowl holding the tomato juices. Seed and derib the bell pepper and jalapeños. Cut the bell pepper into small dice. Mash the jalapeños and taste to determine their heat.

Heat the remaining 2 tablespoons olive oil in a large sauté pan over medium heat until hot. Add the onion, season with salt, and sauté until softened, about 2 minutes. Add the garlic and oregano and stir. Add the tomatoes and their juice and bring to a boil over high heat. Lower the heat to medium and simmer until thickened, about 10 minutes. Add the bell pepper and mashed jalapeño to taste and simmer for another minute. Add the vinegar and stir in the Gorgonzola. Season to taste with salt and pepper. Keep warm.

Meanwhile, bring a large pot of water to a boil and add salt. Add the pasta and cook until al dente, about 12 minutes. Drain and pour into a warm serving bowl. Pour the tomato sauce over the top and add the parsley. Toss well and serve immediately.

Pan Stew *of* Shellfish *and* Tomatoes

Warning! Once you have read this recipe, you can no longer use the excuse that you don't have time to cook. Line up the ingredients by the stove and, if measuring slows you down, just use your judgment. The butter is optional but well worth it. Feel free to double the recipe and serve it as a quick family dinner. Guests will love it, too. Serve with warm crusty bread. To eat this dish, first search your bowl for an empty mussel shell, then use it as tongs to pry the meat from the remaining mussels. Beats a fork every time.

Serves 4 as a first course, 2 as a main course

2 tablespoons extra-virgin olive oil

1½ tablespoons sliced garlic

1½ pounds mussels, scrubbed and debearded

1 cup dry white wine

Salt and freshly ground pepper

3 large yellow tomatoes, peeled and cut
  into chunks about the same size as the mussels

1 tablespoon finely chopped fresh purple
  or green basil

1½ teaspoons finely chopped fresh tarragon

1½ teaspoons finely chopped fresh
  flat-leaf parsley

2 tablespoons unsalted butter (optional)

Heat the olive oil in a large sauté pan over medium-high heat until hot. Add the garlic and sauté briefly until light brown. Add the mussels and white wine and season with salt and pepper. Stir, then cover and cook until the mussels begin to open, about 2 minutes. As they open, transfer them with a slotted spoon to a plate. Discard any that do not open.

Cook the juices over medium-high heat until reduced by about half. Add the tomatoes and cook quickly just until they begin to color the juice, about 30 seconds. Do not overcook or they will melt into the sauce (which is hardly a terrible crime). Add the herbs and the butter, if using. When the butter has melted, return the mussels to the pan with any juices accumulated on the plate. Stir and toss just to reheat. Serve immediately.

CHEF'S NOTE: *For a pretty presentation, garnish with a few whole or halved cherry tomatoes and whole herb leaves.*

bell peppers

The last thing I want to put in my mouth is a raw pepper. Maybe it's because of years of seeing them on salad bars. Sure, when I chop them, I pop a few pieces in my mouth, but eating them on purpose is not something I do. I am adamantly against green bell peppers, which are unripe red bell peppers. I don't like to eat unripe foods. ❧ In my universe, sweet bell peppers—red and yellow—are always cooked and preferably roasted. During the season, Mom—and now my wife, Ines—would roast and can a big supply of sweet peppers. They were then always on hand to whip into a quick sauce for pasta or serve with a grilled flank steak (page 71), one of our family's favorite summertime meals. ❧ A fun idea for roasted peppers is to make "firecrackers." Lay half a roasted pepper on a work counter and spread with a stuffing. One I particularly like is Gorgonzola flavored with toasted pine nuts and thyme. Then roll up the pepper like a cigar, coat it with bread crumbs, and deep fry in olive oil. Serve it, if desired, with the spicy roasted pepper sauce on page 66.

ROASTING BELL PEPPERS AND CHILIES When planning to roast peppers, notice as you shop that some peppers have four lobes on the bottom, some have three, and some come to a point. The more lobes and the more deeply indented they are, the trickier the peppers will be to peel. Look for peppers with thick walls and no soft spots. First brush them all over with olive oil. This carries the heat into any deep crevices and helps the skin blister more evenly. Roast the peppers whole under a broiler or over an open flame or grill, turning occasionally, until the skins blister and char all over. Place in a bowl, cover with a lid, and let steam to loosen the skins. Working over the bowl to catch any juices, peel off the skins. Do not do this under running water, or you will wash the flavor down the drain. It is helpful to occasionally rinse your fingers. Seed the peppers, then tear into long strips and place in a clean bowl. Pour the juices left in the steaming bowl over the peppers and refrigerate for up to several days. You can also add a little vinegar and olive oil. This will extend their shelf life by several days. Figure on about a generous cup roasted peppers per pound of raw peppers. Use the pepper juices in vinaigrettes, soups, stews, even tuna and chicken salads. ❧ If you want a pure, sweet roasted pepper flavor, peel the peppers carefully. Often I like a smokier flavor. To achieve this, simply leave some of the charred skin adhering to the peppers, or, for a very smoky flavor, do not peel them at all. In this case, it is important that the peppers not be blackened but charred a deep brown. ❧ When handling hot chili peppers, take care not to burn your face or eyes: Wear gloves and/or wash your hands and the cutting board immediately after handling them. Do not touch your face or other sensitive parts of your body.

peperoni

Fusilli Salad *with* Roasted Pepper Sauce

This makes a great lunch. The sauce is particularly good for pasta salads, because it doesn't overwhelm the flavor of the pasta. You will find you have more sauce than you need, especially if you sauce your pasta sparingly, as I do. The sauce keeps for several days in the refrigerator, however, and is very handy. Use it as a dip or sauce for boiled artichokes, grilled eggplant, steamed shrimp, salmon, kabobs, or as a sandwich spread.

Serves 4

1 tablespoon plus 1/4 cup extra-virgin olive oil

1 tablespoon minced garlic

1/2 teaspoon red pepper flakes

1 1/2 teaspoons finely chopped fresh thyme

2 cups roasted, peeled, and seeded
red bell peppers (page 64)

Salt and freshly ground pepper

3 tablespoons red wine vinegar

3 ears corn, shucked

3/4 pound dried fusilli

6 ounces snow peas, cut in half crosswise

15 Kalamata olives, pitted and torn
into several pieces

1/2 cup plus 2 tablespoons freshly grated
pecorino cheese

Heat the 1 tablespoon olive oil in a small skillet over medium-high heat until hot. Add the garlic and sauté briefly until light brown. Add the red pepper flakes, stir, remove from the heat, and scrape into a blender. Add the thyme, bell peppers, and salt and pepper to taste and puree until smooth. With the machine running, add the remaining 1/4 cup olive oil in a slow, steady stream. Blend in the vinegar and taste for seasoning. You should have about 2 1/2 cups. (The sauce can be made ahead to this point and kept, covered and refrigerated, for several days.)

Bring a large pot of water to a boil. Add salt and then the corn. Cook until tender, about 5 minutes. Lift out with tongs and reserve. Return the water to a boil and add a little more salt. Add the pasta and cook until al dente, about 12 minutes. While the pasta is cooking, cut the kernels off the cobs and place in a warm serving bowl. When the pasta is done, lift it out with a broad skimmer, and add to the corn. Add 1 generous cup of the pepper sauce and toss well. Add a little pasta cooking water, if necessary, to thin.

Once again, return the water to a boil and add the snow peas. Cook until crisp-tender, about 1 minute. Dip out with a skimmer and add to the pasta. Add the olives and the 1/2 cup pecorino and toss well. Taste for seasoning. Sprinkle the top with the remaining 2 tablespoons cheese. Serve warm or at room temperature.

Variation with Grilled Tomatoes: Substitute grilled tomatoes (see page 61 for technique) for some or all of the roasted peppers.

Rock Shrimp *and* Spicy Roasted Pepper Pasta

This dish has been on Tra Vigne's menu for several years. It looks like a jambalaya and makes a tasty supper with a glass of Sauvignon Blanc. The sauce is one I made for my Tra Vigne "try-out" meal for my prospective partners. It still often appears on our menu. Most rock shrimp are frozen and peeled, so be sure to drain them well after thawing or the finished dish will taste diluted.

Serves 4

¼ cup extra-virgin olive oil

2 jalapeño chilies

1½ cups roasted, peeled, and seeded red
    or yellow bell peppers (page 64)

Salt and freshly ground pepper

1 tablespoon Roasted Garlic Paste (page 197)
    or more to taste (optional)

1 pound rock shrimp

1½ tablespoons minced garlic

1 tablespoon finely chopped fresh oregano

4 cups chicken stock (page 204), canned low-salt
    chicken broth, or half stock or broth
    and half water

¾ pound dried orzo or pastina

2 tablespoons finely chopped fresh
    flat-leaf parsley

1 cup freshly grated Parmesan cheese

Heat 2 tablespoons of the olive oil in a small skillet over medium heat until hot. Tilt the skillet to collect the oil in a small pool against the side of the pan. Drop in the jalapeños and cook until brown all over and cooked through, about 5 minutes. Let cool, then peel and seed (see Chef's Notes).

Place 1 jalapeño and the roasted peppers in a blender with salt and pepper to taste and puree until smooth. Taste and add the second jalapeño, if desired. The sauce should be noticeably spicy, as it will be flavoring ¾ pound pasta. Add the garlic paste, if using. You should have about 1¼ cups sauce. Set aside.

Heat 1 tablespoon of the olive oil in a large sauté pan over medium-high heat until hot. Add the shrimp and spread them out in the pan so they sauté instead of boil. Season well with salt and pepper. Continue to sauté quickly just until they are cooked through and have turned pink, about 3 minutes. Remove to a plate with a slotted spoon. Discard any liquid left in the pan.

Add the remaining 1 tablespoon olive oil to the pan and heat over medium-high heat until hot. Add the garlic and sauté briefly until light brown. Stir in the oregano. Add the chicken stock and bring to a boil. Add the pasta and salt and pepper to taste. Reduce the heat to medium-low and simmer slowly, stirring occasionally so the pasta does not stick to the bottom of the pan, until the pasta is al dente, about 12 minutes.

When the pasta is ready, stir in the pepper puree. Return the shrimp to the pan just to reheat. Add the parsley and all but 1 tablespoon of the Parmesan. Stir again. Pour into a warm serving bowl or individual plates and dust with the remaining 1 tablespoon Parmesan. Serve immediately.

CHEF'S NOTES: *If roasting or grilling bell peppers for this recipe, grill or roast the jalapeños at the same time. Make sure to skewer them so they do not fall through the grate.*

Mom's Meatball-Stuffed Peppers

4 to 6 large yellow bell peppers

1 pound ground sirloin

1 large egg

2 tablespoons freshly grated Parmesan cheese

2 tablespoons finely chopped fresh
    flat-leaf parsley

1 teaspoon dried oregano

2 tablespoons finely chopped fresh basil

1 cup finely chopped onion

1 cup fine dried bread crumbs (see Chef's Notes)

Salt and freshly ground pepper

About 2 cups water

2 cups Quick Tomato Sauce (page 198),
    made without jalapeños

2 tablespoons Gremolata (page 192),
    made without lemon zest

My mother taught my wife, Ines, her meatball recipe. Mom didn't use it to stuff peppers but in a more traditional way: she cooked the meatballs in tomato sauce, then served them on pasta or on their own. She always insisted that the meat mixture be very wet. If you think you've added too much water, you have probably added just enough. She also insisted that the meatballs simmer an hour in the sauce. If you want to serve them that way, set your timer and do something else so you won't be tempted to take them off earlier. At Tra Vigne we do a soup with pastina and meatballs made according to this recipe. We shape the meat into marble-size balls and braise them in the broth. As much as you may want to, resist the desire to fry these meatballs. They need moist-heat cooking. If you need to halve the recipe, you should still use the whole egg.

Serves 4 to 6

Preheat the oven to 350°F. Bring a large pot of water to a boil and add salt. Cut off the lids from the peppers and reserve. Seed and derib the peppers. Cut a small slice from the bottom of each pepper so it will stand upright. Add the peppers and lids to the pot of boiling water and cook until softened, about 10 minutes. Drain and let cool.

In a large bowl, mix together the meat, egg, cheese, parsley, oregano, basil, onion, bread crumbs, 1 tablespoon salt, $^1/_2$ teaspoon pepper, and 1 cup of the water. Knead the water into the meat mixture with your hands. Add another $^1/_2$ cup water and continue to knead. As you knead, the bread crumbs will soften as they absorb the water. Add the remaining $^1/_2$ cup water and knead again. By now the mixture should feel smooth, with no grittiness left, and have a very soft texture.

Season the insides of the peppers with salt and pepper. Spoon a little tomato sauce into the bottom of each pepper and divide the meat mixture among them. Place upright in a flameproof baking dish and pour the remaining tomato sauce over and around the peppers. Top each pepper with its pepper lid. Cover the dish tightly with a lid or foil lined with waxed paper or parchment paper. Bake until the peppers are soft and the filling has cooked through, about 1 hour.

Uncover the dish, remove the pepper lids, and dust the top of each pepper with about 1 teaspoon Gremolata. Turn the oven to broil and place the peppers under the broiler just until browned, about 1 minute. Replace the lids and serve hot, warm, or at room temperature.

CHEF'S NOTES: *Ines will often use Progresso brand plain or seasoned bread crumbs. Even if she uses the seasoned type, she does not change the seasoning in the recipe. The one pound of meat feeds our family: two adults and three growing children.*

Stuffed Chicken Thighs *with* Red Pepper–Tomato Sauce

Every time I work with Jacques Pépin, I learn something. He created this simple sauce, which has a terrific, fresh, clean flavor. Use any extra sauce to poach fish roulades.

Serves 4

For the sauce

1 cup diced red bell peppers
      (about 1 large; ³⁄₄-inch dice)
1 cup diced vine-ripened tomatoes
      (about 2 medium; ³⁄₄-inch dice)
1 cup water
1 teaspoon finely chopped fresh oregano
1 tablespoon unsalted butter, at room temperature
1 tablespoon extra-virgin olive oil
Salt and freshly ground pepper

For the chicken and stuffing

3 garlic cloves
1¹⁄₂ teaspoons finely chopped fresh oregano
1 cup pitted Kalamata olives
4 to 5 tablespoons extra-virgin olive oil
Salt and freshly ground pepper
4 chicken legs and thighs, thighs boned
      and leg bones intact
¹⁄₄ cup water
³⁄₄ pound dried fettuccine
1 tablespoon finely chopped fresh flat-leaf parsley

CHEF'S NOTES: *When tying knots, on the first cross, turn the strings around each other three times. This way the strings won't slip and loosen while you finish the knot. If you have olive paste or tapenade in the fridge, you can use it here instead of making your own.*

To make the sauce, put the bell peppers, tomatoes, and water in a large nonreactive saucepan and bring to a boil over high heat. Lower the heat to medium and simmer until the peppers are tender, about 25 minutes. Add the oregano halfway through cooking. Transfer the mixture to a blender or food processor and add the butter, olive oil, and salt and pepper to taste. Puree until smooth. Return to the pan to keep warm. You should have about 1¹⁄₂ cups. (The sauce can be covered and refrigerated for 1 or 2 days.)

To make the stuffing, drop the garlic, oregano, olives, and 1 tablespoon of the olive oil into a food processor and process until very finely chopped. Season with pepper, pulse again, and scrape into a small bowl. You should have about ¹⁄₂ cup. (The stuffing mixture can be made ahead to this point, covered, and refrigerated for several days.)

Preheat the oven to 400°F. Season the inside of the thighs with salt and pepper. Put about 1¹⁄₂ teaspoons of the olive paste inside each thigh. Tie closed with kitchen string (see Chef's Notes). Season with salt and pepper.

Heat 2 tablespoons of the olive oil in a large, ovenproof skillet over medium-high heat until hot. Lower the heat to medium, add the chicken, and sauté until lightly brown all over. Put in the oven until opaque throughout, about 20 minutes. Transfer to a plate and keep warm.

Pour off the fat from the pan, add the water, place over medium heat, and stir and scrape up all the browned bits from the bottom and sides of the pan. Simmer until slightly reduced. Add 1 cup of the sauce and reheat gently. Add any juices from around the chicken.

Meanwhile, bring a large pot of water to a boil and add salt. Add the pasta and cook until al dente, about 12 minutes. Drain, rinse quickly under cool water, and return to the pot. Toss well with 1 to 2 tablespoons olive oil, the parsley, and salt and pepper to taste.

Divide the fettuccine among 4 plates, and spoon about ¹⁄₄ cup of the sauce on top of each. Slice the thighs and arrange next to the fettuccine. Put a small spoonful of olive paste on the edge of the plate. Serve immediately.

Grilled Flank Steak *with* Roasted Peppers *in* Tomato Sauce

Every summer my mother made this dish: just the steak, crusty bread, and a bowl of her roasted peppers in tomato sauce on the side. All the same ingredients make a great sandwich or piadina the next day. Mom made large batches of her peppers in tomato sauce and canned them to have on hand. This supper would then take very little time to prepare. Refrigerate any surplus peppers for up to several days. They make a terrific addition to many summer meals, served warm or at room temperature.

Serves 4

2 cups peeled, seeded, and chopped
    vine-ripened tomatoes
2 cups roasted, peeled, and seeded red
    and yellow bell peppers (page 64)
1 jalapeño or serrano chili
Salt and cracked black pepper
1 flank steak, about 1 pound
1½ teaspoons dried oregano
3 tablespoons extra-virgin olive oil,
    plus more for brushing on bread
4 large slices bread, cut from a good, crusty loaf
1 teaspoon balsamic vinegar

Prepare the tomatoes and bell peppers, working over a bowl to catch all the juices. Cut or tear the peppers into long strips.

Strain all the juices into a large nonreactive saucepan. Add the chili. Bring to a boil over high heat, reduce the heat to medium, and simmer until the juices reduce to a heavy syrup and the chili is very soft, about 10 minutes. Scoop out the chili, seed if desired, and mince.

Add the peppers and tomatoes to the saucepan and bring to a boil. Lower the heat to medium and simmer for 20 minutes. Stir in the chili and salt and pepper to taste. Keep warm or let cool to room temperature.

Prepare the grill and let it burn down to medium coals. Season the flank steak with salt, pepper, 1 teaspoon of the oregano, and brush with 1 tablespoon of the olive oil. Grill, turning once, until done to your taste, about 10 minutes for rare meat. Transfer to a cutting board, drizzle with another 1 tablespoon olive oil, and crumble the remaining ½ teaspoon oregano over the top. Let rest for about 5 minutes.

Meanwhile, brush the bread on both sides with olive oil and season with salt and pepper. Grill the bread on both sides until brown and crunchy on the outside but still soft within.

Carve the meat on the diagonal into thin slices and arrange on a platter or plates. Top each slice of grilled bread with about ¼ cup of the roasted peppers in sauce and arrange next to the meat. (Reserve any remaining peppers for another use.) Gather all the meat juices (make an effort to scrape the meat juices off the carving board, too) into a small bowl and whisk in the vinegar and the remaining 1 tablespoon olive oil. Drizzle over each portion. Serve immediately.

summer squashes

When prospective cooks interview at Tra Vigne, we ask them to cook a dish with zucchini. Anyone can make foie gras or veal chops taste great. It takes a special cook to understand the delicate nature of zucchini. ❧ The world of summer squashes includes far more than green zucchini. Home gardeners might doubt that for several weeks as they struggle to keep up with their zucchini harvest. It is a terrific vegetable for beginning gardeners because it is fail-safe and provides plenty to give away. Just be sure to give slim, tender, young zucchini away, not the fat baseball bats that somehow manage to hide despite their size. Better yet, make an extra-large batch of Southern Italian Ratatouille (page 76) and give some to neighbors who will appreciate having supper half prepared for them. ❧ Each new summer seems to bring a wider array of summer squashes to market, from pattypan or scallop in yellow or light or dark green to yellow crooknecks and yellow and striped zucchini. The delicate flavor and quick-cooking characteristics of summer squashes make them well-suited to the summer kitchen. Used in combination, their bright, glossy colors add visual interest to summer plates. ❧ Squash flowers turn up more often now at farmers' markets and specialty produce stores. The male flowers grow on a long stem; the females have a small vegetable attached to the base of the flower. You can stuff both kinds with cheese such as mozzarella or goat cheese, then coat them first in flour, then egg, then seasoned dried bread crumbs and panfry them in olive oil. You can also make a squash blossom risotto by cutting the flowers into a chiffonade and stirring them into the rice at the last moment. Make a "triple squash" risotto by using two different-colored summer squashes as well as squash blossoms. The flowers are also a delicious and pretty addition to salads. ❧ Whether you grow squashes or purchase them, choose small to medium vegetables that are firm and without scratches. Larger ones tend to be watery, but are preferable for some preparations such as the saltimbocca on page 80. Salting the vegetable before cooking draws out excess water, adds flavor, and firms up the texture, all positive attributes, especially when you sauté or fry squash. ❧ Summer squashes taste wonderful fried, roasted, grilled, steamed, or sautéed. Teaming squashes with melon (page 75) brings out their sweetness, while their mild flavors mellow strong tastes such as prosciutto and Parmesan cheese (page 80). Because they can be cut into so many shapes—coins, matchsticks, batons, long slices, diagonal slices, long spirals, and cubes of all sizes—summer squashes lend themselves to fun presentations.

zucchine

Sautéed Zucchini Batons
with Melon "Pasta"

Here is good summer food. The dish delivers contrasts—hot and cold, crispy and soft, sweet and salty—and best of all, it can be eaten with the hands. On hot days, serve it on a cold plate, making sure the melon is very cold, and even include a chilled fork, if you like. Another presentation would be to cut thin slices of seedless watermelon and overlap them on a plate for watermelon "carpaccio." Then balance the batons against each other in the middle of the plate. This is a good place to use several drops of your precious *aceto balsamico traditionale*. Or you can serve this with the tomato vinegar on page 79. You can also grill or roast the zucchini. Any kind of melon will work as long as it is ripe (but not overripe and mushy) and fragrant.

Serves 4

1 medium-sized ripe melon
3 zucchini, each about 8 inches long
     and of equal diameter
Salt and freshly ground pepper
24 very thin slices pancetta or prosciutto
1 1/2 teaspoons extra-virgin olive oil
Balsamic vinegar
1 tablespoon finely chopped fresh
     flat-leaf parsley or mint

Halve and seed the melon, then peel. Cut the melon on a mandoline with the julienne blade, or cut by hand into thin slices and then again into flat "noodles" about 1/4 inch wide. Arrange in a pile on a platter or divide among 4 plates and sprinkle with a little salt. Keep refrigerated until needed.

Trim the ends from the zucchini and cut into quarters lengthwise. Season with salt and pepper. Wrap each piece tightly in pancetta, using 2 pieces per quarter. Heat the olive oil in a large sauté pan over medium heat until hot. Add the zucchini and sauté until the pancetta is crispy but the zucchini is still nearly raw, about 5 minutes.

Place 3 zucchini batons on top of each portion of melon, drizzle with balsamic vinegar, and dust with parsley. Serve immediately.

Southern Italian Ratatouille

This dish looks as colorful as confetti. It is my adaptation of a recipe my mother
cooked in a mold, one of those vegetable stews our family lumps together
under the name *tiella*, after the low, wide earthenware baking dish traditionally used.
I call my version ratatouille because it is such a familiar name and the ingredients
are similar. For Tra Vigne's version, the vegetables are separately and quickly cooked
to develop their individual flavors and to maintain their textures and colors.
You can make it ahead of time, but do not refrigerate it. It tends to throw water
and then may need bread crumbs to come together again. Double the recipe
and turn it into a summer staple because it lends itself to so many different dishes.

Makes about 2 ½ cups, serves 4 as a small side dish

3 ½ tablespoons extra-virgin olive oil

1 ½ cups sliced fresh wild
    or domestic mushrooms (¼ inch thick)

½ cup thinly sliced leek, white part only

Salt and freshly ground pepper

1 tablespoon plus 1 teaspoon minced garlic

1 tablespoon finely chopped fresh thyme

¼ cup diced red bell pepper (¼-inch dice)

1 ½ cups diced yellow zucchini or yellow crookneck
    squash (about ½ pound; ¼-inch dice)

1 ½ cups diced green zucchini
    (about ½ pound; ¼-inch dice)

¾ cup peeled, seeded, and chopped vine-ripened
    tomatoes (about ½ pound)

1 cup loosely packed baby spinach,
    cut into a ¼-inch chiffonade

2 tablespoons coarsely chopped fresh basil

2 tablespoons freshly grated Parmesan cheese

Heat 2 tablespoons of the olive oil in a large sauté pan over medium-high heat until hot. Add the mushrooms and cook, without moving them, until brown on one side, about 1 minute. Continue to sauté for another 1 or 2 minutes. Lower the heat to medium, add the leek, season with salt and pepper, and sauté until the leek is soft but not brown, about 2 minutes. Add the 1 tablespoon garlic and sauté for another minute. Add 1 teaspoon of the thyme and stir. Scrape the vegetables into a large bowl. Give the pan a quick rinse and scrub if anything has stuck and burned.

In the same pan, heat another 1 tablespoon of the olive oil over medium-high heat until hot. Add the bell pepper and sauté for about 1 minute. Add the yellow and green zucchini and cook until they release their water and turn translucent but have not colored, about 2 minutes. Add the remaining 2 teaspoons thyme. Season with salt and pepper. Spread the vegetables in the bowl with the mushrooms so they cool quickly and retain their color.

Heat the remaining ½ tablespoon olive oil in the same sauté pan over medium-high heat until hot. Add the remaining 1 teaspoon garlic. Sauté briefly until lightly colored, then add the tomatoes. Season with salt and pepper. Bring to a boil and simmer until the mixture thickens, about 5 minutes. Add the spinach and toss until it wilts into the tomatoes. Scrape into the bowl with the other vegetables and stir so the mixture cools a bit. Add the basil and Parmesan. Toss until well mixed. Serve warm or at room temperature.

Southern Italian Ratatouille Four Ways

Ratatouille Burgers

You can make these "burgers" in the oven or a toaster oven, or heat them in their molds on the grill and grill the bread, too. Serve them for lunch with a glass of Zinfandel on the coolish side.

Serves 4

1 recipe Southern Italian Ratatouille (page 76)

2 tablespoons fine dried bread crumbs

8 slices good, crusty bread such as *ciabatta* (see Chef's Note)

¼ cup Roasted Garlic Paste (page 197) or plain or flavored olive oil such as roasted garlic oil

1 large vine-ripened tomato, thinly sliced

Salt and freshly ground pepper

¼ pound Fontina cheese or other mild cheese, thinly sliced

Preheat the oven to 400°F. In a bowl, mix together the ratatouille and bread crumbs. Spoon into four ½-cup round baking molds such as 3½-inch nonstick tart pans. Place in the oven and bake until hot through, about 10 minutes.

Meanwhile, if you are using *ciabatta*, cut the loaf in half horizontally, then into lengths of 4 to 5 inches. Or cut other bread into thick slices. Toast the bread on both sides (even if one side is a crust). Brush each of 4 slices with 1 tablespoon garlic paste, and top with the tomato. Season with salt and pepper. Unmold the burgers onto the prepared toast, top with the cheese, and close the sandwiches.

CHEF'S NOTE: Ciabatta *means "broken slipper" or "broken heel" in Italian and describes the flattish shape of this traditional Italian peasant bread with a crusty exterior and a chewy, airy interior.*

Ratatouille Pasta

Ratatouille becomes a very pretty, rustic pasta dish with a fresh herb flavor. Serve with a full-bodied, barrel-fermented Sauvignon Blanc.

Serves 4

Salt and freshly ground pepper

¾ pound dried orecchiette

1 recipe Southern Italian Ratatouille (page 76), still warm

2 tablespoons finely chopped fresh flat-leaf parsley

1 tablespoon finely chopped fresh basil

½ cup freshly grated Parmesan cheese

Bring a large pot of water to a boil and add salt. Add the pasta and cook until al dente, about 12 minutes. Drain, reserving about ½ cup of the pasta cooking water.

Pour the pasta into a warm serving bowl and toss well with the ratatouille, parsley, and basil. Season with salt and pepper. Thin with the pasta cooking water as needed. Sprinkle half of the Parmesan on top and toss again. Serve immediately, dusted with a little of the cheese. Pass the remaining cheese at the table.

CHEF'S NOTE: *To reheat ratatouille, put it in a large bowl, then set the bowl over the pasta pot while the pasta is cooking.*

Ratatouille Gratin

This reminds me of a shepherd's pie, but an all-vegetable one. Serve the gratin hot as a side dish for roast chicken or meat or warm or at room temperature as a main dish with crusty bread and a glass of Barbera or Sangiovese.

Serves 4

3 cups mashed potatoes (page 40), warm
1 recipe Southern Italian Ratatouille (page 76), warm
1½ tablespoons Gremolata (page 192)

Preheat the oven to 450°F; preheat the broiler, if a separate unit. Spoon the potatoes into a 1½-quart gratin dish and spoon the vegetable mixture on top. Smooth the top and sprinkle with an even layer of Gremolata.

Bake for about 5 minutes, then place under the boiler until the top is crisp, about 1 minute. You don't want to cook the gratin, just warm it and form a crust. Serve immediately or let cool until just warm.

Ratatouille Risotto

Full-flavored but not rich, this risotto makes a light, satisfying meal. Serve with a Chardonnay. You can cut the amount of wine used in the recipe in half or leave it out altogether. In this case, I like the flavor the whole amount gives.

Serves 3 or 4

4 cups chicken stock (page 204)
    or canned low-salt chicken broth
2 tablespoons extra-virgin olive oil
½ cup diced onion (¼-inch dice)
Salt and freshly ground pepper
1 cup Arborio rice
1 cup dry white wine
1 recipe Southern Italian Ratatouille (page 76),
    warm or at room temperature
1 tablespoon finely chopped fresh flat-leaf parsley
1 cup freshly grated Parmesan cheese

Put the stock in a saucepan and bring to a boil over high heat. Reduce the heat to very low just to keep the stock hot. Heat the olive oil in a heavy saucepan over medium heat until hot. Add the onion, season lightly with salt, and cook until soft but not brown, about 2 minutes. Add the rice and stir and cook for about 1 minute. The center of each grain should look pearly white and the outer layer almost clear.

Add the wine and cook until the pan is nearly dry. Adjust the heat so the rice cooks at a slow simmer. Add ½ cup of the stock, stir, and cook until the pan is nearly dry again. Season lightly with salt and pepper now so the flavor permeates the rice. (Otherwise, if you salt later, you will have a salty broth and flat-tasting rice.) Add another ½ cup of the stock and continue to stir and cook, adding more stock as the previous additions are absorbed, until the rice is cooked, about 18 minutes. Stir in the ratatouille, parsley, and ½ cup of the cheese.

Remove from heat and pour into a warm serving bowl. Dust with a little of the Parmesan and pass the remaining Parmesan at the table.

Crispy Zucchini Salad *with* Tomato Vinegar

Hot, crispy zucchini and cold sauce. With the mint, tomato, and fried flavors, get ready for a quick trip to the streets of Rome. At Tra Vigne, we often serve this salad with our marinated fresh anchovies. We thread several thin fillets into each tangle of zucchini just before serving.

Serves 4

1 cup Summer Tomato Sauce (page 199)
1½ tablespoons red wine vinegar
Salt and freshly ground pepper
4 to 6 cups peanut oil for deep-frying
About ¾ pound zucchini
About 1 cup buttermilk
About 1 cup Arborio Rice Coating (page 193)
2 tablespoons finely chopped fresh mint

Puree the tomato sauce in a blender or with an immersion blender. Whisk in the vinegar and season with salt and pepper. Chill.

Heat the oil in a deep fryer or deep pot to 350°F. Meanwhile, cut the zucchini on a mandoline or by hand into matchsticks about ¼ inch thick and 2½ inches long.

Put the buttermilk in a bowl. Working in small batches, toss the zucchini in the buttermilk. Put them in a sieve and shake off the excess liquid. Holding the sieve over another bowl, pour the rice coating over the zucchini. Toss to coat well and shake off the excess.

Drop a single piece into the oil to test the heat. If it rises immediately to the surface, the oil is ready. Fry the zucchini in small batches until crispy, about 2 minutes. Scoop out with a slotted spoon and drain on paper towels. Put in a slow oven to keep warm.

To serve, spoon the sauce on the bottom of a large platter or 4 plates. Pile the zucchini on top and dust with the mint.

Saltimbocca *of* Zucchini

About 2 pounds zucchini (see Chef's Notes)
Salt and freshly ground pepper
8 thin slices prosciutto (about ¼ pound)
Leaves from 1 bunch fresh sage
About ⅓ pound Fontina cheese, thinly sliced
2 eggs, lightly beaten with a fork
¾ cup all-purpose flour

About ¼ cup pure olive oil
1½ tablespoons finely chopped fresh
    flat-leaf parsley
About 2 tablespoons freshly grated
    Parmesan cheese
1 lemon, cut into wedges

Saltimbocca means "to jump in the mouth," and that's exactly what the flavors in this dish do! Although saltimbocca is classically prepared with milk-fed veal, I like tweaking traditional recipes in an effort to create lighter dishes. Serve this dish as a midweek supper or a weekend starter. It also makes a wonderful accompaniment to roasted meats and poultry. The zucchini taste great at room temperature when all the flavors come through equally. If you plan on serving this as a first course, make a small salad dressed with citrus vinaigrette (page 143) to serve alongside. This is a fun recipe for those overgrown zucchini lurking under the thick leaves in the garden.

Serves 4 as a light main dish, 6 to 8 as a side dish or starter

Cut a thin lengthwise slice off each zucchini so they can then be cut lengthwise into even $^1/_4$- to $^1/_3$-inch-thick slices. This is most easily done on a mandoline. You will need 16 slices total. Lay them out in pairs on paper towels or a clean tea towel and season lightly with salt and pepper.

Arrange the prosciutto slices on half the zucchini slices so none hangs over the edges. Place 2 sage leaves on top. Place the cheese slices on top, taking the same precautions you did with the prosciutto. Finally, lay the remaining zucchini slices on top of each stack. Cover with paper towels or another clean tea towel and press down firmly to extract moisture and firm the zucchini.

Pour the eggs into a deep plate. Season the flour with salt and pepper and put on another plate. Pick up each zucchini stack by both ends and hold it securely closed as you dip it first in the egg and then dredge in the flour until evenly coated.

In a skillet large enough to hold at least 3 zucchini stacks at a time, heat 2 tablespoons of the olive oil over medium-high heat until hot. Cook the zucchini, turning once, until golden brown, about 2 minutes on each side. Remove to a plate and keep warm until all are cooked. Add more oil by tablespoonfuls, if needed.

Add the remaining sage leaves to the hot pan and cook briefly until crisp. Arrange several crisped leaves on top of each saltimbocca. Serve with a sprinkling of parsley, a light dusting of Parmesan, and lemon wedges.

CHEF'S NOTES: *Choose fairly fat, evenly round zucchini that are similar in length and diameter. Those that are about 8 inches long and $1^1/_2$ inches in diameter work well. In addition, the zucchini should be as even in diameter from one end to the other as possible. It is important to work quickly, not hesitating between assembling, coating, and cooking.*

AUTUMN | food hugs

Autumn is my time for rejuvenation and new growth. Activity seems to increase throughout the animal world at this time of year. For instance, if you go fishing, the fish are gorging, getting ready for winter. Food tastes best to me in autumn, perhaps this is my body's atavistic attempt to store calories for the coming winter. ❧ In autumn we can have winter and summer weather within a week. It is the *biga* (a wild yeast starter for bread dough) of the seasons—something you can't control. All that translates to more stimulation in autumn. I think best, teach best, and work hardest this time of year. ❧ Many of my favorite memories and activities are tied to this season. I monitor every rainfall now because twenty-one days after the first cumulative two inches of rain, I begin mushroom hunting. For me, the perfect autumn dish begins with a mushroom hunt in the surrounding hills with a novice hunter from my staff. We pick wild mustard and fennel on the way down and turn our foraged harvest into a pasta dish with stock already on hand. The autumn table is not about long, drawn-out cooking but about quick, big flavor meals. ❧ The flavors of autumn evoke the same feelings as putting on your favorite wool shirt for the first time. They are tastes you can't have other times of the year. Pumpkins don't grow in summer. Peas, tomatoes, and asparagus are available year-round (availability, of course, does not equal quality), but autumn is different. It is persimmons, quinces, nuts picked up off the ground, and fennel, fennel, fennel, and wild fennel seed. (Yes, fennel is my favorite.) ❧ Growing up, life started on the first of September, the opening day of dove season. I haven't missed an opening day since I started shooting when I was about ten years old. I'd hunt from first light until school, dropping any birds off at home and racing my bike as fast as I could so as not to be late. Unlike conventional mothers, Mom thought it was truly a gift that I would take the time to fish or hunt, so she would prepare whatever I brought home. Until I got married, I thought that was a fair arrangement, but my wife disagrees. My daughters and I pluck the birds now, sitting out back and telling stories. ❧ When you watch the landscape of a cornfield every day, waiting for doves to fly over, you notice and are in tune with the season. As a boy, when the second dove season opened at the end of November, I was able to hunt dove, quail, pheasant, duck, and goose and go fishing all in the same day. It was an all-encompassing time, so autumn and I are best friends. ❧ It is the busiest time of year in the kitchen cycle—time to stock the pantry for winter. My family would butcher a pig and make prosciutto and sausage, and the smell of freshly canned tomatoes welcomed me home from school. Great bunches of fennel, oregano, and basil were hung to dry and olives were cured. It was when the family made wine, too. ❧ At the restaurant, we follow these same patterns. We make dried tomatoes and cure olives, and in November, when the weather cools enough, we make our prosciutti, salamis, and sausages. I still find time to hunt and take my staff out to forage for mushrooms, wild mustard, fennel, or the bright orange persimmons that hang so improbably on bare branches. ❧ The reason I love wild fennel is not just because of the flavor. The taste of fennel includes all the times I picked it with my mother and the times I've picked it with my staff and friends. It includes seeing it hanging under the eaves to dry, shaking the bunches gently into a paper bag, and then separating the seeds from the chaff. These events, and the dishes that evoke them, I call food hugs. And autumn has more of them than any other season.

mushrooms

Mushroom hunters know mushrooms are seasonal. For me, the delight and anticipation of wild mushrooms begins with the first rain in October or November. I begin counting the days until the dormant mushroom spores will have had time to become full grown. Then I pull on a pair of boots and hike the hills. Sometimes you can find a patch of chanterelles just by their scent. ❧ On my hunts, I may be accompanied by one of my children as I accompanied my mother. Or I may take one of Tra Vigne's new cooks in order to have them experience how Tra Vigne's food is tied directly to the land and the seasons. I studied mushrooming for years before I foraged on my own, and I don't encourage anyone to go without an expert to identify the edible mushrooms and warn away from poisonous specimens. ❧ Fortunately, the market selection of fresh mushrooms gets better all the time, as the demand for more exotic mushrooms grows and the ability to cultivate new varieties increases. The first commercially grown fresh shiitakes came from Sonoma County in the early 1980s. Now they are almost commonplace here, while the big, broad portobello mushroom has become trendy across the country. ❧ Cultivated or wild, mushrooms should be smooth and firm, never wet or slimy. If I am using domestic mushrooms (white or tan), I prefer those with tightly closed caps. Store mushrooms in a paper sack in the refrigerator. Cultivated mushrooms are grown in sterilized soil and often need no cleaning. If they do, give them a light brushing, or wipe them with a damp towel, or give them a quick rinse and an even faster towel drying. For aesthetic reasons, I do not use mushroom stems unless the recipe calls for dicing the mushrooms. Save the stems for stock. ❧ I always cook mushrooms and prefer techniques that give them a rich, caramelized flavor, such as sautéing, grilling, or roasting. The best way to guarantee a great-tasting mushroom dish is simple: don't crowd the pan! The principle is exactly the same as browning meat for a stew. Leave room between the pieces so the water released by the mushrooms evaporates quickly. Do not move them until they begin to brown on the first side, and only then begin to sauté. ❧ Because mushrooms absorb liquid so quickly, I "marinate" them by spooning the liquid over them and letting it immediately drain away. If they absorbed the marinade, they would not brown. On the other hand, once mushrooms are browned, it is fine to marinate them. ❧ You can make any recipe calling for wild mushrooms with domestic mushrooms. Add a few dried wild mushrooms for greater flavor. It takes about ten pounds of fresh wild mushrooms to make one pound of dried mushrooms, so a few go a long way. Pour boiling water over the dried mushrooms and let sit until soft. Chop the rehydrated mushrooms and strain the soaking liquid. Add them both to the dish after the domestic mushrooms have been well browned. Let cook for several more minutes to allow the flavors to meld.

funghi

Fusilli Michelangelo

In 1985, I was the executive chef of Toby's Bar and Grill in Miami. The restaurant was an early exponent of "new world cuisine." The menu interwove Mediterranean, Latin, and even Asian influences with reinterpretations of regional American classics. This dish began as something I would make for myself and the manager for lunch and was one of the dishes I cooked for my Tra Vigne interview in 1986. It remains on the menu even now. Michelangelo was one of my mother's pet names for me.

Serves 4

⅓ cup dried tomatoes, not packed in oil
  (see Chef's Note)
3 tablespoons boiling water
1½ teaspoons sugar
1½ tablespoons balsamic vinegar
1 teaspoon finely chopped fresh marjoram
¾ pound dried fusilli
¼ cup extra-virgin olive oil
4 cups diced mixed fresh domestic
  and/or wild mushrooms (¾-inch dice)
Salt and freshly ground pepper
1½ tablespoons minced garlic
½ cup loosely packed fresh basil leaves
2 cups Quick Tomato Sauce (page 198)
¾ cup freshly grated Parmesan cheese
4 cups arugula
2 tablespoons pine nuts, toasted
Red pepper flakes (optional)

Combine the tomatoes, boiling water, sugar, vinegar, and marjoram in a small bowl. Let rehydrate until soft, about 10 minutes. Drain well, squeezing out excess liquid. Cut the tomatoes into fine julienne. Set aside. Discard marinade.

Bring a large pot of water to a boil. Add salt and the pasta and cook until al dente, about 10 minutes. Drain, reserving about ½ cup of the pasta cooking water.

While the pasta is cooking, heat the olive oil in a large sauté pan over medium-high heat until hot. Add the mushrooms and do not move them until they begin to brown, about 1 minute. Then sauté until brown all over, about 5 minutes. Season with salt and pepper. Add the garlic and sauté briefly until light brown. Add the basil and julienned tomatoes and cook quickly, pulling the pan off the heat as necessary so the tomatoes do not burn.

Add the tomato sauce and bring to a simmer. If you chose to add jalapeños to the tomato sauce, seed, mash, and reserve them. As soon as the pasta is done, add it to the tomato-mushroom mixture and toss well with ½ cup of the cheese and the reserved pasta cooking water. Add 3 cups of the arugula and toss until barely wilted.

Pour into a warm serving bowl or onto a platter and scatter the remaining 1 cup arugula on top. Sprinkle with the nuts and dust with a little cheese. Serve immediately and pass the remaining cheese at the table with a shaker of red pepper flakes, if using, or a small bowl of the mashed jalapeños.

CHEF'S NOTE: *You can substitute ½ cup drained, oil-packed dried tomatoes or Oven-Dried Tomatoes (page 199) and omit the rehydration step.*

Grilled Chicken *with* Grilled Mushroom Vinaigrette

This was the first chicken dish I put on the Tra Vigne menu. It's just as good today and would make a great one-plate Friday-night supper. The vinaigrette is really more of a mushroom salsa or salad than a dressing. If you don't want to light the grill, this can be done on the stove-top or in the broiler with the shelf positioned far from the element.

Serves 4

4 thick slices bread, cut from a good, crusty loaf
Extra-virgin olive oil for brushing on bread,
    plus ½ to ¾ cup
Salt and freshly ground pepper
4 boneless chicken breast halves, skin on
About 2 tablespoons Fennel Spice (page 193)
1 pound mixed fresh mushrooms such as shiitake,
    morel, chanterelle, and domestic
2 teaspoons finely chopped fresh thyme
1 tablespoon minced garlic
1 tablespoon minced shallot
2 tablespoons sherry vinegar
2 tablespoons finely chopped fresh
    flat-leaf parsley
3 to 4 cups arugula or watercress
About 2 tablespoons Whole Citrus Vinaigrette
    (page 143) or other vinaigrette of choice

Brush the bread on both sides with olive oil and season with salt and pepper. Place on a baking sheet and set aside. Coat the chicken well with the Fennel Spice and set aside until ready to cook.

Prepare the grill and let it burn down to medium-hot coals. Place the bread on the grill, away from direct heat, and grill on both sides until brown and crispy on the outside but still soft within, about 5 minutes.

Leave the mushrooms whole and toss in a bowl with ½ cup of the olive oil, 1 teaspoon of the thyme, the garlic, and salt and pepper to taste. Immediately grill the mushrooms (be careful not to allow the flames to flare up and burn the mushrooms), turning at least once, until browned and cooked through, about 5 minutes. As the mushrooms are done, return them to the marinade in the bowl. Let cool, finely chop, and return to the marinade.

Add the shallot, vinegar, parsley, the remaining 1 teaspoon thyme, and salt and pepper to taste to the mushrooms. Toss well and add the remaining ¼ cup olive oil, if necessary for balance. Toss well again. (The mushroom vinaigrette may be made a day ahead, covered, and refrigerated, and then returned to room temperature before serving.)

When the coals have burned down to a medium fire, place the chicken, skin side down, on the grill and cook until browned, about 2 minutes. Turn over, move to the edge of the grill away from direct heat, and continue to cook until opaque throughout, about 7 minutes. Remove to a plate.

In a bowl, toss the arugula with the citrus vinaigrette. Place a grilled bread slice on each of 4 plates. Slice the chicken breasts crosswise and arrange on top of the bread. Pour any accumulated chicken juices into the mushrooms and stir. Spoon the mushrooms over and alongside the chicken. Divide the arugula among the plates. Serve immediately.

Portobello Mushroom
Cooked *like a* Steak

1/2 cup extra-virgin olive oil, plus 2 tablespoons
2 tablespoons minced shallot
2 teaspoons finely chopped fresh thyme
1 cup dry red wine
1 1/2 cups double-strength chicken stock
    (page 204), or 3 cups canned low-salt chicken
    broth boiled until reduced by half
Salt and freshly ground pepper

1 tablespoon red wine vinegar
1 tablespoon unsalted butter
1/4 cup balsamic vinegar
1 1/2 teaspoons minced garlic
4 large fresh portobello mushrooms, gills removed
4 good handfuls baby spinach
1 recipe garlic mashed potatoes (page 40)
    or Soft Polenta (page 201), hot

This is a meatless dish, but it is not a vegetarian one. You could substitute vegetable stock, but I prefer the richness and natural thickness given the sauce by a double-strength or roasted chicken stock. If you happen to have veal stock, you will have an incredible dish, especially if you make some roasted winter squash (page 152) to fold into the mashed potatoes. You can treat large shiitake mushrooms, porcini, and thick slices of puff ball mushrooms in the same way.

Serves 4

Prepare the grill and let it burn down to medium-hot coals. While waiting for the grill to be ready, make the sauce. Heat 1 tablespoon of the olive oil in a medium saucepan over medium-high heat until hot. Add the shallot and cook briefly until soft and light brown. Add 1 teaspoon of the thyme and stir. Then add the red wine, bring to a boil, and cook until reduced to about $^1/_4$ cup. Add the stock, return to a boil, and continue to cook until reduced to about $^3/_4$ cup. Season with salt and pepper.

Measure 2 tablespoons sauce into a medium bowl and whisk in the red wine vinegar. While whisking rapidly, drizzle in 1 tablespoon of the olive oil. Taste for salt and pepper. Set the vinaigrette aside until ready to assemble the dish. Whisk the butter into the remaining sauce, season with salt and pepper to taste, and keep warm.

In a medium bowl, whisk together the remaining $^1/_2$ cup olive oil, the balsamic vinegar, the garlic, and the remaining 1 teaspoon thyme. Holding the mushrooms one at a time over the bowl, spoon the marinade over them and let the excess run back into the bowl. Repeat until the mushrooms have been well coated all over. (This method prevents the mushrooms from absorbing too much marinade.) Lay the mushrooms on a plate and season both sides with salt and pepper.

Place the mushrooms, gill side down, on the grill and cook, turning once, until browned on both sides and cooked through, about 4 minutes total. Remove and keep warm.

Add the spinach to the vinaigrette and toss well. Divide the potatoes among 4 warm plates. Top with the mushrooms, gill side up, and spoon the sauce onto the mushrooms and over the potatoes. Top with the spinach salad and serve immediately.

CHEF'S NOTES: *If the olive oil flares up and burns the mushrooms, it creates a petroleum flavor. So make sure the oil doesn't drip from the mushrooms when you put them on the grill.*

If you don't care to start the grill, you can cook the mushrooms indoors on a ridged stove-top grill. Oil it lightly and preheat it before cooking the mushrooms. Or you can use a heavy sauté pan with a little olive oil, preheated over medium-high heat, then turned down to medium to cook the mushrooms through.

Lamb Shanks
with Mushroom Bolognese

6 tablespoons extra-virgin olive oil

4 lamb shanks

Salt and freshly ground pepper

³/₄ pound mixed fresh mushrooms such
    as morel, shiitake, chanterelle,
    and domestic, roughly chopped

1 tablespoon minced garlic

1 cup diced onion (¹/₄-inch dice)

¹/₂ cup diced carrot (¹/₄-inch dice)

¹/₂ cup diced celery (¹/₄-inch dice)

2 cups dry red wine

1 bay leaf

3 cups chicken stock (page 204)
    or canned low-salt chicken broth

3 cups peeled, seeded, and chopped tomatoes
    (fresh or canned, depending on season)

¹/₂ pound dried orecchiette

3 tablespoons finely chopped fresh basil

1 tablespoon finely chopped fresh oregano

I grew up eating cuts such as shank, short ribs, and oxtails. And I love the flavor imparted by the slow braising these cuts require. Lamb shanks were the first meat I put on Tra Vigne's menu, even before a steak. If you like to smoke foods, try smoking your lamb shanks in a covered grill for 45 minutes to add yet another layer of flavor.

Serves 4

Preheat the oven to 300°F. Heat 3 tablespoons of the olive oil in a large, deep ovenproof pot over medium heat until hot. Season the shanks with salt and pepper and brown on all sides, about 10 minutes. Remove to a plate.

Raise the heat to medium-high, add the mushrooms, and do not move them until they begin to brown, about 1 minute. Season with salt and pepper and sauté until brown all over, about 5 minutes. Remove to another plate and reserve for final assembly.

Reduce the heat to medium, add the remaining 3 tablespoons olive oil to the pot, and heat until hot. Add the garlic and sauté briefly until light brown. Add the onion, carrot, and celery, season with salt and pepper, and sauté until light brown, about 8 minutes.

Add the wine and bay leaf, bring to a boil over high heat, and cook until reduced by half. Add the stock and tomatoes and bring to a boil again. Season with salt and pepper. Return the meat to the pot, cover, and place in the oven to braise until fork tender. Test at 2 hours, but the shanks may take as long as 4 hours.

Let the meat cool in the liquid to room temperature. Remove from the braising liquid and reserve separately. Skim off and discard the fat from the braising liquids. (The recipe may be made to this point a day ahead, covered, and refrigerated. See Chef's Notes.)

Bring a large pot of water to a boil. Add salt and the pasta and cook until al dente, about 12 minutes. Drain.

Meanwhile, pour the defatted braising liquids into a saucepan and bring to a boil over high heat. Reduce the heat and simmer for about 10 minutes, skimming the surface all the while. Add the basil and oregano.

Return the shanks to the sauce and simmer gently just until heated through, then remove and keep warm. (To serve the meat off the bones, see the variation, below.) Add the mushrooms and pasta to the sauce and heat gently until warm through. Pour onto a large, deep platter or divide among plates and top with the shanks. Serve immediately.

Variation: If you wish to serve the meat off the bone (which turns this into a pasta dish rather than meat on a bed of pasta), tear the meat into big chunks and return it to the sauce with the mushrooms. Cook just until reheated. Add the pasta, stir, and heat through. Taste for seasoning and serve immediately.

CHEF'S NOTES:
It is acceptable and even preferable to do this dish a day ahead. It is much easier to defat the braising liquid after it has been refrigerated. The meat can even cook while you sleep. For example, from midnight to 6:00 a.m. at 250°F. You can also cook the whole dish in a covered pot on the stove-top. There is a caramelization of flavors in oven braising that stove-top cooking does not replicate. If the shanks are cracked—cut through the bone in the middle— they will cook through to tenderness more rapidly, closer to 2 hours than 4 hours.

Do not serve cheese with this pasta. The subtle gaminess of the cheese emphasizes the gaminess of the lamb.

greens

Some growing things—humans and vegetables—thrive in heat. Others flourish as the sunlight begins to slant and turn golden and the air freshens. Greens, spinach, chard, kale, and mustard greens fall into this latter group. ❧ When I think of greens, my mind turns to wild fennel. In the autumn it sets seeds, which my mother would collect, dry under the eaves, and sort. My family and I still follow the same tradition. Later in the autumn, after the rains commence, soft, feathery fennel fronds begin to grow from the bottom of the dried stalks. The fronds flavor menisha (page 100), a hearty vegetable soup of greens and potatoes that my brothers and I were raised on. In fact, many of the greens dishes I like best would fall into the comfort-food category. ❧ In the late autumn and winter, mustard blooms throughout the valley and we celebrate the event with a mustard festival. I love the small, bright yellow flowers in salads and the leaves in quick sautés, while I use the biggest, more bitter leaves in ribollita, a Tuscan bean soup. ❧ Bitterness distinguishes, but doesn't define, greens for me. All greens taste somewhat bitter, but how bitter depends on the amount of heat during the growing season (the hotter, the more bitter), the age (the older, the more bitter), and the type (mustard greens tend to be very bitter, while chard and spinach, by comparison, border on sweetness). ❧ I like greens especially because their flavors are bold and distinct. They can be cooked with other strong flavors such as toasted garlic, prosciutto and pancetta, vinegar, blue cheeses, and anchovies (try spinach or radicchio Caesar salad, page 94). Pasta and polenta make great foils for greens' strength of character, softening their nature to create soul-satisfying supper dishes (page 97). ❧ Be sure to nibble a leaf before cooking to determine its taste. A soak in ice water, especially recommended for radicchio, will refresh and sweeten greens. If they are very bitter, blanch quickly in salted water and shock in ice water to stop the cooking. This will knock out some of the bitterness. ❧ Greens tend to fall into two categories. Tender greens, such as spinach, beet tops, chard, arugula, and watercress, can be eaten raw (especially when young) or cooked only long enough to wilt in hot pasta or in the rinsing water clinging to the leaves. Coarser greens, such as kale, turnip greens, and collard greens, require longer cooking and are usually not eaten raw, although very young kale makes a colorful addition to salads. When you buy them, all greens should look as vigorous and alive as your child rushing inside after playing in a pile of leaves. Pass wilted greens by.

verdura

Radicchio Caesar Salad

Tra Vigne's Caesar salad—with the traditional romaine lettuce—is served on a ten-inch plate with two crostini spread with roasted garlic and topped with our house-cured anchovies. Radicchio makes not only a delicious Caesar—the bitterness of the vegetable tastes great against the creamy cheese richness of the dressing— but it is practical, too. It doesn't get soggy when tossed with dressings ahead of time, so the salad can be fully assembled, ready and waiting for you and your guests.

Serves 4

2 heads radicchio, about ¾ pound total
8 long thin slices bread, about 2 by 6 inches,
    cut from a good, crusty loaf
Extra-virgin olive oil for brushing on bread
Salt and freshly ground pepper
1 garlic clove
About ¼ cup freshly grated Parmesan cheese
1 recipe Caesar Mayonnaise Dressing (page 23)

Preheat the oven to 375°F. Core the heads of radicchio and separate the leaves. Tear into bite-size pieces. Make an ice bath and soak the radicchio for about 15 minutes. Then drain and spin or pat dry.

Meanwhile, brush the bread on both sides with the olive oil and season with salt and pepper. Rub one side of each slice all over with the garlic clove. Place on a baking sheet and bake until about half done, about 7 minutes. Turn, dust lightly with some of the Parmesan, and bake until crisp, about 8 minutes longer.

In a large bowl, toss the radicchio with about ⅔ cup of the dressing and season with salt and pepper to taste. Divide among individual plates and dust each salad with a little more Parmesan. Top each salad with two crostini. Pass any remaining cheese at the table.

CHEF'S NOTES: *It won't be hard to use up any extra Caesar dressing. You may decide to have another Caesar salad the very next night, or use the dressing as a sandwich spread, with the last of the season's tomatoes, or perhaps as a dressing for a white bean salad.*

For me, the difference between crostini and bruschetta is the thickness of the bread. See the recipe on page 194 for a full explanation.

Autumn Fruit *and* Frisée Salad *with* Panettone Croutons

Serve this festive-looking salad for a Thanksgiving starter or to accompany a roast chicken on a Sunday. If you have a whole loaf of panettone, you could make bruschetta to serve with the salad and omit the croutons. To give the salad more substance to serve as a light lunch, you might want to add crumbled feta or finely grated aged goat cheese.

Serves 4

1 cup diced Panettone (¹⁄₂-inch dice; page 184)

2 tablespoons dried cherries

2 tablespoons diced dried apricots (¹⁄₄-inch dice)

2 tablespoons golden raisins

2 tablespoons honey

2 tablespoons champagne vinegar

4 to 5 tablespoons extra-virgin olive oil

1 large pear, about ¹⁄₂ pound, peeled, cored, and cut into slivers about ¹⁄₄ inch by 1¹⁄₂ inches

¹⁄₄ large fennel bulb, about 3 ounces, cut into slivers the same size as the pear

Salt and freshly ground pepper

4 cups roughly torn frisée or curly endive

Preheat the oven to 250°F. Scatter the panettone cubes on a baking sheet and bake, tossing occasionally, until crisp and brown, about 1 hour. Be careful that they do not burn. Set aside.

Put the cherries, apricots, and raisins in a medium bowl. Measure the honey and vinegar into a small pan or microwave-safe bowl. Heat together just until warm. Whisk in 4 tablespoons olive oil and taste for balance. Add the remaining 1 tablespoon oil, if necessary. Pour over the dried fruits. Add the pear, fennel, and salt and pepper to taste.

Pour the fruits and dressing over the greens in a salad bowl and toss well. Add the croutons and toss again. Serve immediately.

CHEF'S NOTE: *Add croutons only when ready to serve so they stay crisp.*

Sicilian Harvest Salad

With the addition of a grilled chicken breast, this unusual appetizer salad would be a great main course. The fruit mixture on its own makes a wonderful little "chutney" to serve alongside a piece of grilled chicken or swordfish or to scatter across the top of focaccia before baking. The dried fruit adds richness, so don't leave it out. In the autumn and winter you can use figs, apples, pears, or persimmons in place of the grapes, while in summer you can use plums, apricots, and peaches.

Serves 4

1/2 cup raisins

Boiling water

1 cup halved large seedless grapes

1 tablespoon diced dried apricots (1/4-inch dice)

1 1/2 tablespoons fried rosemary (see Chef's Notes)

1/4 large red onion, cut into small slivers

Juice of 1 large lemon

5 tablespoons extra-virgin olive oil

Salt and freshly ground pepper

1 large head radicchio, about 3/4 pound

2 cups loosely packed baby spinach

12 thin slices prosciutto, 1/4 cup Prosciutto Bits
     (page 192), or 1/4 pound sausage,
     grilled and cubed (optional)

1 tablespoon pine nuts, toasted

Put the raisins in a small bowl and pour boiling water over them to cover. Let stand until plump and soft, about 10 minutes. Drain.

Put the raisins, grapes, apricots, rosemary, and onion in a large bowl. Add the lemon juice and stir in the olive oil. Season with salt and pepper.

Separate the radicchio into leaves, saving the heart for another use. Tear into bite-size pieces and add to the dried fruit mixture along with the spinach. Toss well. Divide among 4 plates and top with the prosciutto, if using. Scatter the pine nuts over the top.

CHEF'S NOTES: *Frying rosemary on the branch removes its slightly soapy, bitter flavor, so you can use more. Deep-fry the rosemary for 30 seconds and drain on paper towels. Strip the leaves off the stems and crush the leaves in the paper towels to remove any excess oil. Mince and store in a clean, tightly sealed container. Use the fried rosemary to make a seasoned salt by adding it to a mixture of black pepper, dried lemon zest, and salt. Or use it with Fennel Spice (page 193) or Roasted Garlic Paste (page 197) as a seasoning for lamb and pork.*

Fettuccine *with* Mustard Greens *and* Mushrooms

Morels begin to grow in Napa Valley's surrounding mountains after the autumn rains begin. I get a sense of cooking straight off the land when my friends and I take time to go mushroom hunting in the hills. We pick wild mustard on the way down, then our hunger marches us straight into Tra Vigne's kitchen to cook a dish very like this one.

Serves 4

5 tablespoons extra-virgin olive oil,
    plus a little more as necessary
4 cups roughly chopped fresh mushrooms
    such as shiitake or morel
Salt and freshly ground pepper
1 tablespoon minced garlic
1 tablespoon finely chopped fresh thyme
½ teaspoon fennel seeds
2 cups double-strength chicken broth (page 204),
    or 4 cups canned low-salt chicken broth boiled
    until reduced by half
4 cups packed roughly chopped mustard greens,
    green chard, or spinach
¾ pound dried fettuccine
2 tablespoons unsalted butter
2 tablespoons finely chopped fresh
    flat-leaf parsley
About 1 cup freshly grated Parmesan cheese

Heat ¼ cup of the olive oil in a large sauté pan over medium-high heat until hot. Add the mushrooms and do not move them until they begin to brown, about 1 minute. Then sauté until brown all over, about 5 minutes. Add another tablespoon olive oil if the pan is too dry. Season with salt and pepper. Add the garlic and cook quickly until light brown. Add the thyme, fennel seeds, and stock and bring to a boil. Add the greens, season with salt and pepper, and simmer until tender, about 5 minutes.

Meanwhile, bring a large pot of water to a boil and add salt. Add the pasta and cook until al dente, about 12 minutes. Drain, refresh quickly under cool running water, and toss with the remaining 1 tablespoon olive oil.

Stir the butter into the greens and add the pasta and parsley. Toss to heat through and add ½ cup of the Parmesan. Toss well again and pour onto a heated serving platter. Dust with another 1 to 2 tablespoons Parmesan and pass the remaining cheese at the table.

Chicken Piadine *with* Baby Spinach

Piadine are actually unleavened breads cooked on a stove-top, but I've translated that idea into these addictive sandwiches made with a pizzalike dough. If you have some dough in the freezer, you can assemble them out of any manner of ingredients. This sandwich is a great excuse to make sure you are getting your proper quotient of spinach.

Serves 6

1 recipe Piadine Dough (page 194)

All-purpose flour for dusting work surface

2 ¼ cups roasted, peeled, and seeded
 red bell peppers (page 64)

3 tablespoons Roasted Garlic Paste (page 197)

Salt and freshly ground pepper

⅓ cup freshly grated Parmesan cheese

3 tablespoons finely chopped fresh oregano

Coarse cornmeal for sprinkling on baking sheets

9 cups loosely packed baby spinach

About ½ cup Whole Citrus Vinaigrette (page 143)

1 ½ cups diced fresh mozzarella cheese
 (½-inch dice)

3 chicken breast halves, cooked, boned,
 and torn into shreds (see Chef's Note)

Position the oven racks on the lowest and uppermost rungs of the oven. Place 2 large baking sheets in the oven and preheat to 500°F.

Divide the dough into 6 balls. Working on a surface free of flour, roll each ball under your palm. As it rolls, it will stick slightly to the surface, creating tension that helps form a tight, round ball. Dust the work surface with flour, pat each ball down lightly, dust the tops with flour, cover with a towel, and let rise for about 15 minutes.

Combine 1½ cups of the roasted peppers, the garlic paste, and salt and pepper to taste in a blender or food processor and puree until smooth. Cut the remaining ¾ cup peppers into long, narrow strips. Set aside.

With a rolling pin, roll each ball into a circle 8 or 9 inches in diameter and about ⅛ inch thick. Spread each round with about 3 tablespoons of the red pepper puree, then sprinkle with 1 tablespoon Parmesan and 1½ teaspoons oregano.

Remove the baking sheets from the oven, sprinkle evenly with cornmeal, and transfer the rounds to the sheets. Bake until slightly underdone (they will be lightly browned around the edges but still pliable), 8 to 12 minutes.

While the crusts are baking, in a bowl, toss together the spinach, vinaigrette, mozzarella, reserved pepper strips, and chicken. Taste for seasoning. Let the crusts cool very briefly so they won't cook the greens when filled. Transfer the crusts to plates and divide the salad among them. Serve "open face." Diners fold their piadine in half.

CHEF'S NOTE: *You can poach, sauté, roast, or grill the chicken. We grill it at the restaurant because that adds the most flavor. You can also save time by using purchased rotisserie chicken.*

Menisha

In Calabrian dialect, menisha means "soup." This is a sort of green minestrone, very rustic and home style, and satisfying as a main dish with some good, crusty bread. The dish is meant to use up bolting greens from the garden and such cool-weather fall greens as kale and chard. If you have a garden, look for Italian wild kale mix in seed catalogs and then look forward to this soup. This would also be a good place to use the mixed braising greens I see in supermarkets next to the salad mix. The version here is not mine but my wife's, who learned it from my mother. It is the ideal food for bringing up children. My mother would add a prosciutto bone if she had one. I will add fennel as well as fennel tops, but this is not acceptable to my children. Perhaps it will be to yours. Read the Chef's Notes at the end of the recipe for some tips from Ines.

Serves 8

About ½ cup extra-virgin olive oil

1 cup diced onion (¼-inch dice)

1 cup diced celery (¼-inch dice)

2 tablespoons minced garlic

Salt and freshly ground pepper

4 cups chicken stock (page 204),
    canned low-salt chicken broth, or water

2 ounces prosciutto, finely chopped (optional)

1 bay leaf (optional)

2 cups cut-up green beans (½-inch lengths)

2 cups diced zucchini (½-inch dice)

8 cups water

4 cups packed roughly chopped Napa cabbage

4 cups packed roughly chopped spinach
    or chard (about 1 bunch)

2 cups packed roughly chopped mixed
    "wild" greens such as kale, escarole,
    curly endive, dandelion, chicory,
    and bok choy, in any combination

3 cups diced potatoes (½-inch dice)

1 to 2 tablespoons finely chopped fennel leaves

Heat ¼ cup of the olive oil in a large soup pot over medium heat until hot. Add the onion, celery, garlic, and a pinch of salt and cook slowly until very tender but not colored, about 10 minutes. Add the stock, prosciutto and the bay leaf, if using, raise the heat to high, and bring to a boil. Add the green beans and zucchini and lower the heat to a simmer. Cook until the vegetables are tender, about 10 minutes.

Add the water and all the greens and bring to a boil. Simmer slowly until the greens begin to turn from bright to dark (army) green, about 10 minutes. Add the potatoes and salt and pepper to taste and simmer until the potatoes are tender, about 20 minutes longer. Taste for salt, as the potatoes will absorb much of the salt flavor. Just before serving, stir in the fennel leaves using 1 tablespoon if children are eating and 2 tablespoons if the soup is for adults. Serve the remaining ¼ cup or so olive oil at the table for drizzling over individual portions.

INES'S NOTES: *There are few rules for making this soup, but some general guidelines may help. It should include either cabbage or Brussels sprouts and either spinach or chard. I include one strong green and one mild green. It is best to cook the soup in the morning and let it "age" to develop flavor. It also freezes well. For my girls and myself, I usually make it as a vegetarian dish with all water and no prosciutto. I also omit the bay leaf. Late in the season, it seems green beans and zucchini take the longest to cook, thus their order in the recipe. When the soup is army green, you know you have done it right.*

Chard, White Bean, *and* Tubbetini Soup

This can be either a thick soup or a brothy pasta, depending on how much liquid is added. Either way, it is a hearty dish of the kind traditionally eaten by Italian laborers (and kitchen workers) as a midmorning snack to carry them through to a late lunch hour. Once the beans are cooked, the dish goes together rapidly, yet has a soul-satisfying long-cooked flavor.

Serves 4 to 6

½ pound dried white beans (about 1 ¼ cups)

½ small onion

¼ carrot

½ celery stalk

1 bay leaf

4 cups chicken stock (page 204), canned low-salt chicken broth, or water and a prosciutto or ham bone

Salt and freshly ground pepper

½ pound dried tubbetini or other medium-size pasta shape

About ½ cup extra-virgin olive oil

2 tablespoons thinly sliced garlic

½ teaspoon red pepper flakes

1 cup roughly chopped chard stems (see Chef's Notes)

4 cups roughly chopped chard greens, still wet from rinsing

¾ teaspoon finely chopped fresh rosemary

2 tablespoons finely chopped fresh flat-leaf parsley

About ½ cup freshly grated Parmesan cheese

CHEF'S NOTES: *These amounts of chard are equal to about 1 large bunch. Use white or golden chard, as red chard will stain everything pink-red.*

The onion, carrot, and celery are discarded after cooking, so cut them into big pieces. This is an unchopped mirepoix. *It is traditionally two parts onion, one part carrot, and one part celery.*

Pick over the beans to remove any small stones. Rinse and put in a small saucepan, add water to cover, and place over high heat. As soon as the beans begin to boil, remove from the heat and let cool for about 1 hour.

Drain the soaked beans, rinse, and return to the pan with the onion, carrot, celery, and bay leaf. Add the stock, bring to a boil over high heat, reduce the heat to low, cover loosely, and simmer, until beans are tender, 45 to 60 minutes. Add salt and pepper to taste only during the last half of cooking time. (Salting too early toughens the skins of the beans and lengthens cooking time.) Add more water if the beans absorb all the liquid before they cook through, but don't drown them. When the beans are cooked, drain, reserving the cooking liquid, and discard the onion, carrot, celery, and bay leaf.

Bring a large pot of water to a boil. Add salt and the pasta and cook until al dente, about 12 minutes. Drain, refresh quickly under cool running water, and toss with about 1 tablespoon of the olive oil. Set aside.

Heat 2 tablespoons of the olive oil in a large sauté pan over medium heat until hot. Add the garlic and sauté briefly until light brown. Add the red pepper flakes, stir, and add the chard stems. Sauté for about 2 minutes. Add the chard, season with salt and pepper to taste, and cook until wilted, about 3 minutes. Add 3 cups of the reserved bean broth (add water to make up the amount, if necessary), bring to a simmer, and cook until the chard is tender, about 3 more minutes.

Add the beans and rosemary and cook until the beans are heated through. Add the pasta and continue to cook until hot through. Taste for salt and pepper and stir in the parsley. Pass the Parmesan and the remaining olive oil at the table.

onions

Pity the poor onion, always taken for granted. Even in the most poorly supplied kitchen, an onion probably lurks somewhere. With an onion, you are on your way to dinner. ❧ Onions and all their relatives—yellow, white, sweet, red, shallots, scallions, leeks, and garlic—usually perform supporting roles in the kitchen. But given a chance to star, they reward with delicious flavors of varying degrees of intensity and pack a nutritional wallop. ❧ Picked early, onions taste sweet and less pungent than later in their season, when they have been dried off to form their papery coats and stored. I rarely eat any member of the onion family raw with the exception of tiny leeks thinned from rows in midsummer, scallions, marinated red onions, and red torpedo onions, an onion frequently grown by old Italian men. I am not sure why the torpedo is so beloved by them, but it is good enough reason for me to make torpedo onions my favorite. If you grill them, they will probably become your favorite, too. ❧ The onion harvest in California begins as early as the spring and continues through the autumn. By then, the freshly dried onions have reached the market, as have bundles of fat leeks. Now is the time to buy onions by the pound and caramelize them for schiacciata (page 104), bruschetta, and soup. You can freeze well-caramelized onions, so make a huge batch and freeze some to keep on hand. ❧ To use onions in abundance, you will need to cut, slice, dice, and chop them. That may mean some tears. Freshly dried onions have fewer of the tear-causing sulfur compounds than long-stored ones. In addition, a very sharp, stainless steel knife (carbon steel will react with the onions, discoloring both the knife and the onion) will cut cleanly and get the job done faster, causing fewer tears. Are tears the snubbed onion's revenge? No doubt you will chalk this up to my being a chef, but I do believe in chopping onions with a knife instead of a machine. The pieces are even, which means they cook evenly, and the juices stay inside the onion. ❧ I do not cook with white onions. Yellow onions are my usual cooking onion. I like red onions for salads and marinate them in vinegar for several minutes first to soften their flavor. My Italian roots mean I also love the small, flattish, sweet cipolline variety that crops up more frequently now in markets. If you find them, try roasting them with balsamic vinegar (page 105). The double dose of sweet and sour is addictive.

SLICING ONIONS FOR SOUPS AND STEWS When you want onion slices to float nicely in soup and stay on the spoon when scooped from the bowl, peel the onion and halve lengthwise through the stem end. Cut two long notches on each of the rounded sides so you don't get a thick rounded end slice. Cut each half lengthwise into thin slices.

cipolle

Schiacciata *with* Caramelized Onions

Schiaciatta has been a favorite appetizer on Tra Vigne's menu for years. We use a paper-thin cracker crust and mince the onions. Or we might leave off the onions, spread the crust with Gorgonzola, and serve it with a whole head of roasted garlic. Cut it into small squares for hors d'oeuvre or into slices for a light lunch, brunch, or appetizer. If you don't want to make your own dough, buy plain focaccia or even a prepared pizza crust.

Serves 6 as an appetizer

3 tablespoons extra-virgin olive oil
5 cups thinly sliced onions (page 102)
Salt
1/2 cup water
1 1/2 teaspoons finely chopped fresh thyme
Freshly ground pepper
Cornmeal for dusting baking sheets
1/2 recipe Piadine Dough (page 194)
All-purpose flour for dusting dough
    and work surface
About 15 oil-cured olives, pitted
    and torn into pieces
About 3 tablespoons Gorgonzola, or 6 anchovy
    fillets, torn into little pieces (optional)
3 small handfuls fresh flat-leaf
    parsley leaves (optional)
Sherry vinegar (optional)

Heat 2 tablespoons of the olive oil in a large sauté pan over medium heat until hot. Add the onions, season with salt so the onions release their liquid, and reduce the heat to medium-low. Cook until the onions stop releasing water and the pan is nearly dry again, about 4 minutes. Do not allow the onions to brown. Add the water, stir, cover, and cook until softened, about 10 minutes. Uncover, stir in the thyme, and cook over medium heat until the onions are light brown, about 10 minutes longer. Season lightly with pepper. Do not cook the onions too long now as they will brown further in the oven. Let cool for several minutes.

Preheat the oven to 500°F. Dust 2 baking sheets with cornmeal. Cut the dough into 3 equal pieces. Working on a floured surface, shape each piece of dough by hand or with a rolling pin into an 8-inch round, keeping the edges a little thicker than the center. Transfer the rounds to the prepared baking sheets. Brush each round with 1 teaspoon of the olive oil and divide the onions evenly among them. Let rise for about 20 minutes.

Scatter olives over each round and push them into the dough with your fingers. Dot rounds with about 1 tablespoon cheese or with the anchovies (or make one or more of each flavor). Bake until light brown all around the edges and on the bottom, about 12 minutes. Let cool for a minute, then, if desired, pile a handful of parsley leaves on top of each. If using, put the vinegar in a spray bottle and mist the parsley.

CHEF'S NOTES: *If you use Gorgonzola, omit the anchovies and vice versa. Diced cooked potatoes are also a good addition to the onions.*

At Tra Vigne, we keep several types of vinegar in different spray bottles for just such a purpose as this garnish. A quick mist of vinegar adds a hint of freshness and moistness to all kinds of dishes.

Bistecca *with* Balsamic-Roasted Onions

Use the best meat, the best salt, and the best balsamic vinegar you can afford for this dish. In order to cook the meat in the shortest amount of time and thus extract the most flavor, the meat must be at room temperature. Afterward, the meat must rest before carving. If this procedure is followed, the carving knife glides right through the steak.

Serves 3 or 4

3 large red onions or 15 cipolline or boiling onions
¼ cup plus 1 tablespoon extra-virgin olive oil
Salt, preferably gray salt,
    and freshly ground pepper
1 tablespoon minced garlic
1 tablespoon finely chopped fresh thyme
¼ cup balsamic vinegar
1 large porterhouse steak, about 1½ pounds
    and 2 inches thick
1 tablespoon unsalted butter, cut into bits

CHEF'S NOTES: *I would not butter prime meat, but that quality is not usually available for purchase. The butter goes on the steak while it's still in the oven to give the butter a cooked versus a melted flavor.*

A 1½ pound porterhouse should give you about 14 ounces of meat off the bone, enough for three or even four people. However, if you are steak lovers, you might want to buy two steaks of that size for four people.

Preheat the oven to 450°F. If using large onions, peel them and cut into quarters or wedges. Leave as much root on as possible to keep the wedges from falling apart. If using boiling onions, peel and leave whole.

Heat the ¼ cup olive oil in a large, ovenproof sauté pan over medium-high heat until hot. Add the onions, reduce the heat to medium, and cook until brown on all sides, about 5 minutes. Season with salt and pepper. Add the garlic and cook briefly until light brown. Add the thyme and stir. Regulate the heat, as necessary, by moving the pan on and off the heat. Add 2 tablespoons of the vinegar (stand back so as not to get splattered) and toss well with the onions. Place the onions in the oven and roast until tender and very browned (the wedges will tend to char along the edges), about 30 minutes. Stir gently at least once during roasting. Do not stress out if the wedges separate into pieces. Remove to a plate. While the pan is still hot, add the remaining 2 tablespoons balsamic vinegar to the pan and stir and scrape up all the browned bits clinging to the bottom of the pan. Pour over the onions. Leave the oven on at the same heat.

Heat the remaining 1 tablespoon olive oil in a heavy sauté pan over medium-high heat until very hot. Season the steak with salt and pepper. Turn on the exhaust fan and place the steak in the pan. Stand back to prevent being splattered. Cook until brown on the first side, about 2 minutes. Turn and place in the oven to roast until done as desired, about 4 minutes for rare meat. Just before removing from the oven, dot the top of the steak with the butter. Remove the steak to a carving board and let rest for about 5 minutes.

Return the onions to the sauté pan and reheat by tossing over medium heat. To serve, cut the meat off the bone, then carve into thin slices. Arrange the meat on plates and top with the onions. Pour any juices from the carving board over the meat. Serve immediately.

Crispy Onion Salad

I love to contrast hot and cold and sweet and sour in all sorts of dishes at
Tra Vigne. Fun and clever, this salad will take your guests by surprise.
If you prefer a slightly tarter flavor, cut back on the oil in the marinated onions.

Serves 4 to 6

2 ½ cups thinly sliced red onions

¼ cup champagne vinegar

Salt

10 oil-cured olives, pitted and halved

12 very thin lemon slices, preferably cut
  on a mandoline, seeded

3 tablespoons extra-virgin olive oil

4 to 6 cups peanut oil for deep-frying

About ½ cup buttermilk

2 large red onions, thinly sliced and separated
  into rounds

About 2 cups Arborio Rice Coating (page 193)

2 tablespoons finely julienned fresh mint

In a large nonreactive bowl, toss together the 2 ½ cups onions, vinegar, salt to taste, olives, lemon slices, and olive oil. Set aside.

Heat the peanut oil in a deep fryer or deep pot to 350°F. Meanwhile, put the buttermilk in a bowl. Working in small batches, toss the onion rounds in the buttermilk. Put them in a sieve to shake off the excess liquid. Holding the sieve over another bowl, pour the rice coating over the onions. Toss to coat well and shake off the excess.

Drop a single piece in the oil to test the heat. If it rises immediately to the surface, the oil is ready. Fry the onion rounds in small batches until crispy, about 2 minutes. Scoop out with a slotted spoon and drain on paper towels. Put in a low oven to keep warm.

To serve, using a slotted spoon, remove the marinated onions from the marinade and divide among salad plates. Pile the crispy onions on top. For a pretty presentation, tuck the lemon slices and olives from the marinated onions throughout each portion. Dust each with mint and serve.

Swordfish *with* Onion, Raisin, *and* Tomato Agrodolce

3 1/2 tablespoons extra-virgin olive oil
5 cups thinly sliced onions (page 102)
Salt
1/2 cup water
Freshly ground pepper
1 teaspoon finely chopped fresh rosemary
1 can (14 1/2 ounces) chopped tomatoes, or 1 1/2 cups
    peeled and chopped vine-ripened tomatoes
1 tablespoon sugar
1/2 cup golden raisins

Freshly grated zest of 1 lemon
Juice of 1/2 lemon
2 tablespoons finely chopped fresh
    flat-leaf parsley
4 swordfish steaks, about 7 ounces each,
    at least 1 inch thick
2 tablespoons *panko* (see Chef's Notes)
    or other dried bread crumbs
Lemon wedges

Mariano Orlando has inspired the food of our Cantinetta for the last eight years. He loves hungry people, and it is rare for anyone talking with him to leave the shop without "a little something." Mariano is Sicilian and often makes savory dishes that include raisins and other dried fruits. This agrodolce, a sweet-and-sour sauce, is a classic Sicilian flavoring, a neat package of sun-drenched flavors: caramelized onions, tomatoes, and lemons. Together fish and sauce make a full meal. If the sauce is done ahead, you can have a fabulous dish on the table in fewer than fifteen minutes.

Serves 4

Heat 2 tablespoons of the olive oil in a large sauté pan over medium heat until hot. Add the onions and a little salt so the onions release their liquid. Reduce the heat to medium-low and sauté until the onions stop releasing liquid and the pan is nearly dry again, about 4 minutes. Do not allow the onions to brown. Add the water, cover, and cook, stirring occasionally, until the onions are very soft, about 10 minutes.

Uncover, season with pepper, add the rosemary, and increase the heat to medium-high. Sauté until the onions are very lightly browned, about 10 minutes. Remove half of the onions to a plate and set aside.

Add the tomatoes and their juice to the onions remaining in the pan. Bring to a boil over high heat, season with salt and pepper, lower the heat and simmer until thick, about 4 minutes. Add the sugar and the raisins and stir in the lemon zest and lemon juice. Remove from the heat and let cool for a bit. Stir in 1 tablespoon of the parsley. Keep warm. (The recipe may be completed up to this point a day ahead. Cover and refrigerate the reserved onions and sauce separately.)

Preheat the oven to 450°F. Turn on the broiler, if a separate unit. Heat the remaining 1½ tablespoons olive oil in a large, ovenproof sauté pan over medium-high heat until hot. Season the fish steaks with salt and pepper and place in the pan. Lower the heat to medium and cook until the fish is browned on the underside, about 1½ minutes. Turn and top evenly with the reserved onions. Sprinkle each steak with the bread crumbs and place in the oven just until cooked through, about 5 minutes. Run the fish under the broiler to brown the crumbs.

To serve, reheat the sauce, if necessary. It should be warm, not blistering hot. Pour the sauce onto a serving platter or divide among 4 plates. Top with the fish, dust with the remaining 1 tablespoon parsley, and serve immediately with lemon wedges.

CHEF'S NOTES:
Panko *are terrific, very crisp, white, unseasoned bread crumbs from Japan.*

The caramelization of onions here differs from others in this chapter because my intent with fish is to have a lighter flavor.

If fresh tomatoes have disappeared from your markets, a good brand of canned tomatoes makes a very successful dish.

eggplants

If an eggplant were a person, it would be diagnosed as a multiple personality. Botanically, it is a fruit. In the kitchen, it is cooked and eaten as a vegetable, and if you are a vegetarian, it can be looked upon as a meat substitute. (Without realizing it, all the recipes I chose to include here are made without meat.) Eggplant's harvest season begins in mid- to late summer. Yet it takes on such robust flavors when cooked that it is just the thing for crisp fall weather. ❦ Globe eggplants are the most readily available and recognizable type and adapt themselves to any type of preparation, from sautéing, baking, smoking, roasting, and grilling to stuffing. This versatility is one of the eggplant's best features. You can intensify its flavors depending on how it is cooked. Steaming gives the most delicate flavor, grilling the most intense. Without learning a new recipe, you can give your favorite recipe a new twist simply by changing the cooking technique. For instance, you can substitute oven-roasted eggplant for sautéed, or grilled eggplant for smoked eggplant. ❦ As more people become interested in eggplant, more varieties are becoming available, especially at farmers' markets. They range from tiny white eggs to purple-and-cream-striped slim eggplants, to all-purple, slender, and elegant Japanese eggplants. Their flavor is usually milder than globe eggplant and they lend themselves especially well to dishes where presentation is important. They can be served whole or thinly sliced lengthwise, leaving the slices attached at the stem end, then fanned. ❦ In season and freshly picked, eggplants have a firm, glossy skin and need neither peeling nor salting to remove bitterness (see below). If shriveled or brown in spots, the eggplants have been stored too long. There are all sorts of stories about how to choose an eggplant with few seeds. I have not found any tricks that work reliably, however. Perhaps the best advice is to choose smaller rather than larger eggplants and to cook and eat them in season.

A NOTE ABOUT SALTING Globe eggplants are normally salted to remove their bitterness. There is another reason to salt, however. Not only does the salt flavor permeate the dense flesh, but it also removes excess moisture and firms the texture. A salted and dried eggplant will need less oil when cooked. A dish based on salted eggplant may not need another addition of salt. To salt eggplant, slice or cube the vegetable, sprinkle the pieces all over with a generous amount of salt, then let drain in a colander. After 20 to 30 minutes, depending on the thickness of the slices or cubes, rinse quickly under running water, then dry by pressing firmly between sheets of paper towels or tea towels.

melanzane

Lasagnette *of* Eggplant *and* Goat Cheese

2 eggplants, about 2½ pounds total
Salt
2 to 4 cups pure olive oil or peanut oil for frying
1 cup all-purpose flour
½ teaspoon freshly ground pepper
1 recipe Thick Tomato Sauce (page 197)

Generous ½ cup freshly grated
    Parmesan cheese
Generous ½ cup finely chopped fresh
    flat-leaf parsley
½ pound chabis (fresh goat cheese)
3 tablespoons fine dried bread crumbs

This is a terrific example of that anti-intuitive thing Italians sometimes do with fried foods. First you fry the eggplant and it gets deliciously crisp. Then you layer it with tomato sauce and cheese and it gets soft. Why bother? Because the frying here is used for the flavor it imparts, not for the texture. It is the first dish for the restaurant I tried with goat cheese made by Laura Chenel, the famed Sonoma County goat cheese producer and a personal friend since I came to Tra Vigne. If you are not a goat cheese lover, you could use ricotta salata or provolone.

Serves 6 as a main course, 8 to 10 as an appetizer

Do not peel the eggplants. Cut them lengthwise into 1/8-inch-thick slices. A mandoline is a great tool for this. Salt for 20 minutes, then rinse and dry (page 110).

Pour the olive oil into a large skillet to a depth of 1 inch and place over medium-high heat until hot, about 350°F. Meanwhile, season the flour with the pepper (since the eggplant is salted, no more is necessary). Dredge the slices in the flour and fry, turning once, until browned, about 2 minutes total. Drain on paper towels. The oil should be hot enough to bubble gaily while the eggplant is cooking. Add more oil as necessary to maintain the oil at a depth of about 1 inch.

Preheat the oven to 375°F. Spread a thin layer of the tomato sauce in the bottom of a 2 1/2-quart baking dish. A shallow dish (about 2 inches deep) is best. Arrange a layer of eggplant in the dish to cover the bottom completely. Spoon on another layer of sauce, and sprinkle with 2 tablespoons of the Parmesan, 1 tablespoon of the parsley, and dot with one-third of the chabis. Repeat the layering twice, beginning with eggplant and ending with chabis. Do not press down on the layers. Top with the remaining eggplant and then another thin layer of sauce. Sprinkle with the remaining Parmesan (you should have about 3 tablespoons), parsley (about 2 tablespoons), and the bread crumbs. (The dish can be made to this point a day ahead, covered and refrigerated. Return to room temperature before baking, or add another 10 minutes or so if baking straight from the refrigerator.)

Bake until browned and bubbling, about 30 minutes. Do not overbrown. Let rest a few minutes before cutting into squares to serve. Serve hot or warm.

CHEF'S NOTES: *You will be glad to have left-over lasagnette. Just reheat it in a slow oven or cover and microwave. If you have any leftover sauce, refrigerate it and use as an addition to soups, stews, or pasta sauce. If you have used a deeper baking dish, you will need to determine if the lasagnette is hot in the middle. Use an old chef's trick: Insert a knife or metal skewer into the center of the dish, then withdraw it and lay it on your tongue. If it is hot, the dish is done. (This method is recommended only for those cooks sensible enough not to burn their tongues!)*

Caponata *with* Polenta Crackers

I am no longer sure where the idea for this recipe originated. It has very intense flavors with a vinegar tang. The making of it is a lesson in browning. Do serve it at room temperature to allow all its flavors to show to best advantage.

Makes about 2 cups caponata and about 4 dozen 1 1/2-by-3 1/2-inch crackers

1 recipe focaccia dough (page 41), rolled
    according to pizzette instructions (page 196)
About 1/4 cup fine polenta (see Chef's Notes)
Salt and freshly ground pepper
About 1 teaspoon red pepper flakes (optional)
2 tablespoons freshly grated orange zest
About 1/3 cup extra-virgin olive oil
1 eggplant, about 1 pound, peeled and
    cut into small dice (see Chef's Notes)
1 tablespoon minced garlic
1 1/2 cups diced onion (1/4-inch dice)
1 tablespoon finely chopped fresh thyme
2 anchovy fillets, chopped
2 tablespoons caper juice
1/4 cup balsamic vinegar
1 tablespoon roughly chopped capers
1/2 cup roasted, peeled, seeded, and diced red bell
    peppers (1/4-inch dice; page 64)
1 tablespoon finely chopped fresh flat-leaf parsley

CHEF'S NOTES: *If you plan to serve the caponata as part of an elegant appetizer, cut the eggplant into 1/4-inch dice. If your style is more casual, the dice can be as large as 3/4 inch. The caponata also makes a wonderful sandwich filling or stuffing for a chicken paillard.*

Depending on the fineness of the polenta and your pasta machine, you can press the polenta into the dough and then pass the dough through the pasta machine. Sometimes the polenta may cause the dough to tear, however. If so, back up to a wider setting to reroll the dough, then finish rolling out by hand.

Preheat the oven to 375°F. Cut each strip of dough in half crosswise for easier handling. Scatter some polenta on several baking sheets and on the work surface. Lay strips of dough on the polenta, scatter more polenta on top of the dough, and press down with your hands so the polenta is pressed into the dough. You can also do this with a rolling pin. Transfer to the prepared baking sheets.

Mist the dough with water, then sprinkle with salt and pepper to taste, the red pepper flakes, if using, and the orange zest. Press down lightly again to help seasonings adhere to the dough. Score into generous rectangular crackers with a rolling ravioli cutter or sharp knife.

Bake until browned and crisp, about 12 minutes. Let cool, then break along marked lines. (The crackers will keep, stored airtight, for a week or more.)

Heat 2 tablespoons of the olive oil in a large sauté pan over medium-high heat until hot. Add the eggplant and sauté until browned and cooked through, about 6 minutes. Add more olive oil as the cooking progresses if the pan becomes too dry. If you add more early on, the eggplant will absorb all of it and still need more. Make sure to scrape the bottom of the pan well so nothing burns. Season with salt and pepper. Scrape into a bowl.

In the same pan, heat another 2 tablespoons olive oil over medium-high heat until hot. Add the garlic and sauté briefly until brown. Add the onion and cook until beginning to brown, about 3 minutes. Reduce the heat to medium, and add the thyme and a pinch each of salt and pepper. Go easy on the salt because of the anchovies. Continue to cook until the onion is well browned, about 5 minutes. Add the anchovies and cook and stir until they melt into the onion. Add the caper juice and stand back to avoid getting splattered. Stir and scrape all around the pan. Add the vinegar, return the heat to high, and boil until reduced and thick, 1 to 2 minutes. Add the eggplant and capers, stir well, then scrape into a bowl. Stir in the roasted peppers and parsley and taste again for seasoning. Let cool to room temperature before serving. Serve with the polenta crackers.

Fusilli *with* Roasted Eggplant, Fall Vegetables, *and* Balsamic-Dijon Vinaigrette

Years ago, I cooked a special dinner at Mark's Place in Miami, a restaurant owned by Mark Militello. While there, I met his pastry chef, Ana Pineda, and hired her on the spot—with Mark's permission—to be Tra Vigne's pastry chef. Later, she became our Cantinetta manager. This is one of her Cantinetta recipes. We serve it as a warm pasta salad accompanied with a salad.

Serves 4

For the vinaigrette
2 tablespoons Dijon mustard

3 tablespoons balsamic vinegar

1 teaspoon finely chopped fresh thyme

Salt and freshly ground pepper

³/₄ cup extra-virgin olive oil

1 eggplant, about 1 pound, sliced
about ³/₄ inch thick

Salt

5 tablespoons extra-virgin olive oil

2 teaspoons finely chopped fresh thyme

2 teaspoons minced garlic

Freshly ground pepper

1 large fennel bulb, sliced about ¹/₂ inch thick

1 large zucchini, about ¹/₂ pound,
sliced diagonally about ¹/₂ inch thick

1 pint basket pearl onions, peeled

1 large red bell pepper, roasted, peeled, seeded,
and cut into ¹/₂-inch dice (page 64)

³/₄ pound dried fusilli

3 tablespoons finely chopped fresh
flat-leaf parsley

3 tablespoons freshly grated Parmesan cheese

To make the vinaigrette, combine the mustard, vinegar, thyme, and salt and pepper to taste in a bowl or blender and whisk or blend to mix. While whisking vigorously or with the machine running, add the oil in a thin, steady stream so the mixture emulsifies. You should have about 1 cup. (The vinaigrette can be made 1 to 2 days ahead.)

Preheat the oven to 475°F. Salt the eggplant for 30 minutes, then rinse and dry (page 110). Toss the eggplant with 1¹/₂ tablespoons of the olive oil, 1 teaspoon of the thyme, 1 teaspoon of the garlic, and a little pepper. Place on a baking sheet and roast in the oven until brown on both sides and tender, about 30 minutes. Toss the fennel, zucchini, and onions in a bowl with 3 tablespoons of the olive oil, the remaining 1 teaspoon thyme, the remaining 1 teaspoon garlic, and salt and pepper to taste. Place on a baking sheet and roast in the oven until brown and tender, about 20 minutes. While the vegetables are roasting, check and turn them occasionally and remove any pieces that are done before the others. Let the vegetables cool, then dice into ¹/₂-inch pieces. Place in a large bowl with the roasted pepper.

Meanwhile, bring a large pot of water to a boil and add salt. Add the pasta and cook until al dente, about 12 minutes. Place the bowl with the vegetables on top of the pasta pot to reheat, if necessary. When the pasta is done, drain and add to the bowl with the vegetables. Toss well with about ¹/₂ cup vinaigrette. Taste and add more if needed. Add the parsley and Parmesan and toss again. Taste for seasoning.

Serve warm or at room temperature.

Grilled Eggplant Pizza

3 eggplants, about 3 pounds total,
    sliced ³/₄ inch thick

Salt

Extra-virgin olive oil for brushing on
    vegetables, plus about ¼ cup

Freshly ground pepper

2 large red or yellow bell peppers

1 recipe Piadine Dough (page 194)

All-purpose flour for dusting work surface

1 tablespoon minced garlic

2 tablespoons finely chopped fresh oregano

1 teaspoon red pepper flakes (optional)

About 1 cup pitted Kalamata olives

About ½ pound buffalo mozzarella cheese
    or provolone cheese, coarsely shredded

About 3 cups packed arugula

Balsamic vinegar

Since you've gone to the trouble to light the grill for the eggplant, why not grill the whole thing, pizza dough included? This is what is called a "dry" pie, meaning it has no tomato sauce, but it does not taste dry. I like the brininess of buffalo mozzarella here, but any fresh mozzarella will do. Provolone is also a good choice. You might find it more convenient to grill just one or two larger pies rather than six individual ones.

Serves 6

Prepare the grill and let burn down to medium coals. Salt the eggplant for 30 minutes, then rinse and dry (page 110).

Brush the eggplant slices with olive oil and season with pepper. Toss the peppers with a little olive oil. Place both on the grill and cook the eggplant until browned on the first side, about 3 minutes. The slices should be browned between the grill marks when ready to turn. Move them away from direct heat and cook on the second side until tender, about 10 minutes total. Cut the slices into ½-inch dice.

Cook the peppers, turning as necessary, until charred all over. Remove the peppers to a bowl. Cover and let the peppers steam to loosen the skins. When cool enough to handle, peel, seed, and tear into long, thin strips.

Divide the dough into 6 equal balls. Working on a surface free of flour, roll each ball under your palm. As it rolls, it will stick slightly to the surface, creating tension that helps form a tight, round ball. Dust the work surface lightly with flour, pat each ball down lightly, dust the tops with flour, cover with a towel, and let rise for about 15 minutes. With a rolling pin, roll out each ball into a circle 8 or 9 inches in diameter and about ⅛ inch thick.

Have the grill ready at medium heat. Have the ¼ cup olive oil, eggplant, peppers, garlic, oregano, red pepper flakes (if using), olives, and cheese in bowls and ready by the side of the grill.

Brush each dough round with about 1 teaspoon of the olive oil. Place on the grill, oiled side up, and cook until browned on the underside, about 2 minutes. Turn and, working quickly, brush each round with another 1 teaspoon olive oil. Then scatter each with one-sixth each of the garlic, oregano, red pepper flakes (if using), eggplant, bell peppers, olives, and cheese. Cover the grill and cook until the rounds are browned on the bottom and the cheese has softened, about 7 minutes.

Transfer to plates and top each with an equal amount of the arugula. Spritz lightly with vinegar. Serve immediately.

CHEF'S NOTES: *To cook in the oven, position the racks on the lowest and uppermost rungs, place 2 large baking sheets on the racks, and preheat to 500°F. Remove the sheets, dust them with cornmeal, and transfer the dough rounds to them. Brush each round with about 1 teaspoon olive oil. Scatter the ingredients evenly over the rounds. Bake until the crusts are light brown on the bottom, 8 to 12 minutes.*

Roasted Eggplant *and* Onion Ravioloni *with* Roasted Tomato Sauce

This is a wonderful dish, homey tasting but refined looking. You can grill or sauté the vegetables for the filling instead of roasting them. In summer, you might want to grill everything, including the tomatoes for the sauce. I recommend serving the ravioloni as a main course, because when it comes to food hugs like this dish, a small portion may not be enough. They would also taste great next to a piece of lamb.

Makes about 16 ravioloni; serves about 8 as an appetizer, or 3 or 4 as a main course

1 eggplant, about 1 pound, sliced ½ inch thick
Salt
1 large red or yellow onion, sliced ½ inch thick
1½ pounds vine-ripened tomatoes, cored
Extra-virgin olive oil for brushing on vegetables,
    plus 3 tablespoons
4 teaspoons finely chopped fresh thyme
Freshly ground pepper
About 6 ounces provolone cheese
1 can (28 ounces) whole tomatoes
    (see Chef's Notes)
1 tablespoon minced garlic
1 cup minced onion
1 recipe Pasta Dough,
    rolled to ravioli thickness (page 195)
All-purpose flour for dusting work surface
2 tablespoons unsalted butter
1 tablespoon freshly grated Parmesan cheese
1 tablespoon finely chopped fresh
    flat-leaf parsley

Preheat the oven to 475°F. Salt the eggplant for 30 minutes, then rinse and dry (page 110).

Brush the eggplant, sliced onion, and fresh tomatoes with olive oil and sprinkle each with 1 teaspoon of the thyme. Season the eggplant with pepper and the onion and tomatoes with salt and pepper. Pour each vegetable into a separate baking dish and roast, turning occasionally, until browned on both sides and tender, about 30 minutes for the eggplant and about 35 minutes for the onions and tomatoes.

When the vegetables are cool enough to handle, finely chop the eggplant and onion and scrape into a bowl. Peel the tomatoes. Chop the tomatoes and put in a sieve over a bowl. Reserve the juices for another use (or add to the sauce). Add the tomatoes to the eggplant and onion. Using the coarse holes of a grater, grate enough provolone to measure ½ cup. Cut the remaining cheese into ¾-inch chunks and set aside. Add the grated cheese to the vegetables and toss well. Taste for salt and pepper. Reserve to use as the raviolini filling.

Preheat the broiler. Pour the canned tomatoes and their juice into a flameproof baking dish and add 1 tablespoon of the olive oil, the remaining 1 teaspoon thyme, and salt and pepper to taste. Run the tomatoes under the broiler until brown on top, about 5 minutes, then stir. Repeat the browning and stirring as often as needed until the tomatoes develop a roasted flavor, about 30 minutes. Remove from the broiler and put in a sieve over a bowl. Chop the tomatoes if they have not broken down, and set the tomatoes and juice aside separately.

Heat the remaining 2 tablespoons of the olive oil in a nonreactive saucepan over medium-high heat. Add the garlic and sauté briefly until light brown. Add the minced onion and a pinch of salt and sauté until the onion begins to brown, about 3 minutes. Lower the heat to medium and continue to sauté until cooked through and well browned, about 6 minutes. Add the juice from the canned broiled tomatoes (and the reserved roasted fresh tomato juice, if desired) and bring to a boil. Cook several minutes to thicken. Add the canned broiled tomatoes and season with salt and pepper to taste. Simmer until thickened, about 10 minutes. Set aside.

With a ravioli cutter or sharp knife, cut the pasta sheets into large rectangles, about 3 inches by 4 inches. Reroll and cut the scraps, if desired. Top half of the pasta pieces with a rounded spoonful of filling. Brush around the filling with water and top with the remaining pasta pieces. Close by working from the center toward the edges to press out air bubbles. Press the dough edges so they are the thickness of a single sheet of dough. Dust with flour and cover with a tea towel until ready to cook.

Bring a large pot of water to a boil and add salt. Add the ravioloni and simmer gently until al dente, about 3 minutes after they return to the top of the water. It is important to simmer gently, so they do not pop open. Drain.

While the ravioloni are cooking, finish the tomato sauce. Add the provolone chunks to the simmering sauce so they soften but do not melt into the sauce (you should have about 2 chunks per person). Stir in the butter and keep warm until ready to serve.

Divide the ravioloni among warm soup plates. Spoon the tomato sauce over and around the pasta. (Do not drown the ravioloni in sauce.) Garnish with a dusting of Parmesan and parsley.

Variation with Beurre Noisette: To gild the lily, heat about 4 tablespoons ($^1/_2$ stick) unsalted butter over medium heat until it stops foaming and turns light brown. Pour a spoonful over each portion of the ravioloni and then spoon on the sauce.

CHEF'S NOTES: *If you are going to the trouble of making ravioloni, you might as well double the pasta dough and freeze any ravioloni you do not need. Extra filling is delicious on its own or wrapped in wonton wrappers or phyllo.*

If good tomatoes are still in season, you can make the sauce with fresh tomatoes, roasting them with the tomatoes that are tossed with the eggplant. You will need about 4 cups peeled, seeded, and chopped tomatoes to replace the canned tomatoes. This technique of roasting canned tomatoes allows you to add rich flavor to dishes when tomatoes are out of season.

WINTER

storytelling time

Whenever my family gets together, we tell stories. But winter is prime storytelling time. From the time I was young, we visited our grandparents, aunts, and uncles in the mountains of Northern California, where my parents were born. In winter we would gather around the big wood stove in Nonna's kitchen and listen to family tales. The older we children became, the more details our parents and grandparents added to their telling. ❧ Winter is also a time of magical meals. Aunt Mary, my mother's sister, will call to say, "When are you coming up? I'll boil a chicken." On the face of it, not a very enticing invitation. But taste the soup from that boiled chicken, and it is the most incredible bowl of soup you've ever had. Then there is the poached chicken. Finally, her whole pantry opens up and a parade of tastes occupies the rest of the afternoon: prosciutto, salami, breads, sardines. All are as varied, rich, familiar, and surprising as the voices and laughter that accompany each course. ❧ Three flavors come to mind when I think of winter. Olive pressing takes place in late fall and winter. Until we got our new equipment, chefs Michael Laukert, Carmen Quagliata, and I would cook all day, then press all night with our little olive mill and press. It would get so cold, we'd come into the kitchen to warm up by the stoves. Because new-pressed oil is so fresh and its flavor is so particular and vibrant, it is not really a fat but a flavor, a major presence in a dish, used as a condiment at the very end of cooking. And I love oranges. Mom and I would often eat oranges together in the evening, then she would put the peels in a paper bag and put them in the fire. We also gathered walnuts to dry in the sun or in front of the fireplace. I remember my mother and I sitting on the floor of the garage with a bucket of walnuts. We'd crack them with hammers, laughing when they'd fly like shot into the air. ❧ For Tra Vigne's kitchen staff, winter is about recuperating from the rushing swirl of summer. The winter is when we restore our bonds, when we can explore food together and shake things up. ❧ Week long food festivals create excitement for the cooks and our diners. We make everything we can think of with truffles. We stage a gnocchi week to see and understand the many faces of this pasta—*alla romana*, crispy, potato, and all flour. In 1997, my partner Kevin Cronin, then Tra Vigne's general manager and now our director of operations at Real Restaurants, returned from our trip to Italy with gnocchi boards for all the chefs. Now they compete for the title of fastest gnocchi maker. ❧ When the restaurant is less busy, we may sell just ten or twenty orders of a special. That allows us to indulge in such handmade pastas as bow ties that are twisted, not squeezed, or garganelli, a pennelike pasta wrapped around a dowel, then rolled on a gnocchi board to mark them with ridges. ❧ I also want to be at home more in the winter, to spend more time around my personal table. The cooks at Tra Vigne have an open invitation to my house on Sundays, and Ines and I invite people over several times a week. ❧ In winter, my personal taste turns to long-cooked flavors and multiple-step cooking methods. For instance, I like to brine oxtails, then smoke them, braise them, pick the meat off the bone, and stuff it in chard leaves to serve in a jus of reduced cooking liquids. I believe that more complicated cooking is necessary, because the choice of ingredients narrows in this season. You have to create and vary flavor through cooking techniques. There is more time for cooking and, I think, people just want to be where it is warm, in the kitchen. It's Sunday, you're at home, and it's raining hard.

broccoli

Say broccoli and my mind turns not to the all-American, tightly clustered, dark green heads of broccoli, but to broccoli rabe, an Italian green with a distinctive bitter flavor. Both broccoli and broccoli rabe are members of the large cabbage family. This fact is important to keep in mind when cooking broccoli, because when overcooked, broccoli smells, well, like cabbage and is unappealing. Cooked just until bright green and tender, its flavor remains its own. ❦ The culinary difference between broccoli and broccoli rabe is that broccoli is mainly about the florets and broccoli rabe is about leaves and stems. A bunch of broccoli rabe looks similar to the wild mustard that blankets Napa Valley in winter. It has tiny yellow flowers, moss green stems, and leaves that look like overblown broccoli leaves. Broccoli may always be substituted for broccoli rabe, as well as mustard greens. (This equation does not move in the opposite direction, however, because of broccoli rabe's bitter edge.) Once known and grown only by Italians, broccoli rabe is becoming more common at farmers' markets and good produce markets in fall and winter. ❦ While I can say that I love the taste of broccoli rabe, I wonder how many people would say broccoli is their favorite vegetable. It is too dependable and available all year in supermarkets to arouse a passionate response. But eating broccoli in season reinstates it as a vegetable to look forward to. Who could say no to a quick supper of pasta with sautéed broccoli florets, toasted garlic, and red pepper flakes? The flavor of broccoli adapts particularly well to cheeses, and I like to serve it in ways that make it taste sumptuous—as a course all on its own coated with butter and toasted Parmesan cheese (page 125) or with a decadent sauce of Cambozola cheese and cream (page 129).

TRIMMING BROCCOLI When preparing broccoli, cut the stem from the flower head in one long piece. Cut a slice from the stem and taste the heart to make sure it is tender. If so, cut off and discard the stem end and peel the tough outer skin from the stem down to the pale green, tender heart. If the stem is fibrous, discard it. ❦ Cut the peeled stem in half unless very slim, and then cut crosswise into slices of equal size. Cook them, uncovered, in boiling salted water for about 3 minutes and then add the florets. Any time a recipe calls for florets only, you can always use the stems, too. Using florets only is usually a matter of looks, not taste or nutrition.

broccoli

Broccoli *and* Cauliflower *with* Shell Pasta

The combination of orange zest and raisins with red pepper flakes and pine nuts in a savory dish may at first seem unusual, but it is actually part of traditional Italian cooking, fairly typical of some old recipes of Venice and Sicily. The ingredients are probably vestiges of the Moorish conquests and occupations of much of the Mediterranean.

Serves 4

¾ pound broccoli florets

¾ pound cauliflower florets

¾ pound small dried pasta shells

¼ cup diced pancetta or thickly sliced bacon
(¼-inch dice; about 3 ounces)

About 3 tablespoons extra-virgin olive oil

1 tablespoon minced garlic, plus 1 teaspoon

½ teaspoon red pepper flakes

1 teaspoon finely chopped fresh rosemary

1½ cups chicken stock (page 204)
or canned low-salt chicken broth

Salt and freshly ground pepper

2 teaspoons freshly grated orange zest

½ cup raisins

¼ cup finely chopped fresh flat-leaf parsley

2 tablespoons pine nuts, toasted

½ cup freshly grated Parmesan, ricotta salata,
dry Jack, or aged goat cheese

Bring a large pot of water to a boil and add salt. Add the broccoli florets and cook quickly until just tender and still bright green, about 4 minutes. Dip the broccoli out with a sieve, shake off the excess water, and scatter on a baking sheet to cool. Repeat with the cauliflower. Reserve the water for cooking the pasta.

Return the vegetable cooking water to a rolling boil, add more salt and the pasta, and cook until al dente, about 12 minutes.

While the pasta is cooking, make the sauce: Heat together the pancetta and 1 tablespoon of the olive oil in a skillet over medium heat. Cook slowly until well browned and crisp. Tilt the pan to collect the fat in a little pool against the side and scrape the pancetta into the fat. Cook for another minute to make sure the pancetta is very crisp. Remove with a slotted spoon to paper towels to drain. Set the pancetta aside.

Add olive oil to the pan as needed to make about ¼ cup fat. Heat over medium-high heat until hot. Working quickly, add the garlic and cook until light brown. While standing back to avoid inhaling fumes and being splattered, add the red pepper flakes, rosemary, and stock. Bring to a boil, season with salt and pepper, and cook, stirring and scraping up all the browned bits that cling to the bottom and sides of the pan, to concentrate flavors a bit, about 2 minutes. Add the orange zest, raisins, parsley, and reserved pancetta and cook for another minute or so. Add the broccoli and cauliflower and stir and toss several minutes until heated through. Season with salt and pepper.

When the pasta is done, drain and, if there is room, turn it into the sauté pan holding the vegetables and toss. If not, pour the pasta into a warm serving bowl, immediately add the contents of the sauté pan, and toss well. Sprinkle with the pine nuts and serve immediately. Pass the cheese at the table.

Broccoli *with* Parmesan Fritelle

Here is one of those vegetable dishes in which the vegetable gets thoroughly cooked. The broccoli must be soft enough for a spoon to slice through easily, as if through soft butter. Sunday dinner traditions are based on this kind of dish: simple and unpretentious in looks and flavors and at the same time a celebration of that simplicity. Buy broccoli with the largest heads on the stalks you can find. Serve as a side vegetable with a roasted whole fish, chicken, or leg of lamb and steamed potatoes.

Serves 4

Unsalted butter for the baking sheet,
    plus 4 tablespoons (½ stick)
1 cup freshly grated Parmesan cheese
1 large bunch broccoli, about 1½ pounds
Salt and freshly ground pepper
2 tablespoons freshly squeezed lemon juice
1 tablespoon coarsely chopped fresh sage (optional)

CHEF'S NOTES: *The fritelle is reason enough to make this recipe. The taste of toasted Parmesan never fails to evoke memories of my mother and how she gave us tastes of the warm toasted cheese. I do the same with my daughters, so they will share that taste memory. You will have more fritelle than you need, which allows you plenty for snacking and for sprinkling on salads, soups, and pastas.*

Preheat the oven to 350°F. To make Parmesan fritelle (toasted Parmesan), line a baking sheet with aluminum foil and butter the foil well. Sprinkle the cheese in an even, thin layer over the whole baking sheet and place in the oven. Cook until lightly browned, about 5 minutes. The cheese will continue to cook even as you remove the baking sheet from the oven, so be sure to watch carefully. If some parts brown before others, you can remove these and replace the pan in the oven.

Quickly slide the foil off the baking sheet and let cool on a counter. When cool, pry the cheese off the foil and crumble into bits. You should have about 1 cup. (The recipe can be made to this point several days ahead and stored in an airtight container in the refrigerator. To serve, briefly recrisp, if necessary, in a nonstick skillet over medium heat.)

Bring a large pot of water to a boil and add salt. Cut the broccoli florets from the stems in one large piece, leaving an inch or more of stem attached. Peel the tough outer skin from the broccoli stems and trim off the fibrous ends. Cut the stems in half lengthwise. (This will allow heads and stems to cook in the same amount of time.) Cook the broccoli in the boiling water until very tender, about 8 minutes. Drain the florets and stand them stem end up on a warm serving platter. Scatter the stems around the florets and season with salt and pepper.

Melt the remaining 4 tablespoons butter in a medium skillet over medium-high heat. When the butter stops foaming and turns light brown, add the lemon juice and the sage, if using. Cook, swirling the pan, for about 30 seconds, to cook off some of the sharpness of the lemon juice. Immediately pour over the broccoli and sprinkle with ¼ cup of the fritelle. Serve at once.

Very Green Broccoli Soup

1½ pounds broccoli
2 tablespoons extra-virgin olive oil
1 tablespoon unsalted butter
1 tablespoon minced garlic
1 cup diced onion (¼-inch dice)
½ cup diced celery (¼-inch dice)
Salt and freshly ground pepper
2 teaspoons finely chopped fresh thyme

5 cups chicken stock (page 204)
    or canned low-salt chicken broth
2 cups packed spinach
2 teaspoons freshly grated lemon zest
1 cup heavy cream or buttermilk (if using
    buttermilk, cut the lemon zest in half)
¼ cup Gremolata (page 192)

Has soup become too old-fashioned? I hope not, because I love making soup. It can be served in far more ways than in a bowl, too. At Tra Vigne, we use soups as sauces for pasta and rice and even as the foundation for a dish. For example, we might ladle this soup in the bottom of a deep plate and top it with a piece of roasted fish and steamed potatoes. Soup is one of the best things in the world to freeze. And if you are in a hurry, just cut the ingredients into smaller pieces so they cook faster. This is a thick soup that would easily make a satisfying supper, especially if served with the Gorgonzola crostini suggested in the variation.

Makes about 8 cups; serves 6

Cut the broccoli florets from the stems. Peel the tough outer skin from the stems and trim off the fibrous ends. Cut the stems lengthwise into slices about $\frac{1}{2}$ inch thick and then crosswise into $\frac{1}{2}$-inch pieces.

Heat the olive oil and butter in a soup pot over medium-high heat until hot. Add the garlic and cook until light brown. Add the onion and celery, lower the heat to medium, and season with salt. Cook the vegetables slowly until tender, about 10 minutes. Regulate the heat so the vegetables cook without taking on color.

Add the thyme and stir. Add the broccoli stems, stock, and salt and pepper to taste and bring to a boil. Cook, uncovered, for about 3 minutes. Add the florets and continue to cook until very tender, about 7 minutes more. Stir in the spinach and lemon zest. The spinach will wilt into the soup. Puree the soup in a blender in small batches. (The soup can be made to this point, covered, and refrigerated for up to 1 day or frozen for up to 1 month.)

Return the soup to the pan and reheat over gentle heat. Stir in the cream. Taste and adjust the seasoning with salt and pepper. Ladle into warm bowls and sprinkle a teaspoonful of Gremolata on top of each bowl. Pass the remaining Gremolata at the table.

Variation with Gorgonzola Crostini: Another delicious garnish would be Gorgonzola crostini. If you make large ones, soup becomes dinner. Cut thin slices from good, crusty bread. Butter the slices on both sides and toast in a 375°F oven until brown and crisp on the outside but still soft within, about 12 minutes. Mash together equal amounts of Gorgonzola and unsalted butter (or to taste) and spread on the toasts. Return to a warm oven just before serving to allow the cheese to soften and warm, but not run.

CHEF'S NOTE: *When I plan on finishing a dish with the addition of a dairy product, as I do here with cream, I often add a dairy product early in the cooking, too, as I do with the butter in the initial cooking of the vegetables. It melds the flavors.*

Soft Polenta *with* Pancetta *and* Broccoli Rabe

How about a food hug? Just try this dish and see if you don't agree it's that kind of comfort food. The taste of bitter greens against the richness of the polenta makes a great combination. It can be a supper dish on its own and it also makes a wonderful pillow for roast chicken. This recipe is really more a technique than a recipe specific to broccoli rabe. You can use any winter green—mustard greens, kale, chard, spinach—or any vegetable that tastes good when cooked with garlic and thyme. I'm not sure I can name one that wouldn't.

Serves 4

1 recipe Soft Polenta (page 201)
1 slice pancetta, ¼ inch thick
About 1 tablespoon extra-virgin olive oil
1 tablespoon minced garlic
1 tablespoon finely chopped fresh thyme
1½ cups chicken stock (page 204)
 or canned low-salt chicken broth
4 cups packed roughly chopped broccoli rabe
 or mustard greens
Salt and freshly ground pepper

CHEF'S NOTE: *If the broccoli rabe is bitter, soak it in ice water for 30 minutes before cooking. If it looks as if it has bolted, blanch and drain it before continuing with the recipe.*

Make the polenta and keep warm. Unwind the pancetta into a long strip and cut crosswise into ¼-inch-wide pieces. Heat together the pancetta and the 1 tablespoon olive oil in a skillet over medium heat. Cook slowly until well browned and crisp. Tilt the pan to collect the fat in a little pool against the side and scrape the pancetta into the fat. Cook for another minute to make sure the pancetta is very crisp. Remove with a slotted spoon to paper towels to drain. Set the pancetta aside.

There should be about 2 tablespoons fat remaining in the pan. If not, add a little olive oil. Turn the heat to medium-high and heat until hot. Add the garlic and sauté briefly until light brown. Add the thyme, stir, add the stock, and bring to a boil. Cook until reduced by about half. Add the broccoli rabe, season with salt and pepper, toss well, cover, reduce the heat to low, and cook until tender, about 5 minutes.

Pour the polenta into a warm serving dish or bowl and pour the vegetables over it. Sprinkle with the reserved pancetta.

Broccoli *with* Cambozola Sauce

The sauce is so delicious, you might want to make this the main event for a party with salad and bread and perhaps a fruit tart for dessert. Otherwise, it's a spectacular first course. You could add other vegetables such as carrots. And when spring rolls around, you won't have to give up your newest favorite recipe. Use asparagus.

Serves 4

½ loaf good, crusty bread
2 tablespoons unsalted butter
Salt and freshly ground pepper
2 tablespoons extra-virgin olive oil
½ cup water
1½ pounds broccoli
¼ pound Cambozola cheese
½ cup heavy cream
1 teaspoon finely chopped fresh thyme
2 tablespoons pine nuts, toasted

Preheat the oven to 375°F. Cut the bread into thick slices about 1½ inches wide and 5 inches long. You will need at least 1 slice per person. Melt the butter in an ovenproof skillet, add the bread, and toss to coat well. Season with salt and pepper. Toss again and bake until browned and crisp outside but still soft within, about 15 minutes. Drain on paper towels and keep warm.

Combine the olive oil, water, and salt and pepper to taste in a large sauté pan and bring to a boil. Cut the broccoli florets from the stems, leaving about 2 inches of stem attached to the florets. Save the stems for another use. Add the florets to the sauté pan, cover, and cook for 5 minutes. Uncover and raise the heat to boil off any remaining water. Sauté the broccoli in the olive oil remaining in the pan until cooked through and light brown, about 5 minutes longer.

While the broccoli is cooking, slowly melt the Cambozola with the cream in a saucepan. Add the thyme and season well with pepper. Place 1 or more slices of bread on each of 4 warm plates. Arrange the broccoli on the bread and pour the sauce over the top. Sprinkle each serving with pine nuts. Serve immediately.

artichokes

Originally a North African native and a member of the thistle family, artichokes need the cool and damp of the northern end of California's Salinas Valley, or the plants bolt and flower before they form artichokes. The beautiful plant, with its long, curving, silvery green, thick leaves, is often grown in the Napa Valley as an ornamental. Our farmers' markets are full of the large, blue, thistlelike flowers in the fall. Artichokes are now available year-round, but the Monterey crop, planted in May through August, begins its harvest in September and gets into full swing about December. By May the crop is tapering off. Look for artichokes with tightly closed leaves. It seems that the more tightly closed the leaves, the larger the heart. If you are in a place that allows discreet squeezing, go ahead. The vegetable should feel firm, not squishy, and heavy in your hand. Check the stem to see if it has been freshly cut. "The lighter the color, the sweeter the choke" is an old saying. Dark green artichokes will have seen more sun and can be fibrous. Instead, choose those that are medium green. Sometimes the tips of artichoke leaves carry sharp thorns. If so, and if I plan to serve the artichoke whole, I clip the thorns, but normally I don't bother. The thorns soften when cooked and no longer pose a threat. I'm a "heart" man, however. I cook artichokes mainly for the heart and rarely serve the vegetable whole. I do like to stew baby artichokes whole when they are very tender and sweet. The hearts can also be thinly sliced and eaten raw. I often make a salad of raw artichoke hearts, sliced as thinly as possible, with a dressing of lemon juice, gray salt, and extra-virgin olive oil.

PREPARING ARTICHOKE HEARTS If you plan on doing a number of artichokes, it is a good idea to wear surgical gloves. The oils work into your hands and under your nails and everything you touch afterward will taste bitter. Use stainless steel knives. Make sure you have a bowl of water ready into which you have squeezed the juice of 2 lemons. Drop the lemon rinds into the water as well. Prepare 1 artichoke at a time. As you work, dip it into the lemon water occasionally to prevent darkening. When the heart is fully trimmed, drop it immediately into the bowl. Preparing artichoke hearts correctly is one of the hardest things to teach people. But once you get the hang of it, it is very simple. My method results in more of the meat at the base of each leaf being left on the artichoke, so the heart ends up slightly larger than it would by other methods. But it is a small percentage, important in the restaurant industry, less so at home. Begin by pulling off the tiny leaves around the base and stem and discard. Trim the stem to within about an inch of the base. Then, instead of simply snapping off the larger leaves any which way, hold the artichoke stem down in your left hand (if you are right-handed). Hold your left thumb against the base of each leaf as you grasp its top between your right thumb and forefinger. Pull down and the leaf will snap off above your left thumb. The fat flesh you would normally eat from a cooked leaf stays behind on the artichoke. Continue snapping until only pale yellow-green leaves remain. You will know when you have taken off enough of the leaves not just from the color, but from the feel as well. As you work toward the center of the artichoke, the leaves become more pliable and tender and you will suddenly discover that there is no effort needed to snap off the leaves. Cut off and discard the top third of the artichoke. Turn the artichoke so you can see the cut surface of the stem. You will notice a light-colored inner circle. Trim away all the stem to this circle, the tender core. Trim the artichoke bottom of any remaining dark green parts. Cut the artichoke lengthwise into quarters and cut out the choke with the paring knife. At this point follow the chosen recipe.

carciofi

Lemon-Braised Artichokes

This recipe came into Tra Vigne's repertoire more than nine years ago. Brent Brassotti, reaching back into his family's Tuscan roots, prepared these artichokes when he interviewed for a chef's position with us. This dish is a great example of what I call a master recipe. Artichokes prepared by this method lend themselves to dozens of uses, and they are one of my very favorite flavors, whether served as an appetizer salad on their own, in a pasta (page 133), or under fish or meat (page 134). A few additional ideas appear at the end of the recipe. Wait until artichokes are in full season before delving into this recipe. Yes, it takes some work to trim the hearts, but think of it as a little winter therapy. If preparing a larger number of artichokes, just increase the marinade proportionately. If you like spicy food, add a pinch of red pepper flakes to the marinade.

Makes 4 braised hearts

1/2 cup extra-virgin olive oil

1/4 cup freshly squeezed lemon juice

1 1/2 teaspoons finely chopped fresh thyme,
   or 3/4 teaspoon herbes de Provence

1 1/2 teaspoons minced garlic

1 1/2 teaspoons kosher salt

Small pinch freshly ground pepper

4 medium or large artichoke hearts (page 130)

1/2 lemon

Preheat the oven to 375°F. Combine the olive oil, lemon juice, thyme, garlic, salt, and pepper in a medium nonreactive saucepan. Mix well and set aside while preparing the artichokes.

As each artichoke heart quarter is completed, immediately turn it in the marinade to coat completely. When all the artichokes are trimmed, put the pan over high heat and bring to a boil. (This step may be omitted, but it gets the cooking process off to a rapid start.) Pour the artichokes and marinade into a baking dish (or cook them in the saucepan if it is ovenproof), cover, and cook until the artichokes test tender when pierced with a fork, about 1 hour. Remove from the oven and let cool in the cooking liquid.

Ideas for Serving and Cooking with Lemon-Braised Artichoke Hearts:

Serve them as an appetizer salad on their own with their braising liquid. Make sure to have crusty bread on hand to sop up the juices.

Slice or roughly chop and scatter across a cheese pizza. Be sure to drizzle some of the braising liquid on the pizza as well.

Roughly chop and add to a risotto at the last minute just to heat through. Add some of the braising liquid, too, to flavor the risotto.

Season a nice piece of fish with salt and pepper and place on top of the artichokes to cook with them the last 10 to 15 minutes of their cooking time.

Fettuccine *with* Lemon-Braised Artichokes

Call it homemade convenience food: this very simple dish tastes complex because you are capitalizing on work already done. The flavor is in the artichokes. This is almost a pasta *in brodo*; I find the brothiness appealing, and the dish would be nice topped with a sautéed chicken breast. Feel free to substitute *orecchiette* for the fettuccine.

Serves 4 as a first course or light supper dish

½ pound dried fettuccine

2 tablespoons extra-virgin olive oil

12 garlic cloves, lightly crushed with the
    side of a knife

4 cups double-strength chicken stock
    (page 204), or 8 cups canned low-salt chicken
    broth boiled until reduced by half

Salt and freshly ground pepper

3 tablespoons unsalted butter (optional)

2 tablespoons finely chopped fresh chervil
    (optional)

2 tablespoons finely chopped fresh marjoram
    or oregano

1 recipe Lemon-Braised Artichokes (page 132),
    thinly sliced (reserve cooking liquid
    for another use)

¼ cup freshly grated Parmesan cheese,
    plus 2 tablespoons

Bring a large pot of water to a boil and add salt. Add the pasta and cook until al dente, about 12 minutes.

Meanwhile, heat the olive oil in a large sauté pan over medium-high heat until hot. Add the garlic and tilt the pan to collect the oil in a little pool against the side. Push the garlic into the oil and cook until golden brown, about 2 minutes. Move the pan on and off the heat to regulate the temperature so the garlic does not burn. Taking care to stand out of the way of spatters, add the chicken stock. Bring to a boil, reduce the heat to a gentle simmer, and cook until the garlic is cooked through, about 5 minutes. Taste for salt and pepper.

Add the butter and chervil, if using, the marjoram, and the artichokes. The pasta should now be done, so drain and add to the sauté pan with the ¼ cup Parmesan.

Toss well and pour into a warm serving bowl. Scatter the remaining 2 tablespoons Parmesan on top and serve immediately.

Lemon-Braised Artichokes *and* White Beans *with* Pan-Seared Lamb Loin

The spicing in this dish is Italian, but by adding other spices such as cumin it could easily take on flavors characteristic of other Mediterranean countries. To save yourself time, make sure your butcher does the work of trimming the lamb of all fat and silver skin. The various parts of this dish can be completed well ahead of time, then reheated for a few minutes while the lamb finishes cooking. Potatoes can replace the beans, or you can use any type of bean you prefer or have on hand: lentils, split peas, even black beans. They would make a great contrast with the spice coating on the lamb. If you have trouble finding lamb loins, use loin lamb chops, serving one or two per person.

Serves 4

1 cup dried white beans such as
   Great Northern beans or navy beans
2 lamb loins, about ½ pound each, trimmed
   of fat and silver skin
2 tablespoons Toasted Spice Rub (page 192)
2 tablespoons finely chopped carrot
2 tablespoons finely chopped celery
¼ cup finely chopped onion
2 garlic cloves
1 bay leaf
1 teaspoon finely chopped fresh thyme
2 cups water
Salt and freshly ground pepper
1 recipe Lemon-Braised Artichokes
   with their cooking liquid (page 132)
2 tablespoons extra-virgin olive oil
3 tablespoons finely chopped fresh
   flat-leaf parsley

Pick over the beans to remove any small stones. Rinse, put in a medium pot, add water to cover, and place over high heat. As soon as the beans begin to boil, remove from the heat and let cool for about 1 hour.

Season the lamb well with the spice rub and let sit for 30 to 60 minutes, or refrigerate for several hours or as long as overnight. As the meat sits, the rub draws out some of the moisture and forms a crust. The longer the meat sits with the seasoning, the more the crust adheres to the meat.

Drain the soaked beans, rinse, and return to the pot with the carrot, celery, onion, garlic, bay leaf, and thyme. Add the water, bring to a boil over high heat, reduce the heat to low, cover partially, and simmer until the beans are tender, 45 to 60 minutes. Add salt and pepper to taste only during the last half of the cooking time. (Early salting toughens the skins of the beans and lengthens cooking time.) Add more water if the beans absorb all the liquid before they are tender.

When the beans are cooked, drain and reserve the cooking liquid. Set aside several tablespoons artichoke braising liquid for use in the lamb pan sauce. Puree the beans in a food processor with 2 of the braised artichoke hearts. Unless you prefer a smooth puree, leave some texture. Thin with the remaining liquid from the braised chokes and some of the bean stock, if necessary. The puree should be the texture of soft mashed potatoes. Season with salt and pepper. Keep warm. (The recipe can be made to this point, covered, and refrigerated for 1 to 2 days.

Reheat, covered, in a microwave oven.) Coarsely chop and reserve the remaining 2 artichoke hearts.

When ready to complete the dish, preheat the oven to 450°F. Heat the olive oil in a heavy, ovenproof sauté pan over medium-high heat until very hot. Add the meat and cook on one side until brown, 1 to 2 minutes. Turn the meat and immediately place in the oven to finish cooking, about 5 minutes. (If using chops, they will take an extra 2 minutes or so for rare meat.) If the meat is at room temperature, it will cook very rapidly at this heat. Check at 2 minutes. (The meat may be browned several hours ahead of time, then cooked in the preheated oven just before serving.)

When the meat is cooked, transfer to a carving board and let rest for 3 to 4 minutes. To make the sauce, place the pan in which the lamb was cooked over medium heat. Add ½ cup reserved bean cooking liquid and stir and scrape up all the browned bits from the bottom and sides of the pan. Add the reserved artichoke braising liquid, chopped artichoke hearts, and 2 tablespoons of the parsley. Taste and season with salt and pepper.

To serve, mound the bean puree in the center of a warm platter or divide among 4 warm dinner plates. Cut each loin in half crosswise, then into thin slices lengthwise. Arrange on top of the bean puree. Spoon the sauce around the puree and garnish with the remaining 1 tablespoon parsley.

CHEF'S NOTE: *I suspect some people may feel letting meat rest is an affectation, especially in the case of a piece as small as a lamb loin. But here it is more important than ever. Resting allows the juices to be reabsorbed into the meat. When it is carved or sliced after resting, the meat remains juicy and moist.*

Roasted Artichokes, Carrots, *and* Fennel *with* Pan-Roasted Halibut

2 lemons

3 large artichoke hearts (page 130), halved
  instead of quartered

16 baby-cut carrots

1 small fennel bulb, halved lengthwise, then each
  half cut into quarters (or use 1/2 large bulb)

4 halibut or sea bass steaks, about 6 ounces each

Salt and freshly ground pepper

2 1/4 teaspoons herbes de Provence

2 tablespoons extra-virgin olive oil

1 cup dry white wine, fish or chicken stock
  (page 204), or canned low-salt chicken broth

1 1/2 tablespoons finely chopped fennel leaves

3 tablespoons unsalted butter (optional)

This is a great one-pot dish that is more a method than a recipe. I've kept the seasonings simple. For a heartier dish, you could substitute meat or poultry for the fish, use other vegetables such as potatoes, add garlic, and finish the sauce with red wine instead of white. For a spring feast, you could use fat asparagus in place of the artichokes and add English peas at the very end to cook briefly. If you want to stay away from butter, use olive oil to finish the sauce, although I do prefer the taste of butter here. And if you happen to have baby artichokes in your market, use them. Leave them whole and use three per person.

Serves 4

Preheat the oven to 400°F. Bring a large pot of water to a boil and add salt. Cut the lemons in half and squeeze the juice into the salted water. Drop in the shells. Add the artichoke hearts, carrots, and fennel. Cook until all the vegetables are tender, about 12 minutes. Drain and spread on a baking sheet to cool.

Season the fish steaks on both sides with salt and pepper and then season each steak with $1/2$ teaspoon of the herbs. Heat the olive oil in a heavy, ovenproof sauté pan over medium-high heat until hot. Add the fish and sear for about 2 minutes on each side. Remove the fish to a plate.

Replace the pan over medium-high heat and add the artichokes, carrots, and fennel. Season with salt and pepper and the remaining $1/4$ teaspoon herbes de Provence. Sauté until brown, about 3 minutes.

Arrange the fish on top of the vegetables and place the pan, uncovered, in the oven to finish cooking, about 10 minutes.

When cooked, remove the fish and vegetables to a warm platter and keep warm while you make the sauce. Place the sauté pan over medium-high heat and add the wine. Bring to a boil, stirring and scraping all the browned bits from the bottom and sides of the pan. Cook until reduced by about two-thirds (this is a brothy sauce).

Stir in the fennel leaves and the butter, if using. Taste for seasoning and pour over the fish. Serve immediately.

CHEF'S NOTE: *Do not make a habit of blanching all vegetables with lemon juice. It is necessary here to prevent the artichokes from darkening and adds a wonderful contrasting tang to fennel's sweetness. Vegetables full of chlorophyll such as asparagus and green beans will immediately turn brown if in contact with lemon juice or vinegar, however. So, if you are planning a pretty green bean or asparagus salad, drizzle the dressing over the vegetables just before serving.*

Crispy Artichoke *and* Baby Spinach Salad *with* Creamy Tarragon Dressing

For the creamy tarragon dressing
$^1/_2$ cup buttermilk
$^1/_4$ cup sour cream
2 tablespoons roughly chopped fresh tarragon
1 tablespoon capers
$^1/_4$ teaspoon salt
$^1/_4$ teaspoon freshly ground pepper
$^1/_2$ cup extra-virgin olive oil
1 tablespoon champagne vinegar

4 to 6 cups peanut oil for deep-frying
About $^1/_2$ cup buttermilk
1 large artichoke heart (page 130), sliced about $^1/_{16}$ inch thick
About 1 cup Arborio Rice Coating (page 193)
Salt and freshly ground pepper
1 large lemon, very thinly sliced and seeded
16 Kalamata olives
8 cups baby spinach
Long curls of lemon zest

Who says you can't fry ahead of time. The coating I suggest here, made with Arborio rice flour (nothing so very exotic, just rice pulverized in a blender), stays crisp and has a wonderful, sweet crunchiness. Served as is, the salad makes a great lunch. Add calamari or rock shrimp that have been dipped in buttermilk, dredged in the same coating as the vegetables, and fried, and the salad easily becomes a substantial main dish. You will have more of the light, bright-tasting dressing than you will need. You can use the remainder as a dip for crudités, a sauce for crab cakes, or as a substitute for tartar sauce. If possible, make the dressing an hour or more ahead of time to give it an opportunity to thicken up in the refrigerator. It will keep for several days in a tightly sealed nonreactive container.

Serves 4

To make the dressing, combine the buttermilk, sour cream, tarragon, and capers in a blender. Puree until smooth. Season with the salt and pepper. With the machine running, add the olive oil and vinegar. Blend until smooth. Taste for seasoning. Pour into a clean glass jar, cover, and refrigerate. You should have about 1 cup.

Heat the oil in a deep fryer or deep pot to 350°F. Meanwhile, put the buttermilk in a bowl. Working in small batches, toss the artichoke hearts in the buttermilk. Put them in a sieve and shake off the excess liquid. Holding the sieve over another bowl, pour the rice coating over the artichoke slices. Toss to coat well and shake to remove excess.

Drop a single artichoke slice in the oil to test the heat. If it rises immediately to the top, the oil is ready. Fry the artichokes in small batches until crusty and golden brown, a very few minutes. Scoop out with a slotted spoon and drain on a paper towel-lined baking sheet. Taste and sprinkle with salt if desired. Put in a slow oven to keep warm.

Dip the lemon slices in the buttermilk and toss with the coating. Deep-fry until golden, about 1 minute. Put on the baking sheet with the artichoke hearts. Repeat the dipping and dredging with the olives, then fry them for less than a minute. Add to the baking sheet.

Toss the spinach with ¹/₃ cup of the dressing in a large bowl until well dressed. Season with salt and pepper to taste. Pile the spinach on 4 salad plates (it also looks attractive on larger plates). Spoon a border of dressing around each salad, and arrange the artichokes, lemons, and olives on this border, dividing them evenly among the plates. Garnish the salads with the lemon zest.

CHEF'S NOTES: *If you like to deep-fry, I strongly recommend an electric deep fryer. For a small investment you have the safety of temperature-controlled oil. And oil of even temperature is the secret to the best fried foods: crisp, not oily or soggy. Even temperature control also prevents oil from boiling over. If health is a concern, fry in pure olive oil. Also, be sure to put the fryer under the stove hood or as close to it as you can get. The exhaust will remove fumes, but there is another safety reason as well. If you have children in the house, they are accustomed to being warned away from the stove. If you fry on an open countertop, you run the risk of a curious child pulling on the handle of the fryer. Add only a few pieces of food at a time to the hot oil and don't drop them from any height. You don't want to get splattered.*

citrus

To me, citrus evokes memories of sticky hands on bicycle handlebars and bits of pith lodged between my teeth. When I was in junior high school, a buddy and I would ride our bikes home past a neighbor's orange tree. In December and January, we often parked ourselves under her tree, eating ripe oranges until we became too cold to sit anymore. Occasionally, the owner would chase us away, but she never frightened us enough to scare us off for long. At church one day years later, my mom began chatting with the tree's owner. She confessed she had seen us every time we robbed the branches. But because she understood that stolen pleasures sometimes taste sweeter, she would occasionally act the part of outraged owner and chase us away. ✦ Unless you live in a citrus-growing region, it may seem strange to consider citrus a seasonal crop. When you visit good produce or farmers' markets in California from late December through March, the variety of citrus fruits available could well bowl you over: thick-skinned navel oranges, juicy Valencias, Satsumas, Clementines, tangerines, pink grapefruit, white grapefruit, ugli fruits, pomelos, blood oranges, bitter Sevilles and Bergamots, iridescent yellow Meyer lemons, kumquats, and recently, limequats. Each of these will be the product of one of a variety of agricultural practices, including pesticide-free, organic, or commercial. To sample them is to experience firsthand why particular places become famous for the quality of their citrus. ✦ Grapefruit is to citrus what lamb is to meat. Its flavor has a pithiness that gives the fruit and juice a refreshing tang, but makes it difficult to use in cooking. I prefer to cook with oranges and lemons, especially Meyers. Roasting lemons until they lightly caramelize is a taste treat you will not soon forget (page 145). And one of the most delicious and versatile dressings I have ever created is a mayonnaiselike concoction of whole oranges and lemons put through a juicer (page 143). ✦ Various types of citrus are fairly interchangeable in recipes. Degrees of sweetness, acidity, and bitterness will affect the taste balance of recipes, however, so be sure to taste, taste, taste.

agrumi

Fennel-Spiced Prawns *with* Citrus Salad

In a sea of wintry dishes, citrus adds spark, so make this salad in winter, when your palate deserves a refreshing blast. Make it in summer, too, when citrus bears again and your tongue's hanging out from the heat. In winter, cook the prawns on the stove and finish in the oven. In summer, grill them. It's never more than a matter of minutes. Use any combination of citrus for the salad: pomelos, grapefruit, several varieties of orange, kumquats, Meyer lemons. Buy the largest prawns you can afford for a spectacular presentation. The taste is equally delicious with smaller prawns.

Serves 4

12 jumbo prawns or shrimp, about ½ pound total, shells on
1 tablespoon Fennel Spice (page 193)
1 blood orange
½ large grapefruit
2 navel or other large oranges
Salt and freshly ground pepper
¼ cup extra-virgin olive oil
1 large bunch watercress

Split the prawns open like a book, slitting from the head down the back to the tail but not quite cutting all the way through. Do not worry about pulling off the legs. Devein the prawns. Sprinkle the spice mix evenly over the flesh side of the prawns and let sit, covered and refrigerated, for up to 6 hours.

Cut the skin and white pith off all the citrus fruits and segment the fruits over a bowl to catch both the segments and the juices. Squeeze the cores to extract any extra juice. Season with salt and pepper and add 2 tablespoons of the olive oil. Toss well, taste for balance, and reserve.

Preheat the oven to 400°F. Heat the remaining 2 tablespoons olive oil in a large skillet with an even curved edge over medium-high heat until hot. Lay the prawns, flesh down, against the curved sides of the pan, tails up and heads toward the center of the pan. Press them down with a spatula or rest a slightly smaller pan on top of the prawns as a weight, so they cook evenly and rapidly. This will give them a gently curled shape. Cook until they begin to turn pink around the edges, about 2 minutes. Place the pan in the oven until the prawns are evenly pink, about 2 minutes longer.

To serve, place one-fourth of the watercress on each of 4 plates. Toss the citrus mixture again and spoon around and over the watercress, making sure to moisten the watercress well with juices. Arrange 3 prawns around each salad, standing them in a circle, tails up, and serve hot, warm, or at room temperature.

CHEF'S NOTE: *These prawns are delicious cold the next day, too. The texture is not quite as nice, however, so don't try to make them ahead and reheat them.*

Mixed Green Salad
with Whole Citrus Vinaigrette

We use citrus vinaigrette regularly at Tra Vigne and in our Cantinetta. In my opinion, citrus vinaigrettes often disappoint. Here, I use the whole fruit, a trick I learned from Alain Ducasse, the three-star French chef of Louis XV in Monte Carlo. It makes a delicious and sunny yellow vinaigrette. When I have it around, I use it on everything. You can spoon it over a piece of cooked fish, use it as a dip, or use it to dress a spinach salad slipped inside piadine (page 99). This salad easily becomes a main dish, great for lunch or supper, by adding grilled or sautéed chicken breast or shrimp or grilled or deep-fried calamari. I prefer to use a juice extractor for this recipe, but I have made it successfully in a blender as well (see variation).

Serves 4

2 lemons
$\frac{1}{2}$ navel orange or 1 small orange
1 shallot
$1\frac{1}{2}$ cups pure olive oil
1 teaspoon salt
$\frac{1}{2}$ teaspoon freshly ground pepper
8 cups mixed young green lettuces

Juice the lemons, orange, and shallot in a juice extractor. Put the juices in a bowl and whisk in the olive oil in a slow stream to form an emulsion. Season with the salt and pepper. Taste and adjust the seasoning. Whisk again, cover, and refrigerate for up to 3 days. You should have about 2 cups.

Just before serving, place the greens in a salad bowl, add about $\frac{1}{2}$ cup vinaigrette, and toss well. Add more to taste and adjust the seasoning.

Variation for Blender: Use 3 lemons, 2 small oranges, 1 shallot, 1 teaspoon salt, $\frac{1}{2}$ teaspoon pepper, and $1\frac{1}{2}$ cups pure olive oil. Cut off and discard the stem ends of 2 lemons and 1 orange. Cut into quarters, cut out the core, and deseed. Place in a blender. Squeeze the juice from the remaining lemon and orange; add to the blender with the shallot, salt, and pepper. Pulse and then blend the fruit until as smooth as possible. With the machine running, add the olive oil in a thin, steady stream. The vinaigrette will be thick like a mayonnaise. If it is too thick, with the machine still on, thin with a little hot water. Taste for seasoning. Cover and refrigerate for up to 3 days. If the vinaigrette separates, return it to the blender and blend until smooth again. Makes about 3 cups.

Chicken *with* Roasted Lemon *and* Rosemary Sauce

In 1997, my Tra Vigne crew and I cooked for a week at the Mandarin-Oriental in Bangkok, Thailand. Norbert A. Kostner, the hotel's head chef, would not let me leave without giving him this recipe. It's a dish that will look familiar to everyone—chicken and potatoes—but just wait until you taste it.

Serves 4

1 1/2 pounds small new potatoes such as Red Bliss

2 large lemons

Extra-virgin olive oil for brushing on lemons, plus 1/4 cup

Salt and freshly ground pepper

4 boneless chicken breast halves, skin on

1 tablespoon minced garlic

1 cup double-strength chicken stock (page 204), or 2 cups canned low-salt chicken broth boiled until reduced by half

1 teaspoon finely chopped fresh rosemary

1 tablespoon finely chopped fresh flat-leaf parsley

1 tablespoon unsalted butter (optional)

Put the potatoes in a pot of salted cold water and bring to a boil. Cook until just tender, about 20 minutes. Drain and let cool, but do not peel. Cut in half and set aside.

Preheat the broiler. Cut a small slice off both ends of each lemon, then cut in half crosswise. Arrange the lemons, flesh side up, in a flameproof nonreactive baking dish, brush with olive oil, and season with salt and pepper. Broil 6 inches or more from the heat until browned and soft, about 10 minutes. Let cool. Squeeze the lemon halves over a sieve suspended over a bowl. Push and stir the pulp through the sieve with a rubber spatula or wooden spoon. Discard the lemon shells.

Preheat the oven to 450°F. Season the chicken with salt and pepper. Heat the remaining 1/4 cup olive oil in a large ovenproof sauté pan over medium-high heat until hot. Add the chicken, lower the heat to medium, and cook, turning once, until brown on both sides, about 5 minutes. Remove to a platter.

Return the pan to medium-high heat, add the potatoes, season with salt and pepper, and cook, stirring and tossing, until brown all over, about 5 minutes. Drain off the excess oil. Arrange the chicken breasts on top of the potatoes and place in the oven to reheat and cook through, about 10 minutes. When done, remove the chicken to a platter and put the pan with the potatoes over medium-high heat. Toss well so the pan juices are absorbed into the potatoes. Scrape the potatoes out of the pan onto the platter around the chicken.

Return the pan to medium-high heat and add the garlic. Sauté briefly until light brown. Immediately add the reserved roasted lemon juice (this final flash of heat will cook off any residual acid flavor), stock, rosemary, and parsley. Stir and scrape up all the browned bits that cling to the bottom and sides of the pan. Season to taste with salt and pepper. If the sauce tastes too lemony, stir in the optional butter. Pour the sauce over the chicken and potatoes and serve immediately.

Lemon-Baked Sea Bass
with Spinach Salad

4 lemons

1 tablespoon minced shallot

2 tablespoons finely chopped fresh
    flat-leaf parsley

About 1 cup extra-virgin olive oil

4 sea bass fillets, about 6 ounces each and ¾ inch
    thick (if thicker, butterfly)

Salt and freshly ground pepper

2 tablespoons red onion slivers (see Chef's Notes)

2 cups packed baby spinach

The distinctly lemony tang of this dish strongly reminds me of parts of the Mediterranean. Don't let any fear of folding parchment paper into baking containers for the fish prevent you from making this recipe. You can use aluminum foil lined with waxed paper in place of the parchment. Even a paper bag will work, simply folded over like a school lunch bag.

Serves 4

Preheat the oven to 450°F. Squeeze the juice of 2 lemons into a nonreactive baking dish and whisk in the shallot, parsley, and about ¾ cup of the olive oil. Taste for balance; it should taste moderately tart. Add another 1 to 2 tablespoons olive oil, if necessary. Add the fish to the marinade and turn to coat well. Leave to marinate for 10 minutes.

Fold 4 large sheets of parchment paper in half. Beginning at one end of the fold, cut a point, then around into as wide a semicircle as possible, ending at the opposite end of the fold with a rounded point. When opened out, the paper will resemble a heart. Center the fish on one side of the heart, season with salt and pepper, and spoon a generous tablespoon marinade over each fillet. Cut 1 lemon into very thin slices. Overlap 3 or 4 lemon slices along the length of each fillet.

Seal the packets by folding the second side of the paper over the fish, then starting at the blunt end, make a sharp, small fold toward the fish. Continue making small folds around the open edge, refold the last tuck in upon itself several times to make a tight closure, and fold it under the packet. Transfer the packets to a baking sheet. Bake in the preheated oven until cooked through, about 12 minutes, depending on the thickness of the fillets.

While the fish bakes, make the spinach salad. In a bowl, soak the red onion slivers in the juice of the remaining lemon for several minutes. The onions will turn a pale pink. Whisk in the remaining ¼ cup olive oil and season to taste with salt and pepper. Add the spinach and toss well.

When the fish is done, remove from the oven and place on 4 warm dinner plates. Cut open the packets and spread back the paper. Quickly divide the salad among the packets. The spinach will wilt across the top. Serve immediately.

CHEF'S NOTE: *Cut the onion in half lengthwise, and cut each half in half again crosswise. Cut the slivers lengthwise from each half. They will have an attractive crescent shape. You can also simply cut the onions into ¼-inch dice.*

Roasted Beet, Onion, *and* Orange Salad

1 pound beets, preferably very small ones
20 large pearl onions, about ½ pound
1 tablespoon extra-virgin olive oil
Salt and freshly ground pepper
2 tablespoons hazelnuts
2 tablespoons hazelnut oil

1 tablespoon coarsely chopped fresh
    coriander
¼ cup freshly squeezed orange juice
2 oranges
1 ounce aged crottin or pecorino (optional),
    grated on medium-sized holes of box grater

This dish, for me, embodies the contradictions of late winter in Northern California. The deep, sweet flavors of the roasted beets and onions contrast with the freshness of orange and fresh coriander. Adding an earthy cheese such as crottin (from goats) or pecorino (from sheep) acts as a subtle reminder that this is also the season of newborn kids and lambs.

Serves 4

Preheat the oven to 400°F. Cut the stems and tails off the beets and trim both ends off the onions. Do not peel. In a baking dish, toss the beets and onions with the olive oil and season with salt and pepper. Roast until tender, about 30 minutes for small beets or about 1½ hours for large beets and 30 minutes for the onions.

Arrange the hazelnuts in a small baking dish and place in the oven with the vegetables. Cook, shaking the pan occasionally, until the nuts are lightly browned and fragrant, about 20 minutes. Fold the nuts into a tea towel and let sit about 5 minutes, then rub them vigorously with the towel to loosen and remove the skins. Chop the nuts coarsely and reserve.

As the vegetables are done, remove them to a plate, let cool, then peel. Depending on their size, cut the beets in half or into thin slices. Cut the onions in half lengthwise.

In a medium bowl, combine the hazelnut oil, coriander, and orange juice. Whisk until well combined and season with salt and pepper.

Peel and remove the membranes from the oranges with a sharp paring knife. Cut the oranges in half lengthwise, and then crosswise into thin slices. Seed the slices and add to the bowl containing the dressing. Add the onions and toss well. Divide the orange slices and onions among 4 plates. Scatter the beets around the oranges and onions and drizzle the salads with any juices left in the mixing bowl. Sprinkle some of the grated cheese over each salad, if desired, and sprinkle with the reserved nuts. Serve immediately.

winter squashes

When the yellows, oranges, and mossy greens of hard squashes cascade over tables at farmers' markets, Thanksgiving, family holidays, and seasonal treats cannot be far behind. At Tra Vigne, we roast the squashes in our wood-fired oven and then make a rich-tasting puree that we serve as a ravioli stuffing, a thick, rich soup, and stirred into polenta and pastina. ❧ Whether called pumpkin or squash, these delicious and versatile vegetables share characteristically hard shells that allow them to be stored in cool places for long periods. They are not indestructible, however, and when kept at room temperature will tend to dry out and/or rot. Their orange flesh is fairly dense and moist, very much like sweet potato or yam, and they can, in fact, be used interchangeably with them. Individual squashes and pumpkins can also be substituted for one another. If you shop at farmers' markets, ask the growers for cooking tips and ideas for particular varieties. ❧ The mild, sweet flavor of hard squashes calls for punching up with intense flavors, such as a glaze of butter, balsamic vinegar, and molasses (page 152). I rub the glaze over the cut surfaces, then bake the squash in a medium-hot oven. I prefer the flavor roasting gives to squashes over other cooking methods. It tends to caramelize and sweeten their flavors. But if it is a question of not cooking hard squashes or microwaving, then microwave. ❧ One of the reasons I use pumpkin and squash purees so often is that hard squashes, as their name implies, are hard to peel. For recipes requiring peeled squash, my best advice is to use butternut squash, the easiest of them all to peel. It has the added advantage of having the most intense flavor of the winter squashes. Otherwise, cut the squash in half or in slices and rub with the glaze before baking, then scrape the cooked squash off the skin. Use a very heavy knife and be careful. You can also buy precut chunks of banana squash in markets. These give you a head start toward peeling and baking. ❧ Spaghetti squash will intrigue your children as you loosen its long, spaghetti-like strands from the shell, and may convince the children to eat squash, especially if you treat it just like pasta (page 157). If the squash is large, cut it in half crosswise and bake or microwave cut side down so it doesn't lose its moisture.

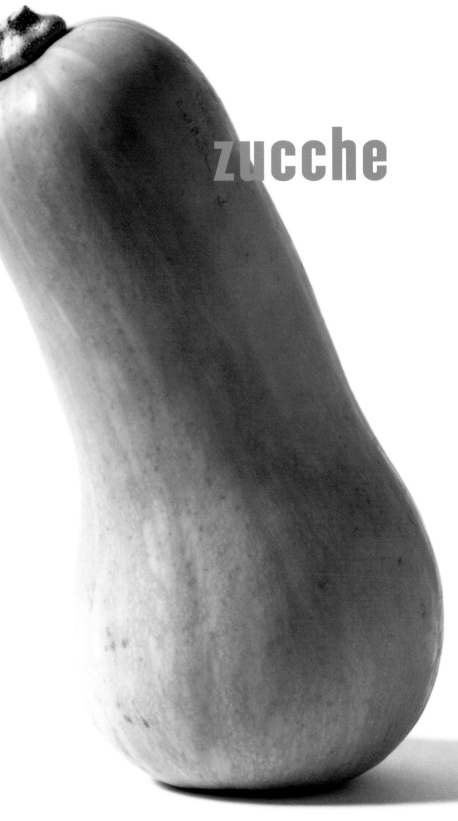

zucche

Roasted Winter Squash

I love the seasonal flavor of winter squash roasted with molasses and balsamic vinegar. To give the puree a hit of heat and spice, add some Fennel Spice (page 193) or a tablespoon of Toasted Spice Rub (page 192). You can cook any winter squash—or a mixture of squash—by this method and each squash will contribute its particular sweetness.

Makes about 4 cups puree

About 3 pounds butternut squash
  (preferably 1 large squash)
Salt and freshly ground pepper
1/2 cup (1 stick) unsalted butter
2 tablespoons finely chopped fresh sage
2 tablespoons granulated sugar
1/4 cup balsamic vinegar
1/4 cup dark unsulfured molasses

Preheat the oven to 400°F. Peel the squash with a vegetable peeler. Halve lengthwise, discard the seeds, then cut into 1-inch dice. Place in a large bowl and season with salt and pepper.

Heat the butter in a medium skillet over medium-high heat. When the butter ceases to foam and has turned a light brown, pull the pan off the heat and immediately add the sage, sugar, vinegar (stand back so as not to get splattered), and molasses. Mix well and let simmer over medium-low heat for 1 to 2 minutes to meld the flavors.

Pour the vinegar mixture over the squash and toss well, then transfer to a heavy rimmed baking sheet or baking dish large enough to hold the squash in a single layer. Place in the oven and roast, tossing at least once, until very tender and caramelized, about 1 hour. Set aside until cool enough to handle but still warm, so the liquids are runny.

Working in batches if necessary, transfer the warm squash and all the cooking liquids to a food processor and process until smooth. Use immediately, refrigerate for up to 5 days, or freeze for up to 2 months.

Suggested Uses: Serve the puree on its own as a side dish for roast chicken, turkey, or pork; stir into polenta just before the end of cooking (page 201); use as a stuffing for ravioli (page 156); make into a soup (page 153); or use to flavor pastina (page 159). Or omit the sage, season with ground cinnamon and freshly grated nutmeg to taste, and use as a substitute for canned pumpkin in your favorite pumpkin pie recipe.

Variation for Smoky Butternut Squash: Cook the prepared squash on a baking sheet in a covered grill with soaked chips to give a slightly smoky taste. Substitute in any of the recipes that call for roasted squash.

CHEF'S NOTE: *If cooking kabocha, acorn, or other difficult-to-peel squash, cut in half, scoop out the seeds, and rub the insides and cut edges with the molasses mixture. Place on a baking sheet, cut sides up, and roast at 400°F until tender. Scoop out and puree.*

Roasted Butternut Squash Soup

With a green salad, this rich, wintry soup is supper. Or use it as a sauce: serve in a deep plate topped with sliced pork tenderloin and wilted greens or with veal or turkey scaloppini. It would make a pretty terrific sauce for ravioli or pasta as well. The coriander is optional but tastes great.

Makes about 4½ cups, serves 4

2 tablespoons extra-virgin olive oil
½ cup diced onion (¼-inch dice)
¼ cup diced celery (¼-inch dice)
¼ cup diced carrot (¼-inch dice)
1 cinnamon stick
Salt and freshly ground pepper
About 4 cups chicken stock (page 204)
    or canned low-salt chicken broth
½ teaspoon ground toasted coriander (optional)
1½ cups Roasted Winter Squash (page 152)
½ cup half-and-half (optional)
¼ cup mascarpone cheese (optional)
2 tablespoons Toasted Pumpkin Seeds
    (page 192; optional)

Heat the olive oil in a large saucepan over medium heat until hot. Add the onion, celery, carrot, and cinnamon stick and sauté until soft but not brown, about 10 minutes. Season with salt and pepper.

Add the chicken stock and the coriander, if using, and bring to a boil. Simmer for several minutes. Stir in the squash until smooth, then simmer gently to let the flavors meld, about 10 minutes. Discard the cinnamon stick.

Puree the soup in a blender until smooth. (The soup can be made ahead to this point, cooled, covered, and refrigerated for several days or frozen for about 1 month. It will thicken as it cools and may need thinning with stock or water when reheating.)

Return the soup to the pan and reheat gently. Add the half-and-half, if using. Adjust the seasoning with salt and pepper. Ladle into a warm tureen or 4 soup plates. If desired, garnish with a spoonful of mascarpone and/or a scattering of pumpkin seeds.

"Pumpkin" Polenta
with Medium-Rare Lamb Stew

1 recipe "Pumpkin" Polenta (page 201)

1 pound lamb loin, trimmed of all fat and silver skin

Salt and freshly ground pepper

¼ cup extra-virgin olive oil

3 tablespoons all-purpose flour

1 generous cup pearl onions, peeled

1 generous cup peeled carrot chunks
    (½-inch chunks)

1 generous cup peeled turnip chunks
    (½-inch chunks)

1 tablespoon unsalted butter

1 cup dry red wine (optional)

4 cups double-strength chicken stock (page 204),
    or 8 cups canned low-salt chicken broth boiled
    until reduced by half

1 teaspoon finely chopped fresh rosemary

2 cups packed chard leaves, torn
    or cut into 1-inch pieces

2 tablespoons finely chopped fresh flat-leaf parsley

Here is a stew with deep, rich flavors. Yet the meat remains rare and the dish goes together in under an hour. The trick is to start with tender meat. If you do not care for turnips, try potatoes. If you like parsnips, add them. The flavor of the stew depends on a good caramelization of meat and vegetables. I tend to follow the old adage "The colder it is outside, the thicker the stew." Since it is not often very cold in the Napa Valley, this stew does not coat the tongue. If you prefer a thicker stew, double the flour. You can also serve the stew on white rice or noodles.

Serves 4

Begin by making the polenta and putting it aside. Or you can measure out the ingredients, have them ready, and cook the polenta while the stew simmers.

Cut the lamb loin in half lengthwise, then cut crosswise into 1-inch pieces. The pieces should be fairly large so they do not get overcooked. Season well with salt and pepper. Heat 2 tablespoons of the olive oil in a heavy sauté pan over medium-high heat until hot. Dust the lamb with 2 tablespoons of the flour. Add the lamb to the pan, spreading out the pieces so there is room around them. Do not move the pieces until moisture begins to show on the tops and they have browned on one side, about 2 minutes. Then turn the pieces to continue to brown, about 2 minutes longer. Do not overcook. The lamb should be medium-rare. Remove the meat to a large plate.

Return the pan to medium-high heat and add the remaining 2 tablespoons oil. Add the onions, carrots, and turnips to the pan, season with salt and pepper, and sauté until the vegetables are well caramelized, about 10 minutes. Regulate the heat so the vegetables do not burn. Add the butter and continue to cook for another 2 minutes.

Dust the remaining 1 tablespoon flour over the contents of the pan, stir, and cook over medium heat for another minute. Add the wine, if using, bring to a boil over high heat, and cook until reduced by half. Add the stock, return to a boil, reduce the heat to low, and simmer for 10 minutes. Skim off any foam that forms as the stock comes to a boil. Add the rosemary for the last few minutes. (The stew may be made to this point a day ahead. Refrigerate the liquids and meat separately. Do not freeze, or you will lose the freshness and texture of the meat.)

When ready to eat, bring the liquids to a boil. Return the meat to the pan, add the chard and parsley, and simmer for 1 minute. Season with salt and pepper.

Divide the polenta among soup plates and pour the stew on top. Serve immediately.

CHEF'S NOTES: *Dust meats or other ingredients just before cooking, or the flour will get gummy. The flour needs to cook for a few minutes to lose its raw flavor. It is important when adding liquids to a roux to stir while the mixture comes to a boil. Otherwise, the flour may stick to the bottom of the pan and scorch.*

Butter in a roux serves to bind the flour, so it will not clump with the addition of liquid. Then, as the liquid heats, the butter melts and releases the flour into the liquid. The flour will go into suspension and thicken liquids at just below boiling, so you must bring your stew to a boil after an addition of flour or any ingredient dusted with flour.

Roasted Winter Squash Ravioli

These are delicious and rich, so serve them as a first course. At Tra Vigne, we lighten the squash puree with ricotta and sometimes add diced smoked chicken, duck, or turkey. Don't forget, ravioli freezes well. You can then serve an elegant dinner in minutes.

Makes about 2 dozen ravioli, serves 4

1 cup Roasted Winter Squash (page 152)

¼ cup freshly grated Parmesan cheese

1 recipe Pasta Dough, rolled out
    to ravioli thickness (page 195)

Flour for dusting work surface and ravioli

1 egg beaten with 1½ teaspoons water
    for egg wash or use water only

Salt and freshly ground pepper

½ cup (1 stick) unsalted butter

1½ tablespoons finely chopped fresh sage leaves

2 tablespoons Toasted Pumpkin Seeds (page 192)

Mix together the roasted squash and 2 tablespoons of the Parmesan in a small bowl. Set aside. To fill the ravioli, lay the strips of dough on a lightly floured surface. Cut the pasta into 2½-inch rounds or squares with a ravioli cutter. If you have no ravioli cutter, you can cut the dough into squares with a sharp knife or rolling cutter. Center 1½ teaspoons or so of filling on half the pieces, brush all around the filling with the egg wash, and top with the remaining dough pieces. Seal each ravioli closed, starting from the filling and pressing gently out to the edge to force out all the air.

You may also space spoonfuls of filling a few inches apart down half the length of each dough strip. Brush around the filling with the egg wash, then fold the remaining half of each strip over the filled half. Press down gently around filling mounds to press out the air, then cut between the mounds into ravioli.

Lay the completed ravioli on a baking sheet lined with a flour-dusted tea towel. Lightly dust the tops with flour. Use immediately or cover with tea towels for several hours. (The ravioli may also be frozen at this point for about 1 month. Freeze on the baking sheets, then transfer to a plastic bag or container when they are frozen solid.)

When ready to cook, bring a large pot of water to a boil and add salt. Lower heat to a simmer. Meanwhile, melt the butter in a skillet over medium heat. Heat, without stirring, until the butter stops foaming and turns light brown. Add the sage, salt and pepper to taste, and the pumpkin seeds. Stir and remove from the heat. Keep warm.

Drop the ravioli into the simmering water and cook until they come to the surface, then begin testing for doneness. Pinch their edges; they should be tender. The ravioli will cook in about 6 minutes. To cook frozen ravioli, cook them still frozen and boil about 8 minutes.

When done, drain the ravioli well and blot them dry, if necessary, with a clean tea towel. Divide among 4 individual plates or arrange on a long oval platter and drizzle the browned butter sauce over them. Sprinkle lightly with the remaining 2 tablespoons Parmesan. Serve immediately.

Spaghetti Times Two

One of the things I like about this pasta is that it is vegetables and pasta in one dish. I could play the Italian mama and tell you to eat it because it's good for you: with its red tomatoes and yellow hard squash, it's a micronutrient high. But you will probably enjoy it more if you eat it simply because it's comforting, satisfying, and exactly the way you want home cooking to taste.

Serves 4

1 tablespoon extra-virgin olive oil

1 spaghetti squash, about 2½ pounds

Salt and freshly ground pepper

1 cup water

1 recipe Quick Tomato Sauce (page 198)

¾ pound dried spaghetti

2 tablespoons unsalted butter

¼ cup plus 2 tablespoons freshly grated
    Parmesan cheese

2 tablespoons finely chopped fresh
    flat-leaf parsley

Preheat the oven to 400°F. Oil a rimmed baking sheet with the oil. Cut the squash in half lengthwise and scoop out the seeds and fibers. Season the cut sides with salt and pepper, then place on the prepared baking sheet, cut side down. Add the water to the sheet. (The water will create steam and help the squash cook through.)

Bake until tender—the squash will begin to collapse in on itself—about 1 hour. Remove from the oven and let cool on the baking sheet. When cool enough to handle, scrape the squash out of the shells in long strands and place in a bowl. Season with salt and pepper. (This can be done a day ahead.)

While the squash is baking, prepare the tomato sauce. Meanwhile, bring a large pot of water to a boil and add salt. Add the pasta and cook until al dente, about 12 minutes. While the pasta cooks, put 2 generous cups cooked squash into a large bowl and add the butter. Place the bowl over the pasta pot to reheat the squash, if necessary, and melt the butter. In a small bowl, mash the reserved jalapeño (from the tomato sauce; it is not necessary to seed it) with a large spoonful of the tomato sauce.

When the pasta is done, drain and turn into the bowl holding the squash. Toss well. Pour about two-thirds of the tomato sauce (discard the bay leaf) over the pasta and squash and toss again. Add the ¼ cup Parmesan and the parsley and toss again.

Transfer to a warm serving bowl or 4 warm pasta bowls. Pour the remaining sauce over each portion and sprinkle with the remaining 2 tablespoons Parmesan. Serve immediately. Pass the mashed jalapeño at the table to allow diners to spice their servings as they like. This is a good idea for children who love this dish, but may not care for spice.

"Pumpkin" Pastina
Served Family Style *in a* Pumpkin

Serving the pastina in a pumpkin isn't necessary, but it is appropriate and fun this time of year. And it's simple, too. The hardest part is getting the pumpkin home and resisting the temptation to carve it. You could also make individual tureens with smaller pumpkins and hard squashes such as acorn squash. Use some of their flesh in the pastina. Just make sure you leave enough behind, or the shells will not be sturdy enough to be containers. If you just gave me the pastina in a bowl with a big spoon, I'd be very happy.

Serves 4

1 Jack-o'-Lantern or other large pumpkin, about 6 pounds

Extra-virgin olive oil for oiling pumpkin, plus 2 tablespoons

Salt and freshly ground pepper

About 4 cups chicken stock (page 204) or canned low-salt chicken broth

1 cup finely chopped onion

1 teaspoon finely chopped fresh thyme

3/4 pound dried pastina or other small pasta such as riso

1 cup Roasted Winter Squash (page 152)

1 cup cubed cooked turkey, plain or smoked (about 1/4 pound; optional)

1/2 cup plus 2 tablespoons freshly grated Parmesan cheese

Preheat the oven to 375°F. Cut the lid off the pumpkin and scoop out the seeds and fibers. Scrape away some of the flesh, especially around the top, to form a large, smooth inner cavity. Make sure to leave the shell at least 1 inch thick all around. Oil the pumpkin inside and out and season inside with salt and pepper. Replace the lid. Place on a baking sheet and bake until about two-thirds cooked but still firm enough to stand and act as the soup container, about 40 minutes. Do not overbake. If a good deal of liquid gathers in the bottom, spoon out and discard. Set aside; it will stay warm on its own a good while.

Bring the stock to a low simmer in a saucepan. Heat the remaining 2 tablespoons olive oil in a large sauté pan over medium-high heat until hot. Add the onion and cook until soft but not brown, 2 to 3 minutes. Add the thyme, stir, and add 2 cups of the stock. Bring to a boil. Add the pastina, stir well, and reduce the heat to maintain a slow simmer. Season with salt and pepper. Simmer, adding the stock 1/2 cup at a time as the previous addition is absorbed and stirring occasionally to prevent the pastina from sticking to the bottom of the pan, until the pasta is al dente, about 15 minutes. Add the roasted squash and turkey to reheat. Stir well. The consistency should be quite loose, like a thick soup. Add more stock if necessary. Add the 1/2 cup cheese and let melt for a moment before stirring in. Taste for seasoning.

Ladle the pastina into the reserved pumpkin shell and garnish with the remaining 2 tablespoons Parmesan. Replace the lid and take to the table immediately.

Variation with Greens: For a colorful and nutritious addition, cut several handfuls of winter greens such as spinach or chard into a chiffonade and stir into the pastina just to wilt before serving.

TRA VIGNE

classics

The opportunity to create a way of life that fosters and shelters my family, friends, and coworkers provides my motivation to cook. Tra Vigne is far more than a building or a collection of recipes. It is the creative expression of everyone who works here, including those who have moved on. Tra Vigne is family. ❧ Because we spend so much time at the restaurant, it is important to make room for our families as well. Sometimes my partner's son, Colin, age six, will be at the restaurant for a few minutes early in the morning before school. When he was smaller, his "job" was to look for trash under the tables. Now that he is taller, he is learning to set tables. For several years, my family came at five o'clock every Saturday evening to share a quick supper with me before I went back to cook on the line. When I hear Mariano Orlando in the Cantinetta gently coaxing a cookie into the hand of a guest's shy child, I understand afresh why we all call him "Grandfather." ❧ When we hire new cooks, we tell them, "This will be the hardest job you have ever held." More experienced cooks act the part of older brothers and sisters, supporting the new cooks through the times that require blind faith and celebrating with them when they win recognition. ❧ The cooks—and every other staff member—learn our style of food by the endless repetition of the stories that illuminate the whys and wherefors of each dish. I want the cooks to live Tra Vigne's food, so that when they cook, their heart will be the essential ingredient in every dish. The stories may be about family, a piece of Italian history, or an insight into the nature of seasonal ingredients. If Gravenstein apples are at their peak, a well-trained cook can move beyond apple tarts to savory dishes, perhaps roasting the apples and then making a vinaigrette, folding the apples into risotto, or teaming them with prosciutto. Fish, too, is seasonal, and when we receive local halibut, which is fresher and lower in fat than northern halibut, we make a dish specifically for it, slicing it thin and giving it a fresh lemon juice and olive oil "cure" to serve as a cold antipasto. Or the lesson may be a small thing (because small things add up), for example, the taste of a freshly roasted and peeled bell pepper, a taste that is immediate and direct and irretrievably lost once the pepper has been refrigerated. ❧ All the cooks learn to make mozzarella, and every year we invite a different cook to help make prosciutto, a sort of "family privilege." We create dishes for the nine varieties of table grapes my partner planted around the restaurant and take "family trips" to visit the people who grow our produce and herbs. I want the staff to understand how closely our food is tied to the land, and how strong relationships with the producers play a major role in cooking better food. And I continue to take individual staff members on foraging walks through the vineyards and the surrounding hills. ❧ I learned in the same way, though it took me somewhat longer. In 1982, I had graduated from The Culinary Institute of America with a set of skills, a craft in the same way my grandfather, a carpenter, had a set of skills he used to create something useful. In my first jobs in Florida I tasted the freedom and excitement of the experimental, anything-goes attitude of the emerging American dining scene. Once I got over my liberation-for-the-sake-of-liberation stage, I discovered an emptiness at the center of my food. It was as if I were cooking with one foot off the ground. My technique was solid, but my food told no story. It had no soul. ❧ When I came home to California in 1986 to open Tra Vigne, my cooking came home, too. The food needed to be simple, straightforward, Italian in inspiration, expressive of its location, the Napa Valley, and identifiably Tra Vigne. I saw this as an opportunity to go back to my roots, to explore the rich culinary tradition into which I had been born. It took a few years to hit my stride, but the seeds of what the food would become were apparent in the meal I cooked for my prospective partners as part of my interview. I am grateful they overlooked my irrelevant garnishes and recognized the potential those dishes represented. ❧ My uncle and godfather, John Aiello (like many in my family, he was an avid gardener), provided me with ingredients that had the fresh-from-the-ground flavor I needed. The meal began with "firecrackers" (page 64) served with a spicy roasted pepper sauce and grilled bruschetta. Fusilli Michelangelo (page 86) came next, followed by two-toned shrimp cannelloni in a tomato, basil, and shrimp *brodetto*, garnished with a tuft of basil salad. I flavored and colored half the cannelloni with squid ink and the other half with saffron. The meal ended with my mother's recipe for cannoli with a pistachio filling. ❧ Some of the dishes I cooked that day remain on the menu—the fusilli, the cannoli, variations of cannelloni, and the *brodetto*. That entire menu and the dishes I create today draw on memories of my family's kitchens, not only the food, but their traditional Italian lifestyle that celebrates the bonds of family and land. ❧ Other menu items have evolved as we have grown up. For instance, we have always made our own mozzarella, but we periodically change its presentation. Originally, we served a salad of mozzarella, sliced tomatoes, basil, and extra-virgin olive oil. It evolved into a spiedini similar to the recipe on page 58, but served with basil oil and balsamic essence. Now we make sheets of mozzarella by rolling out the still-warm and pliable cheese between layers of plastic wrap. We use the sheets in a number of ways: folding them around a spoonful of *conserva* (peeled, seeded, and chopped sun-dried tomatoes packed in olive oil) or cutting them into "fettuccine" to be dressed with oven-dried tomatoes (page 199), deep-fried Kalamata olives, and basil oil. ❧ When we opened, we served caponata (page 114) very simply with bruschetta. Now we flavor it with orange zest, roll it in a paillard of tuna, and dust the whole with panko (crisp white Japanese bread crumbs). The fish is seared quickly over high heat to rare and served with a "broken" tomato vinaigrette (page 52) and spiced shoestring potatoes. ❧ While my family heritage continues to inspire Tra Vigne's food, some dishes show their lineage more directly than others. When we first opened, we lacked the experience and techniques necessary to make dishes such as the home-style Gnocchi della Nonna (page 169) on the scale necessary for a restaurant. Now we've added our own twist to gnocchi, browning the little potato dumplings and adding them to salads. ❧ These are weekend recipes. They often require the completion of several subrecipes before the final cooking steps and assembly. For example, for the Monkfish with Roasted Garlic Polenta and Tomato Broth (page 173), you will need to roast the garlic, make the polenta, and then cook the fish. ❧ I've included a mozzarella martini with tomato consommé (page 175) that exemplifies my cooking style: spectacular ingredients (very fresh mozzarella and tomatoes), solid technique (collecting clear, flavorful tomato "water"), and surprising presentations (serving the appetizer in a frosted, oversize martini glass). *Buono appetito!*

i piatti classichi Tra Vigne

Crispy Herb Gnocchi *with* Braised Lamb Shanks *and* Wild Mushrooms

Soul-satisfying earthy flavors infuse this rich dish. When the weather turns cooler, we have lamb shanks on Tra Vigne's menu as often as several times a week, served with risotto, pasta, or gnocchi, as in this recipe. The gnocchi are crisped to a golden brown in butter. This gives them a terrific crunch and another layer of flavor. If you want to reduce the richness of the dish, you can omit this step. You can use all sorts of winter vegetables, including parsnips, carrots, Brussels sprout leaves, and pearl onions, in addition to or in place of the spinach. If you choose to try this dish come spring, lighten the flavors by not browning the shanks as much and by replacing the red wine with white and the spinach with English peas and spring onions. If, on the other hand, it is really, really cold out, you might use equal parts chicken stock and veal stock. The gnocchi may be made after the meat has cooked or prepared ahead of time and frozen. A black cast-iron pan makes a great serving dish.

Serves 4 to 6

4 lamb shanks
Salt and freshly ground pepper
$1/2$ cup extra-virgin olive oil
1 cup diced onion ($1/4$-inch dice)
$1/2$ cup diced carrot ($1/4$-inch dice)
$1/2$ cup diced celery ($1/4$-inch dice)
2 cups full-bodied red wine such as Merlot
6 cups chicken stock (page 204)
     or canned low-salt chicken broth
2 bay leaves
1 teaspoon peppercorns
15 juniper berries
4 cups sliced mixed fresh mushrooms
     such as shiitake, chanterelle,
     and morel ($1/4$ inch thick)
4 shallots, thinly sliced
$1 1/2$ teaspoons minced garlic
1 tablespoon finely chopped fresh thyme
4 cups spinach
3 to 4 tablespoons unsalted butter
1 recipe Herb Gnocchi (page 167)
1 teaspoon finely chopped fresh sage
About 1 ounce ricotta salata cheese (optional)

Preheat the oven to 300°F. Season the lamb very well with salt and pepper. In a deep ovenproof sauté pan or casserole, heat $1/4$ cup of the olive oil over medium-high heat until hot. Add the lamb and sauté until brown all over, about 10 minutes. Take care to regulate the heat to prevent burning. Remove the meat to a plate. Add the onion, carrot, and celery to the pan and continue to sauté over medium heat until well browned, about 8 minutes longer. Add the wine, bring to a boil, and cook until reduced by half.

Add the chicken stock, bay leaves, peppercorns, and juniper berries and return to a boil. Return the shanks to the pan, cover, and place in the oven to braise until fork tender. Test the shanks at 2 hours, but they may take as long as 4 hours.

Let the meat cool in the liquid to room temperature. Pull the meat from the bones and shred. Reserve. Strain the cooking liquid into a bowl. (The recipe may be made to this point a day ahead, covered, and refrigerated.) Defat the cooking liquid, return it to a saucepan, bring to a boil, and cook until reduced to about 3 cups. Reserve.

Heat the remaining $1/4$ cup olive oil in a large sauté pan over medium-high heat until hot. Add the mushrooms and do not move them until they begin to brown, about 1 minute. Then sauté until brown all over, about 5 minutes longer. Season with salt and pepper. Add the shallots and cook until light brown. Add the garlic and cook briefly until pale gold. Stir in the thyme. Add the reserved lamb braising liquid, bring to a boil, and simmer until the sauce thickens and reduces to about 2 cups (see Chef's Notes). Add the reserved lamb and stir and toss until hot. Stir in the spinach until wilted and bright green. Add 1 tablespoon of the butter and reserve.

Bring a large pot of water to a boil and add salt. Drop in the gnocchi. When they return to the surface, cook for another 90 seconds. Meanwhile, heat 2 tablespoons of the butter in a large sauté pan over medium heat until the butter stops foaming and turns light brown. Remove the gnocchi from the water with a slotted spoon or skimmer, drain well, and place in the browned butter. Cook the gnocchi, without moving them, until brown on one side. Add the remaining tablespoon butter if needed. Carefully turn and toss the gnocchi until brown on all sides, about 10 minutes total. Regulate the heat so the butter does not burn. Stir in the sage.

To serve, pour the reserved meat and sauce onto a warm platter or into rimmed soup plates. Using a slotted spoon, arrange the gnocchi around the meat. If desired, use a vegetable peeler to shave curls of cheese over each portion. Serve immediately.

CHEF'S NOTES: *Because the dish is so rich tasting, a little goes a long way. If you plan to include a first course, salad, and dessert, this will serve six comfortably. If you plan on serving only salad, but you know your guests are moderate eaters, this amount will also serve six. If you want to serve the shanks whole, reheat them in a slow oven in a little of the braising liquid. Put a shank in each plate, pour the sauce over, and arrange the gnocchi around the meat. Shave the cheese over the plates. The sauce for this dish is made by a reduction of cooking liquids with no added thickener. If you use homemade stock with its natural body given by the bones, the resulting sauce thickens enough to coat the back of a spoon. If you use canned broth, your sauce, despite reducing to even less volume than one made with homemade stock, will not thicken to the same degree. It will, however, have more than enough rich flavor to satisfy anyone.*

Potato Gnocchi

One of my favorite movie food scenes is in *The Godfather Part 3*, when Andy Garcia shows Sophia Coppola how to shape gnocchi. For me it captures perfectly the implied sensuality and love that goes with making this pasta. I won't guarantee his results every time you make gnocchi, but it will bind you closer to family and friends. I would characterize these gnocchi as medium to light. The more flour you add to potato gnocchi, the heavier they become. That is why I bake my potatoes instead of boiling them. They will need less flour. This is another "master recipe." From here you can go nearly anywhere, from incorporating pureed herbs into the dough, to boiling and then browning the gnocchi, or rolling out the dough and cutting it into circles or squares to make "ravioli." You can serve gnocchi simply, with nothing more than browned butter, sage, and shavings of pecorino cheese. Or you can add them to salads with frisée, crispy pancetta, goat cheese, and dried cherries, as we do at Tra Vigne. Or the gnocchi can be served with rich savory stews.

Serves 4

Kosher salt

1 pound russet potatoes

3 or 4 large egg yolks

1/2 cup freshly grated Parmesan cheese

1/4 teaspoon freshly grated nutmeg

1/2 teaspoon salt

1/4 teaspoon freshly ground pepper

1 cup all-purpose flour, plus more
    for dusting board and dough

Preheat the oven to 450°F. Spread a layer of kosher salt on a baking sheet and arrange the potatoes on top (see Chef's Notes). Bake until a bit overcooked, about 1 hour. Let sit until cool enough to handle, cut in half, and scoop out the flesh. Reserve the potato skins, if desired, for another use.

Pass the potatoes through a potato ricer or grate them on the large holes of a box grater. You should have about 2 cups. In a large bowl, whisk together 3 of the egg yolks, the cheese, nutmeg, salt, and pepper. Add the potatoes and mix well. Sprinkle 1/2 cup of the flour over the potatoes and, using your knuckles, press it into the potatoes. Fold the mass over on itself and press down again. Sprinkle on more flour, little by little, folding and pressing the dough until it just holds together. Work any dough clinging to your fingers back into the dough. If the mixture is too dry, add another egg yolk or a little water. The dough should give under slight pressure. It will feel firm but yielding. To test if the dough is the correct consistency, take a piece and roll it with your hands on a well-floured board into a rope 1/2 inch in diameter. If the dough holds together, it is ready. If not, add more flour, fold and press the dough several more times, and test again.

Keeping your work surface and the dough lightly floured, cut the dough into 4 to 6 pieces. Roll each piece into a rope about 1/2 inch in diameter. Cut into 1/2-inch-long pieces. Lightly flour the gnocchi as you cut them.

You can cook these as is or form them into the classic gnocchi shape with a gnocchi board, ridged butter paddle, or the tines of a large fork turned upside down. Rest the bottom edge of the gnocchi board on the work surface, then tilt it at about a 45-degree angle. Take each piece and squish it lightly with your thumb against the board while simultaneously pushing it away from you. It will roll away and around your thumb, taking on a cupped shape—with ridges on the outer curve from the board and a smooth surface on the inner curve where your thumb was. (Shaping them takes some time and dexterity. You might make a batch just for practice.) The indentation holds the sauce and helps gnocchi cook faster.

As you shape the gnocchi, dust them lightly with flour and scatter them on baking sheets lined with parchment paper or waxed paper. Cover with a kitchen towel and set aside until ready to cook, up to several hours. If you will not cook the gnocchi until the next day or later, freeze them. Alternatively, you can poach them now, drain and toss with a little olive oil, let cool, then refrigerate several hours or overnight. To reheat, dip in hot water for 10 to 15 seconds, then toss with browned butter until hot.

When ready to cook, bring a large pot of water to a boil and add salt. Drop in the gnocchi and cook for about 90 seconds from the time they rise to the surface. Remove the cooked gnocchi with a skimmer, shake off the excess water, and serve as desired (see recipe introduction for suggestions).

Variation for Herb Gnocchi: These are great tossed with tomato *conserva* (peeled, seeded, and chopped sun-dried tomatoes preserved in olive oil), ricotta, and grated Parmesan or with Quick Tomato Sauce (page 198). Blanch 2 cups packed fresh basil or 1 cup packed fresh mint in boiling salted water for 15 seconds. Plunge into an ice bath to stop the cooking, drain well, and squeeze out as much water as you can between your hands. Roughly chop the herbs. Place in a blender with the egg yolks, cheese, nutmeg, salt, pepper, and $\frac{1}{4}$ cup cold water. Puree until smooth. Proceed as directed. Because of the additional water, the gnocchi will need about $\frac{1}{4}$ cup more flour to form a dough. Serves 4 to 6.

CHEF'S NOTES: *Baking potatoes on a layer of salt allows heat to circulate 360 degrees. Scrape the salt into a jar and reuse it again and again. If you do not have time to shape the gnocchi, you can freeze the dough, defrost it in the refrigerator, and then shape it. To freeze shaped gnocchi, line baking sheets with waxed paper and dust with flour. Spread the gnocchi on the prepared sheets and freeze until hard. Remove to individual-portion-size (about 20 gnocchi) freezer bags. Store in the freezer for up to 1 month. To cook, drop the frozen gnocchi into boiling salted water. Cook for about 2 minutes after they come to the surface.*

Warm Basil Gnocchi Salad
with Carpaccio *of* Tomatoes

Here, gnocchi is turned into a summer-supper-on-the-patio type dish, a wonderful palate-twisting combination of different temperatures and textures. Also, if you happen to have some gnocchi in the freezer, the dish goes together in a flash, becoming a great example of it-looks-complicated-but-I-didn't-even-break-a-sweat cooking. It would be particularly pretty if you had tomatoes of several colors and arranged them on a handmade pottery platter. I have incorporated a basil puree in the gnocchi dough. You could also use fresh mint, if you like.

Serves 4

⅓ cup extra-virgin olive oil

2 tablespoons fresh lemon juice

Salt and freshly ground pepper

2 pounds vine-ripened tomatoes, preferably
    a mixture of red, yellow, orange, and variegated

4 handfuls salad greens

½ recipe Herb Gnocchi (page 167)

About 1½ ounces ricotta salata cheese
    or Parmesan cheese

CHEF'S NOTE: *Although you need only a half batch of gnocchi for this recipe, take the time to make a whole batch, freeze half, and reap the rewards of your effort later.*

In a medium or large bowl, whisk together the olive oil, lemon juice, and salt and pepper to taste. Taste for balance and adjust with olive oil or lemon as necessary. Slice the tomatoes as thinly as possible and arrange on a large platter. Season with salt and pepper and spoon a little of the vinaigrette over the tomatoes. Toss the lettuce with a little more of the dressing and arrange on top of the tomatoes.

Bring a large pot of water to a boil and add salt. Add the gnocchi and cook for about 90 seconds from the time they rise to the surface. Remove with a skimmer, drain well, and place in the bowl with the remaining vinaigrette. Toss gently, then scatter the gnocchi on the salad. Using a vegetable peeler, shave the cheese over the salad and serve immediately.

Gnocchi *della* Nonna

Although this is very much a home-style recipe, it is so good that we serve it at the restaurant. My nonna Vicenciana lived about five hours' drive from my family's home. We would leave at about seven in the morning to arrive at my grandparents' house just in time for lunch. This simple sauce is the way Nonna prepared gnocchi. It was my favorite and she prepared it every third visit. On other visits she fixed my brothers' favorites. Nonna's tomato sauce begins with *odori*, the Holy Trinity of Italian cooking. It is the equivalent of a French *mirepoix*, essentially one part celery, one part carrot, and two parts onion. She sweated these slowly with garlic and tomato to make her sauce. Nonna, unlike me, always cooked her vegetables slowly, never allowing them to brown. The dish is simple, yet it is one of the best things you will ever put in your mouth. My hope is that it will become one of your favorites, to be repeated and repeated, much to your children's and grandchildren's delight.

Serves 4

2 tablespoons extra-virgin olive oil

¼ cup finely chopped carrot

¼ cup finely chopped celery

½ cup finely chopped onion

1 bay leaf

Salt and freshly ground pepper

1 tablespoon minced garlic

4 cups peeled, seeded, and finely chopped
  vine-ripened tomatoes, or 1 can (28 ounces)
  whole tomatoes, crushed

1 tablespoon finely chopped fresh flat-leaf parsley

1 tablespoon finely chopped fresh basil

1 recipe Potato Gnocchi (page 166)

1 tablespoon unsalted butter

¼ cup freshly grated Parmesan cheese

Heat the olive oil in a large sauté pan over medium-high heat until hot. Reduce the heat to low and add the carrot, celery, onion, and bay leaf. Season with salt and pepper, cover, and cook, stirring occasionally, until the vegetables are very soft but not brown, about 10 minutes. Uncover, add the garlic, and continue to cook for several minutes. Add the tomatoes, parsley, and basil and bring to a very gentle simmer. Cover and cook until the tomatoes have cooked into a puree, about 1 hour. Make sure to stir occasionally so the sauce does not scorch. Season to taste with salt and pepper. Keep hot until needed.

Bring a large pot of water to a boil and add salt. Drop in gnocchi and cook for about 90 seconds from the time they rise to the surface of the water. Place the butter in the bottom of a wide, shallow serving bowl. Warm the bowl and melt the butter, perhaps by placing it over the pot of boiling water.

Drain the gnocchi and place in the prepared serving bowl. Spoon about half of the sauce over the gnocchi, toss gently, and dust with a fine grating of Parmesan cheese. Pass the remaining sauce and cheese at the table.

CHEF'S NOTE: *You can also use Herb Gnocchi (page 167) in this recipe.*

Braised Rabbit *and* Winter Vegetables

At Tra Vigne I bet we serve more rabbit than almost any other restaurant in America. Indeed, people come here specifically to eat rabbit. This dish has been on our menu almost since the day we opened. It can be served on gnocchi, pasta, or risotto and can be tailored to the weather. In early fall, reduce the sauce less and omit the root vegetables. In the dead of winter, reduce the sauce until it is very intense and serve the rabbit on a bed of "white" risotto (made with onion and chicken stock) with freshly grated Parmesan cheese stirred in at the end of cooking. The sauce can also be reduced until very thick and the dish used as a filling for lasagna. The balsamic vinegar imparts sweetness, color, and a caramelized flavor. Make this on a leisurely weekend. It is not hard, but it is time-consuming. It helps to have roasted chicken stock in the freezer.

Serves 4

1 rabbit, cut into 6 pieces

2 tablespoons balsamic vinegar

Salt and freshly ground pepper

5 1/2 tablespoons extra-virgin olive oil

1 cup diced onion (1/4-inch dice)

1/2 cup diced carrot (1/4-inch dice)

1/2 cup diced celery (1/4-inch dice)

1 cup dry red wine

4 cups roasted chicken stock (page 204)
    or canned low-salt chicken broth

1 bay leaf

4 to 5 fresh thyme sprigs, plus 1 tablespoon
    finely chopped

10 juniper berries

10 peppercorns

3/4 pound spaghettini

1/2 cup pancetta pieces (1/4 by 1/4 by 1 inch)

4 tablespoons (1/2 stick) unsalted butter

1/2 cup diced parsnip (1/2-inch dice)

1/2 cup diced carrot (1/2-inch dice)

1/2 cup diced rutabaga (1/2-inch dice)

1/2 cup diced fennel (1/2-inch dice)

2 cups thickly sliced mixed fresh mushrooms such
    as shiitake, chanterelle, morel, and domestic

1 tablespoon minced garlic

1 1/2 tablespoons finely chopped fresh flat-leaf parsley

1/2 cup freshly grated Parmesan cheese

In a nonreactive dish, toss the rabbit pieces with the balsamic vinegar. Let rest for 15 minutes. Drain the rabbit and reserve the vinegar. Season the rabbit with salt and pepper. Heat 2 1/2 tablespoons of the olive oil in a large sauté pan over medium-high heat until hot. Add the rabbit and cook on all sides until deeply browned, about 5 minutes. Regulate the heat so the rabbit does not burn. Remove and reserve.

Add another 1 tablespoon of the olive oil to the pan, if necessary, and add the 1/4-inch-diced onion, carrot, and the celery. Add a pinch of salt and pepper and cook over medium to medium-high heat until well browned, about 5 minutes. Add the wine and reserved balsamic vinegar and bring to a boil. Stir and scrape all around the bottom and sides of the pan to loosen all the browned bits. Cook until reduced by about half. Add the stock, bay leaf, thyme sprigs, juniper berries, and peppercorns and return to a boil. Reduce the heat to a simmer.

Add the rabbit and simmer gently, uncovered, just until the rabbit is tender, about 7 minutes. (This is just a short braise to cook the rabbit. If the braising liquid boils hard, the rabbit meat will be tough.) Remove the rabbit, let cool, and cut the meat off the bones. Cut the meat into 1/2-inch dice. Reserve. Continue to simmer the cooking liquid until reduced to about 2 cups. Skim the foam as necessary. Strain through a coarse sieve and then through a fine sieve. Reserve.

Bring a large pot of water to a boil and add salt. Add the pasta and cook until al dente, about 12 minutes.

Drain, refresh quickly under cool running water, drain again, and toss with 1 tablespoon of the olive oil. Reserve.

Heat together the pancetta and the remaining 1 tablespoon olive oil in a large skillet over medium heat. Cook slowly until well browned and crisp. Tilt the pan to collect the fat in a little pool against the side and scrape the pancetta into the fat. Cook for another minute to be sure the pancetta is very crisp. Remove with a slotted spoon to paper towels to drain. Reserve.

Add 1 tablespoon of the butter to the skillet and increase heat to medium-high. Add the ½-inch-diced parsnip, carrot, rutabaga, and fennel. Season with salt and pepper and cook until well browned, about 5 minutes. Remove to a plate and reserve.

Add another 1 tablespoon butter to the pan and add the mushrooms. Cook without moving them until they begin to brown, about 1 minute. Then sauté until brown all over, about 5 minutes. Add the garlic and cook briefly until light brown. Add the remaining 1 tablespoon thyme and reduced cooking liquids, and return the root vegetables to the pan. Bring to a boil and simmer gently until the vegetables are tender, about 5 minutes. Return the crisped pancetta to the sauce with the parsley and taste for seasoning. (The dish can be made to this point, covered, and refrigerated for up to a day.)

Return the rabbit to the sauce and heat through. Stir in the remaining 2 tablespoons butter. Add the reserved pasta and toss well until heated through. Turn into a warm serving dish and scatter the cheese over the top.

CHEF'S NOTE: *I like deep, rich flavors, but I don't believe you have to cook for hours to achieve them. Instead, I believe it's more a matter of technique, specifically high heat. If you practice cooking with high heat, you will find that not only will dishes cook faster, but they will take on the rich caramelized flavors that correct browning imparts. High heat does mean being organized, having what you need measured and ready by the side of the stove. If you are not organized, you risk burning something and then you may have to start over or the dish will taste bitter.*

Forever Roasted Pork

It's called Forever Roasted Pork for good reason. It takes forever—about eight hours. But the hardest part of the recipe is dealing with the delicious smells that come from the oven while it cooks. The technique could be called dry braising. The meat is well seasoned with spices and put in a slow oven until it is so tender it shreds. No tending of any kind needed. Long-cooked dishes can be very seductive if handled correctly. They can also be the worst. For instance, if the meat isn't in big pieces or if it is cooked too rapidly, it will dry out and be tasteless. You can make this recipe with any cut. The tougher it is, the longer the cooking time. If you use a cut without an exterior skin and layer of fat, such as a pork "club" roast, cut the meat in half and open it out like a book. Season inside with the Fennel Spice, if desired, and pile the onions on the meat, reclose, tie, season the outside with more spice, and then place in the oven. Once it comes out of the oven, I challenge you not to stand at the kitchen counter and pick.

Serves 6 to 8

2 tablespoons extra-virgin olive oil
2 cups thinly sliced onions
Salt and freshly ground pepper
1 1/2 teaspoons finely chopped fresh sage
1/2 cup water
4 pounds pork leg or shoulder, at room temperature
About 1/4 cup Fennel Spice (page 193)

Heat the olive oil in a large sauté pan over medium heat until hot. Add the onions and a pinch of salt and pepper. Reduce the heat to medium-low and cook for about 1 minute. Add the sage and cook until the onions cease throwing off water, about 3 minutes. Add the water, cover, and cook until the onions are very tender, about 10 minutes. Uncover and sauté until the onions are very soft and the pan is dry again, about 2 minutes. Season well with salt and pepper.

Preheat the oven to 275°F. Peel back the pork skin and spread the onions directly on the fat layer. Fold the skin back over the onions and tie closed with kitchen string. Season well all over with the Fennel Spice.

Arrange the meat on a rack in a roasting pan and cook until the meat is very tender, 6 to 8 hours. It is ready when it pulls away easily if picked at with a pair of tongs. It is often easiest to cook the meat overnight or put it in the oven in the morning and let it cook all day. It does not need to be attended.

Variations: This dish can be simplified or made more elaborate depending on your taste. You can omit the onions and simply season the meat with the Fennel Spice. You can roast aromatic vegetables until caramelized and add them to the bottom of the roasting pan. Or you can add another layer of flavor to the onions: mince fresh rosemary and fruits such as oranges, kumquats, Meyer lemons, apples, pears, or quince and cook with the onions, or make a paste of garlic and fresh or dried chilies and add to the onions.

Monkfish *with* Roasted Garlic Polenta *and* Tomato Broth

This dish may look complex at first glance, but most of its parts can be made ahead, leaving you only the fish to cook at the last minute. You can even sear the fish on top of the stove ahead of time and pop it in the oven at serving time while you reheat the sauce. The amount of roasted garlic you add to the polenta can vary according to your taste and mood, from just a trace to swirling in whole roasted cloves. This is a good showcase for the very best balsamic vinegar you can afford.

Serves 4

1 recipe Soft Polenta (page 201),
    made without Fontina cheese
¼ cup Roasted Garlic Paste,
    or more to taste (page 197)
1 pound monkfish fillets, cut crosswise
    into 1-inch-thick medallions
Salt and freshly ground pepper
2 teaspoons finely chopped fresh thyme
All-purpose flour for dredging
3 tablespoons extra-virgin olive oil
1 cup slivered onion
1½ cups tomato juice (see Chef's Notes)
Balsamic vinegar, preferably *aceto balsamico*
    tradizionale

Make the polenta, stirring in the roasted garlic paste during the last few minutes of cooking. Cover the polenta with plastic wrap and keep warm over hot water.

Preheat the oven to 350°F. Season the fish all over with salt and pepper. Sprinkle with 1 teaspoon of the thyme, then dredge with flour.

Heat 2 tablespoons of the olive oil in a large, oven-proof sauté pan over medium-high heat until hot. Lower the heat to medium, add the fish, and brown on one side until golden, about 1½ minutes. Turn the fish and place in the oven to cook through, about 8 minutes longer, depending on the thickness of the fillets.

Remove the fish to a platter and keep warm. Return the pan to medium heat and add the remaining 1 tablespoon olive oil. Add the onion and sauté until brown, about 4 minutes. Stir in the remaining 1 teaspoon thyme. Add the tomato juice, bring to a boil, and simmer until reduced by about half, about 5 minutes. Season to taste with salt and pepper.

Spoon the polenta onto a warm platter or into rimmed soup plates and arrange the fish on top. Pour the tomato sauce over the fish and drizzle with a little vinegar. Serve immediately.

CHEF'S NOTES: *This is a good use for juices left over from peeling, chopping, and seeding tomatoes. Bottled tomato juice, preferably an organic juice, will do as well, however. To make the sauce ahead, brown the onions in a separate small pan in the olive oil, add the remaining thyme and tomato juice, bring to a simmer and reduce. When ready to serve, reheat the sauce gently.*

Tra Vigne's Fritto Misto *with* Tomato Vinegar

Please stop thinking of frying as a dietary sin. Let it be the accent that it is meant to be. Crispy and fried can act as a supporting flavor, such as a couple of deep-fried shrimp in a tomato salad. Learn to use the method sparingly and, if you must, call it crispy instead of fried. Then add a tiny garnish of fried chiffonadé of leek greens to a piece of fish. Make fritto misto as part of an antipasto or as a first course rather than a main dish. Even a serving of fish and chips was never meant to be a main course—it is street food, a snack. For fried foods, I prefer sauces with vinegar flavors to mayonnaise sauces. The perfect wine is a bone-dry sparkling wine like a blanc de blanc. That is the way we usually serve fritto misto at Tra Vigne—no sauce, not even vinegar, just the wine. Most people do not fry at home anymore, and that is reason enough to do it yourself. Use good-quality oil such as pure olive oil, canola oil, or peanut oil. Of these, canola is the lightest.

Serves 4

1 cup Summer Tomato Sauce (page 199)

1 1/2 tablespoons red wine vinegar

Salt and freshly ground pepper

4 to 6 cups canola oil for deep-frying

1 pound zucchini

1 red onion, thickly sliced and separated into rings

1 pound rock shrimp

3/4 cup buttermilk

About 2 cups Arborio Rice Coating (page 193)

Puree the tomato sauce in a blender or with an immersion blender. Whisk in the vinegar and season with salt and pepper. Taste for balance and chill.

Heat the oil in a deep fryer or deep pot to 350°F. Meanwhile, cut the zucchini into 3-inch lengths, then into 1/8-inch-thick slices, and finally into 1/8-inch-wide sticks. Set aside in a small bowl. Place the onions in another small bowl. Drain the rock shrimp well and place in yet another bowl. Pour 1/4 cup buttermilk each over the zucchini, onions, and shrimp. Toss each well. Put the rice coating in a large bowl. Drain the zucchini well and add to the coating bowl. Toss well, transfer to a sieve, and shake off the excess. Fry in small batches until crisp and pale gold, about 3 minutes. Transfer with a slotted spoon to paper towels to drain and place in a low oven to keep warm. Repeat the process with the onions: cook them for about 2 minutes, drain, and add to the zucchini in the oven. Finally, repeat the process with the shrimp, cooking them for about 3 minutes.

To serve, divide the tomato dipping sauce among 4 small bowls. Pile equal portions of shrimp, zucchini, and onion on each of 4 plates with a bowl of dipping sauce. Serve immediately. Or roll a sheet of waxed paper or doubled newspaper into a cone and place in a tall glass, such as a parfait glass. Fill with the fritto misto and place the bowl of dipping sauce to the side of each serving.

Mozzarella Martini *with* Tomato Consommé

You will want to have everyone's attention when you serve these "martinis." They are stunning when the glasses are heavily frosted. For a real show, use silver skewers and oversized glasses. You can certainly add a splash of vermouth, pepper vodka, or grappa. Make this dish only if you have in-season garden fresh or farmers' market tomatoes. The flavor depends completely on the tomatoes.

Serves 4

3 to 4 pounds vine-ripened tomatoes
     (see Chef's Notes), plus ½ tomato,
     cut into 4 wedges
Salt and freshly ground pepper
4 fresh mozzarella bocconcini,
     each 1 inch in diameter
4 cherry tomatoes
About 1 ½ teaspoons basil-flavored
     olive oil (optional)
8 large fresh basil leaves, cut into very
     fine chiffonade

You will need enough tomato water to fill your martini glasses, so measure their capacity, probably something between 5 and 9 ounces.

Chill the martini glasses in the freezer, if there is room, or refrigerate an hour ahead of serving. (A freezer gives a heavy frost.) Peel, seed, and chop the 3 to 4 pounds tomatoes. Season lightly with salt and pepper, place in a sieve suspended over a bowl and refrigerate for several hours. As the tomatoes release their juice, it will fall into the bowl, giving you an almost gin-clear liquid with lots of flavor. Season the tomato water to taste with salt and pepper and refrigerate until very cold. Reserve the tomato pulp for another use.

Halve or quarter the bocconcini if they are larger than 1 inch in diameter. Thread a tomato wedge, a bocconcini, and a cherry tomato onto each of 4 wooden skewers 4 to 5 inches long. Season with salt and pepper and drizzle with basil oil, if desired. Working quickly, divide the tomato liquid among the chilled martini glasses. Balance the skewers on top of the glasses, then sprinkle the basil chiffonade over the skewers. Serve immediately.

CHEF'S NOTES: *It is impossible to give a specific amount for the tomatoes because how much "water" a tomato releases depends on many factors, including the growing season and the variety. Do not let the tomato pulp go to waste. Use this recipe as an excuse to start your summer tomato sauce season. You can freeze or can your sauce and then have it on hand for quick meals.*

desserts and cookies

Tra Vigne's customers have had a strong influence on our dessert menu. Most traditional Italian desserts do not fit the image of dessert cherished by most Americans. Our challenge at Tra Vigne has been to translate Italian preparations and ingredients into ones our customers would love. ❧ Early on, customers would ask for tiramisù. They assumed that if the restaurant was Italian it must serve tiramisù. After much experimentation, we created one that would meet our guests' desire, surprise them, and fit the style of Tra Vigne. Our Chocolate Tiramisù (page 187) combines layers of zabaglione, chocolate-mascarpone mousse, and a rich chocolate sponge cake. ❧ We also like to take American desserts and give them an Italian twist. For instance, our crostata (page 182), our version of cobbler, is a favorite. We add polenta and aniseeds to the topping for crunch and flavor, while underneath is a seductive mix of seasonal fruits. ❧ As in most kitchens, holidays provide an excuse to bake, bake, bake. Mini and maxi panettones (page 184) parade out of the pastry kitchen and appear in unlikely places on our menu. People love the look of this bread, but usually have no idea what to do with it. Like many Italian foods, the cakey loaf is eaten in stages. First, it is enjoyed fresh; then I love panettone bruschetta in salads. Finally, it makes a terrific dessert bruschetta topped with apricot jam or a great bread pudding. The last dry bits are cut into cubes, slowly dried in the oven until thoroughly toasted, and then added to a holiday turkey stuffing or tossed with a fall fruit salad (page 95). If there are any crumbs left, these can be sprinkled into the bottom of a pie or added to a crostata topping. ❧ My family's traditions and recipes have a direct influence on the cookies we serve. I use my mother's biscotti recipe (page 189), but have substituted crystallized sugar for greater moisture and more "bite." Mom taught her family's collection of holiday treats to my wife. Now Ines comes to the restaurant each year to work with our bakers to turn out batch after batch of Aiello cookies. This often becomes an opportunity for our chefs and bakers to share their grandmothers' versions of these traditional cookies.

dolci e biscotti

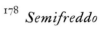

Semifreddo

Hot, cold, sweet, bitter. For such a simple dessert, there is a lot going on here. We had
semifreddo on the Tra Vigne menu for our first four years. I think people loved
it because it combines adult flavors with childhood pleasures—the strong taste of
good espresso and the wonderful texture of melting ice cream. It is also a "small"
dessert, served in small portions, so it fits the bill when you want to indulge in "just a
little something." All you need to do to make it is to fire up your espresso machine.

Serves 1

1 small scoop hazelnut gelato
1 small scoop vanilla gelato
1 shot fresh hot espresso
Spoonful steamed milk froth
Equal parts unsweetened cocoa powder
    and powdered sugar, sifted together

Scoop the gelato into a coffee cup or tempered glass
tumbler. Pour the hot espresso over the gelato and spoon
a little milk froth on top. Dust with the cocoa-sugar mix.

Bugia

"Have you been eating the cookies?" "No! Honest, I haven't." "Then what is all that powdered sugar doing on your chest?" Bugia, or liar's cookies, leave a telltale trail.

Makes 1 1/2 pounds dough, enough for about 6 dozen cookies

2 1/2 cups all-purpose flour, plus more for dusting
work surface

1/2 teaspoon baking powder

1/4 teaspoon salt

2 tablespoons sugar

2 large eggs

1/2 cup (1 stick) unsalted butter, melted
and cooled briefly

1/4 cup freshly squeezed orange juice

1 1/2 tablespoons brandy

1/2 teaspoon vanilla extract

3/4 teaspoon aniseeds, ground

4 to 6 cups peanut or vegetable oil
for deep-frying

About 2 cups powdered sugar

Sift the flour with the baking powder, salt, and sugar and set aside. In the bowl of a stand mixer fitted with paddle attachment, mix together the eggs, butter, orange juice, brandy, vanilla, and aniseeds until well blended. Add the dry ingredients all at once and mix on low speed until the dough cleans the sides of the bowl and adheres to the paddle.

Remove the dough from the bowl onto a floured board. Knead by hand until smooth. Form the dough into a ball, flatten slightly, and place in a bowl. Cover with a tea towel and chill at least 2 hours or up to overnight to allow the dough to relax.

Heat the oil in a deep fryer or deep pot to 350°F. Meanwhile, cut the dough into 4 or 6 equal pieces. Keeping the dough and work surface well floured, pass the dough through the widest setting of a pasta machine 3 or 4 times. Then pass through successively narrower settings until the dough is almost thin enough to see through; depending on your pasta machine, this will probably be the next to thinnest setting.

Cut the dough into long strips 3 inches wide, then cut the strips on the diagonal into pieces about 3 inches long. If the dough tears, cut it off and work it back into the dough. The cookies curl when they fry, so fancier shapes are not important. As the cookies are cut, transfer them to baking sheets lined with flour-dusted tea towels, and cover with tea towels so they won't dry out before frying. Fry in batches, turning once, until puffed and golden brown, about 1 minute. Transfer with a slotted spoon to paper towels to drain.

While the cookies are still hot, dust them well with powdered sugar. Wait for a few minutes while the oil and heat absorb and melt most of this first coating. Dust well a second time until the cookies are quite white. The cookies will keep for a week or so in an airtight container. You may need to redust them with sugar before serving.

CHEF'S NOTES: *Only a few cookies at a time will fit, even in a big pot, so frying takes time. It is best to have company in the kitchen, ready with lots of good talk to keep you amused. And there are always the warm cookies to eat along the way as a reward. You can also dredge the cookies in granulated sugar, crystal sugar, or even a mix of powdered sugar and unsweetened cocoa powder.*

Pastura

3 1/2 cups all-purpose flour (1 pound; see Chef's Notes), plus more for dusting work surface

3 1/2 teaspoons baking powder

1/4 teaspoon baking soda

1/4 teaspoon ground cinnamon

1/4 teaspoon ground cloves

1 1/3 cups honey, warm (1 pound; see Chef's Notes)

1 large egg

2 cups chocolate morsels (12 ounces)

1/4 cup heavy cream

Vegetable spray

About 6 ounces unblanched whole almonds (about 1 1/2 cups)

It didn't matter how much we liked these cookies, Mom made them only once a year. During the holidays she would bake as many as we liked, but once the season was over, we would have to wait for the following year. My children do not care much for nuts, so Ines often leaves them out of half the batch, filling the cookies with chocolate alone or adding raisins. The nuts give the cookies their simple beauty, however. Their forms lined up under the dough give it a subtle pattern, and when the cookies are cut, the exposed shape of the nuts gives a very sophisticated look.

Makes about 2½ dozen cookies

Measure the flour, baking powder, baking soda, cinnamon, and cloves into the bowl of a stand mixer fitted with the paddle attachment. Add the honey and egg and beat on low to medium speed just until mixed. This makes a very sticky dough. You can roll it out immediately or scrape it into a ball, place it in a bowl, cover with a tea towel, and chill for 2 hours or up to overnight.

Preheat the oven to 350°F. Combine the chocolate and cream in a heatproof bowl and place over (but not touching) gently simmering water. Heat, stirring occasionally with a wooden spoon, until melted and smooth. Let cool until warm. (To melt in a microwave, mix the chocolate and cream in a bowl and microwave on high for about 30 seconds. Stir, then repeat.)

Meanwhile, cut 3 sheets of parchment paper large enough to fit your baking sheets. The dough is very sticky and difficult to roll out even on a well-floured board. Lightly spray 2 parchment sheets with vegetable spray. Transfer half the dough to 1 prepared sheet and top with the second. The dough is so easily worked that you can begin to spread it with your hands. Roll the dough into as even a rectangle as you can, about 10 inches by 15 inches. It can easily be pushed and prodded into shape.

Peel off the top sheet of parchment. Spread half the chocolate in a 3- or 4-inch-wide band down the length of the dough, leaving the top half of the dough free and an inch or so border around the remaining 3 sides. Arrange the almonds, side by side, in short rows across the chocolate band. Each row should abut the next to make a regular pattern. Use the parchment to fold the top half of dough over the almonds and chocolate. Carefully peel back the paper and press the edges together to seal. Slide the shaped log, still on the parchment, onto a baking sheet. Lightly spray the third sheet of parchment with vegetable spray and repeat the shaping and filling with the remaining half of the

dough. Slide the log onto the same baking sheet, if there is room. The dough is so soft, it is best to not move it off the parchment until after baking.

Bake until light golden brown, about 20 minutes. Let cool on the baking sheet. If you like softer, chewy cookies, let the logs cool until still slightly warm, then wrap well. If you prefer crispier cookies, let the logs cool completely, then wrap. Using a serrated knife, cut the logs crosswise through the middle of each row of almonds so their rounded shapes show on each side of the cookies. Cut just before serving or the cookies will dry out.

CHEF'S NOTES: *My mother's recipe calls for 1 pound of flour and 1 pound of honey. If you have a scale, put it to use for this project. Use all the honey or the dough won't have the right consistency. Ensure this by buying a 1-pound jar of honey. Microwave it briefly to warm it. Then it will all run out easily and you don't have to fuss with measuring at all. Even then, scrape out all the honey with a rubber spatula.*

Strawberry, Rhubarb, *and* Red Banana Crostata

For the topping
1 1/2 cups pastry flour (1/2 pound)
Scant 3/4 cup polenta (1/4 pound)
1/2 cup granulated sugar (3 1/2 ounces)
Large pinch salt
1 1/2 teaspoons baking powder
1 teaspoon aniseeds, toasted
1/2 cup (1 stick) chilled unsalted butter,
    cut into small pieces
1 large egg, lightly beaten

Vanilla gelato
    or sweetened whipped cream (optional)

For the filling
1 pound rhubarb, cut into 1-inch pieces
1 full pint basket large, ripe strawberries,
    about 1 pound, hulled and halved or quartered
2 large, ripe red bananas, cut into 1-inch pieces
2/3 cup granulated sugar
2/3 cup packed light brown sugar
1/4 teaspoon freshly ground pepper
1 teaspoon ground cinnamon
1 teaspoon salt
1/2 teaspoon aniseeds, toasted
Freshly grated zest of 1/2 orange
Freshly grated zest of 1 lemon
Juice of 1/2 lemon

This is a simple take on the classic American cobbler. As the dessert bakes, the fruit juices bubble up and over the topping in places, making it look homey and luscious. Use any fruit in season, such as peaches, pears, apples, plums, or berries. If the berries are not the best, add a splash of balsamic or mango vinegar to brighten their flavor. How large or small you cut the fruit depends on your preference, but all the pieces should be about the same size. I prefer larger pieces, as they retain more identity in the finished dessert. The rhubarb here acts as a thickener. If it is omitted, I like to add a little tapioca as a thickener because it allows the juices to stay clear. Other thickeners, such as cornstarch or flour, muddy the color of the fruit juices. If you want to avoid the signature tapioca beads in the finished dessert, grind the tapioca in a spice mill or blender to a fine powder. I have given the weights for the dry ingredients because it is often faster to weigh than to measure ingredients. This is also a recipe adapted from our pastry kitchen, where weight rules.

Serves 4 to 6

Preheat the oven to 375°F. *To make the topping,* measure the flour, polenta, sugar, salt, baking powder, and aniseeds into a food processor or a stand mixer fitted with the paddle attachment. Add the butter and pulse or mix on medium-low speed until the mixture resembles coarse crumbs. Transfer the mixture to a bowl and make a well in the center. Pour the egg into the well and toss the egg and flour together lightly and thoroughly with your fingers until evenly mixed. The mixture will not adhere in the manner of a dough but will clump together if pressed in your palm. Set aside until needed.

To make the filling, combine all the ingredients in a large bowl and toss until well mixed. Turn into a 2-quart shallow baking dish. Sprinkle the topping over the filling in an even layer. Do not press down. Place the dish on a baking sheet to catch the drips and place in the oven.

Bake until the juices are bubbling up around the topping and the top is crisp and golden brown, about 1 hour. Serve warm with gelato, if desired.

CHEF'S NOTES: *Red bananas have a red-brown skin and are fairly soft when ripe. They are more aromatic and have a yellower color and a more custardy texture than yellow bananas. If it's allowed where you shop, give the bananas a discreet pinch before you buy. If they are not ripe, they will not soften during baking, but remain fibrous. If you choose to bake the dessert in individual dishes, cut the baking time by about half.*

Panettone

This is a version of the traditional anise-flavored bread that makes its festive appearance in Italian bakeries and specialty food shops for the Christmas holidays. Often it is imported, and when people first taste it, they sometimes wonder what all the excitement is about. To taste it freshly baked is to begin to understand the appeal of this buttery, rich, cakelike bread. At Tra Vigne we add moisture and flavor by brushing still-hot loaves with anise-flavored syrup. The bread is addictive on its own, but if it makes it more than a day in the house, turn it into bruschetta by toasting it with butter and serving it for dessert with apricot jam. Or use it for French toast or bread pudding, or to make small croutons for adding to salads and holiday stuffings. Even the crumbs can be saved for adding to pies and tarts to absorb fruit juices and in crisps and crumbles.

Makes about 4 pounds dough, enough for 2 standard loaves

1 1/2 cups sugar, plus 2/3 cup

1 1/2 cups water

1/3 cup aniseeds

1/2 cup sun-dried cherries

1/2 cup diced dried apricots (1/4-inch dice)

1/3 cup golden raisins

1 1/4 cups whole milk

2 envelopes active dry yeast, or 2 cakes (1/2-ounce each) fresh yeast

4 1/4 cups bread flour, plus more for dusting work surface

4 large eggs

1 1/2 teaspoons freshly grated lemon zest

3/4 cup (1 1/2 sticks) unsalted butter, at room temperature, plus more for buttering pans

Put the 1 1/2 cups sugar, the 1 1/2 cups water, and aniseeds in a small saucepan. Heat over high heat, stirring until the sugar dissolves. Bring to a boil, reduce the heat to low, and simmer gently for 5 minutes to form a syrup.

Put the cherries, apricots, and raisins in a large bowl and pour the hot syrup over them. Mix well and let steep for 10 minutes. Strain the fruits from the syrup, reserving the fruits and syrup separately.

Warm the milk to just below body temperature. Combine the warm milk, yeast and 1/3 cup sugar in the bowl of a stand mixer. Stir well. Whisk in 1 cup of the flour. Cover this sponge with a tea towel and leave in a warm place until tripled in size, about 45 minutes.

Add the eggs and the remaining 3 1/4 cups flour and 1/3 cup sugar to the sponge and mix in with the dough hook attachment. Knead on medium to medium-low speed until the dough begins to clean the sides of the bowl and cling to the dough hook, about 8 minutes.

To make sure the fruit gets evenly distributed throughout the dough, scrape the dough off the dough hook before kneading in the dried fruit and lemon zest on the lowest speed. With the machine running on low, add the butter in about 2-tablespoon chunks. Let each begin to be kneaded in before adding the next. Scrape down the sides and bottom of the bowl to make sure all the butter gets worked into the dough.

Remove the bowl from the machine but leave the dough in the bowl. Cover with a tea towel and leave in a warm place to rise to the top of the bowl, about 1 1/2 hours.

Prepare the molds. You will have enough dough for 2 standard panettone molds, each 7 inches in diameter and 4 1/2 inches high (see Chef's Notes). Butter and flour the molds and line the bottoms with parchment paper.

Dust the dough with flour and, using a pastry scraper, turn it out onto a well-floured board. It will be very sticky, so work quickly and lightly. Knead gently to work the air out of it and to produce a mass a little easier to shape. Divide in half and shape into balls. Place in the prepared molds. Cover with a tea towel and let the dough rise until it reaches the tops of the molds. When touched gently, it should feel light and springy. This may take as long as 2 hours, depending on the temperature of the room. While the dough rises, preheat the oven to 350°F.

Bake until browned and cooked through, about 50 minutes. To check doneness, using thick hot pads, turn a loaf out of its pan. If the bottom and sides are golden tan all over, the bread is done. The tops may be very dark. That is the nature of the bread, and this top becomes the bottom of the bread when presented and served.

Pour the reserved syrup into a cake pan. When the bread is done, working with 1 loaf at a time, turn it out of its pan, peel off the parchment, and sit the loaf in the syrup in the cake pan. Brush the syrup generously up the sides and over the top of the bread and then return it to its mold. Repeat with the second loaf. Let it sit so the warmth of the pan and bread will allow the syrup to be absorbed into the loaves. Brush the top several times more with the syrup as the loaves cool.

CHEF'S NOTES: *Two pounds of dough fits a standard panettone mold. If you do not have a panettone mold, you can use an ovenproof saucepan. One with slightly flared sides is best, as it allows easier unmolding of the bread. You can also use 3 standard loaf pans for this recipe, or make miniature panettones using 2 ounces of dough for each 2 1/2-inch muffin cup. Muffins bake in about 20 minutes. Baste them in syrup as you would a larger bread. It is a good idea to plan ahead how you want to use the loaves. You might want to serve one as a dessert and use the second one for croutons, stuffing, or bread pudding. If so, brush only one loaf with the syrup. Leftover anise-flavored syrup, if any, is delicious stirred into coffee, as a topping for yogurt or ice cream, and as a flavoring for puddings, custards, or Italian meringue. Store in a sealed jar in the refrigerator. It will keep indefinitely.*

Panettone Bread Pudding

Serves 8 to 10

1/2 loaf panettone, preferably one that has not been soaked in anise syrup, thickly sliced or cut into large cubes
8 eggs
1 cup sugar
4 cups whole milk
1 tablespoon vanilla extract

CHEF'S NOTE: *The custard should not taste very sweet, as the bread is already sweet.*

Toast the panettone in a 250°F oven until brown and dry.

Whisk together the eggs and sugar in a large bowl until light. Warm the milk just to a simmer in a large saucepan. Pour a little hot milk into the eggs while whisking vigorously. Slowly pour the rest of the milk into the eggs while whisking all the while. Return the egg mixture to the saucepan and replace over medium-low heat. Cook, stirring constantly, until the mixture coats the back of a spoon, about 20 minutes. Remove from heat and add 1 tablespoon vanilla extract.

Place the toasted bread cubes or slices in a 3-quart baking dish. Pour the custard over the bread. Place the baking dish in a larger baking pan and pour in boiling water to reach halfway up the sides of the pudding mold. Cover and bake in a preheated 350°F oven for about 40 minutes. Remove the cover and bake until set, about 20 minutes longer. Serve with Zabaglione Sauce (page 187), if desired.

Tra Vigne's Chocolate Tiramisù

It looks so innocent: a simple square dusted with cocoa. And then your fork descends through the layers of rich, moist chocolate cake, chocolate mascarpone mousse, zabaglione, more cake. Irresistible. Tra Vigne's tiramisù is actually a triple-decker, but I've made the assembly a little easier here. Serve this for a special occasion. Although it involves several separate steps, all can be completed well ahead of time. Use a decorative glass bowl for a pretty presentation or make individual desserts. We started using this cake recipe for our tiramisù in 1997. We had been searching for a very moist cake and this fit the bill. It is dense (but not fudgy) and rich with a terrific moist crumb. It makes a super birthday cake. Double the recipe for a double-layer cake. It would also be great as a base for a chocolate bread pudding. Both the mousse and the zabaglione may be served as desserts on their own. Garnish the mousse with a scattering of chocolate curls. Traditionally, zabaglione is served warm in a wineglass immediately after it is made. It is an unusual and rich addition to a tiramisù. You could make the zabaglione with half the amount of cream, as a sauce for Panettone Bread Pudding (page 185).

Serves 8 to 10

For the cake
Butter for buttering cake pan
2 cups sifted cake flour
2 teaspoons baking soda
1/2 teaspoon salt
1/3 cup unsweetened cocoa powder
1 cup boiling water
1 teaspoon vanilla extract
3/4 cup real mayonnaise such as Best Foods
    or Hellmann's
1 cup sugar

For the chocolate mascarpone mousse
5 ounces bittersweet chocolate
    such as Valrhona, cut into pieces
1/4 cup heavy cream
1/4 cup cream cheese, at room temperature
1 cup mascarpone cheese, at room temperature
2 large egg yolks, at room temperature
1/4 cup sugar
Pinch salt

For the zabaglione
4 large egg yolks, at room temperature
1 tablespoon light or dark rum
1/4 cup Marsala wine
1/2 cup plus 2 teaspoons sugar
1/2 cup heavy cream

For assembly
1/2 cup sugar
1 cup fresh hot espresso
1/4 cup dark rum
1 ounce bittersweet or semisweet chocolate,
    or 1 tablespoon unsweetened cocoa powder
    or powdered sugar

To make the cake, preheat the oven to 325°F. Butter an 8- or 9-inch cake pan and line the bottom with parchment paper. Butter the parchment (this allows it to peel more easily from the cake bottom).

Sift together the flour, baking soda, and salt and set aside. In a small bowl, whisk together the cocoa and boiling water until smooth. Let cool to room temperature.

Combine the vanilla, mayonnaise, and sugar in a bowl and beat with an electric mixer until light. Start beating on slow speed and increase to medium until the mixture is light and all the sugar has been incorporated. Scrape down the sides of the bowl. Reduce the speed to low and add the cocoa mixture in a slow, steady stream. Add the flour mixture and fold in while turning the bowl to scrape the sides and bottom. Mix just until the flour disappears. You should have a smooth, velvety batter.

Scrape the batter into the prepared pan. With a small, offset spatula, smooth the top. Bake until puffed and a cake tester inserted into the center comes out clean or the top springs back when lightly pressed with a finger, about 50 minutes. Remove from the oven and let cool completely in the pan. Run a knife around the edge to loosen the sides and invert the cake onto a plate. Peel off the parchment. You will have one 8- or 9-inch cake that will serve 6 on its own. (The cake may be made a day ahead. Wrap well.)

To make the mousse, combine the chocolate and cream in a heatproof bowl and place over (but not touching) barely simmering water. Heat, stirring occasionally, until melted, smooth, and shiny. Remove from the heat.

In a large mixing bowl, beat the cream cheese and mascarpone with an electric mixer at medium to medium-high speed until soft and creamy. Pause occasionally to scrape down the sides of the bowl. On low speed, beat in the chocolate mixture.

In another bowl, with clean beaters, whip the egg yolks until frothy. Add the sugar and salt and continue to beat on high speed until the mixture is pale yellow and forms a ribbon when the beaters are lifted.

With a rubber spatula or wooden spoon, mix together the yolks and cheese mixture until smooth. Cover and refrigerate until ready to assemble the tiramisù. You should have about 2 cups mousse. (Served on its own, the mousse will serve 4. The mousse may be made ahead, covered, and refrigerated for up to 1 day.)

To make the zabaglione, prepare an ice water bath. Combine the yolks, rum, and Marsala in the top of a double boiler. Place over (not touching) barely simmering water in the lower pan and whisk vigorously, or beat with an electric mixer, until the mixture begins to foam. Add the ½ cup sugar and whisk continuously until the mixture triples in volume and thickens to form soft mounds when the whisk is lifted, about 7 minutes. Immediately place the top of the double boiler in the ice water bath to stop the cooking. Let cool, stirring occasionally.

In a small bowl, beat the cream until it begins to foam. Add the remaining 2 teaspoons sugar and continue to beat until the cream holds soft peaks. Fold into the zabaglione. Cover and chill for several hours before assembling the tiramisù. You should have about 2 cups, which will serve 4 on its own.

To assemble the dessert, in a small bowl or pitcher, add the sugar to the hot espresso. Stir well to dissolve the sugar, then add the rum. Reserve.

Cut off the top of the cake and reserve for another use (see Chef's Notes). Cut the cake in half horizontally. Arrange a layer of cake, cut side up, in the bottom of a deep 2½-quart bowl. Moisten evenly with some of the espresso syrup. Spread half the mousse on top, and then spread half of the zabaglione on top of the mousse. Arrange the second layer of cake, again cut side up, on the mousse. Moisten well with syrup. Spread the remaining mousse on top in an even layer, followed by the remaining zabaglione. Cover and refrigerate for several hours or overnight before serving. With a vegetable peeler, cut curls of chocolate to garnish the top or dust with cocoa.

CHEF'S NOTES: *The shiny top of the cake will not readily absorb syrup. If you do not cut it off, you might find dry spots in your tiramisù. But don't throw the top out! Crumble it into crumbs and place them in a 150°F to 200°F oven until thoroughly dry and crunchy. Use to decorate the top of the tiramisù, or save them to add to cookie batters or to scatter in pies and tarts to absorb juices.*

If you use an 8-inch pan for the cake, it will rise over the edge by about ¼ inch. If you are planning to use the cake for birthday cake, you will have to trim the cake to get an even edge.

If you are concerned about using raw eggs in the mousse, use pasteurized eggs or a pasteurized egg substitute, using the equivalent of 2 whole eggs. The result will be lighter and delicious.

Tra Vigne's Biscotti

Whenever Mom made biscotti, she always said, "If only we had the black aniseeds we had at home . . ." She meant Calabria. In 1997, on a visit to Calabria, I was served biscotti flavored with black anise. When I asked about the source, I was told to go to the "wild market." It was a small market, perhaps ten booths, the vendors all mountain people who sold an odd assortment of strange-looking roots, mushrooms, cheeses, and various other things. I asked about black anise and the whisperings worked down the row of stalls until the man at the far end presented himself to me. Our negotiations were not about black anise. Instead, we bargained over what else I would buy to convince him to part with a little of the black anise. I came away with prosciutto, cheese, and more, plus a very few grams of the black anise.

Makes about 40 cookies

3 1/2 cups all-purpose flour, plus more
    for dusting work surfaces
1 1/2 teaspoons baking powder
1 teaspoon salt
1/2 cup (1 stick) unsalted butter,
    at room temperature
2/3 cup crystal sugar plus more to roll logs in
    (see Chef's Notes)
1/3 cup packed light brown sugar
5 large eggs
6 tablespoons aniseeds
1 cup unblanched whole almonds, toasted

CHEF'S NOTES: *Crystal, or sparkling, sugar is large-grained, decorative sugar available in both white and colored versions. It gives the cookies a slightly lighter and moister texture since it has a higher moisture content than granulated sugar. You can substitute turbinado sugar, which is also large grained. It gives a slightly coarser texture. You can also use granulated white sugar with very good results.*

You can make biscotti any size you like. The 3-inch-diameter log makes cookies about 4 1/2 inches long. If you prefer a more delicate cookie, divide the dough into thirds and roll into logs just 2 inches or less in diameter, then slice more thinly for the second baking. For a more elegant cookie, cut the logs on a slight diagonal.

Sift together the flour, baking powder, and salt and set aside. In the bowl of a stand mixer fitted with the paddle attachment, cream together the butter, crystal sugar, and brown sugar until light and fluffy. Add the eggs, flour mixture, and aniseeds. Beat on low just until the dough begins to come together. Add the almonds and mix just until distributed. Do not overwork. On a floured board, shape the dough into a ball, flatten, put in a bowl, and chill for 2 hours to allow the dough to relax.

Preheat the oven to 325°F. Line a baking sheet with parchment paper. Divide the dough into 2 equal portions on a lightly floured work surface. Using your hands, roll each portion into a log about 3 inches in diameter. Roll the logs in crystal sugar to coat well. Place the logs on the prepared baking sheet and press down lightly to flatten slightly. Logs should be several inches apart.

Bake until firm and light brown, about 1 hour. When poked with a finger, the dough should feel firm to the touch and not collapse or cave in. Remove from the oven, then lower the oven temperature to 300°F.

Let the logs cool completely. Carefully move them, still on the parchment, to a cutting board, then peel off the parchment. Cut the logs with a sharp serrated knife into 1/2-inch-thick slices. Lay the slices down on a baking sheet and return to the oven. Bake until toasted to a golden brown on both sides, about 50 minutes. Turn the cookies during toasting, as needed, to brown evenly on both sides. Let cool completely, then store in an airtight container.

pantry

When I was a child, our family honored guests with a tour through the cellar. The heart of the house, the pride of the household, was the quality and abundance stored in this underground pantry. ✎ Because the visit created a special occasion, an uncut prosciutto might be brought up to the kitchen. Anxiety would spice anticipation of the first cut. Curing is always unpredictable: the prosciutto might not have hung long enough, or the cure might not have penetrated evenly throughout the meat. It is impossible to know without cutting into the meat, and then, of course, it is too late to let it hang longer. There would be a collective and audible sigh of pleasure from all as the knife glided through the silken, deep rose flesh. My paternal grandfather still has the reputation of making the best prosciutto in the family. Just why is a mystery, although it may be because of the mountain air and the native flora of his cellar. ✎ In the days of my parents and grandparents, a full pantry was a natural byproduct of a way of life. Tomatoes are a good example. Early in the summer, we made cured green tomatoes from thinnings, then the time arrived to eat tomatoes fresh from the vine. At the end of summer, we made canned tomatoes, tomato sauce, dried tomatoes, and tomato *conserva*. Grapes became wine. Some of that wine became vinegar. Pigs were fattened all summer to become prosciutto and sausage in the fall. Extra milk in the summer was turned into cheese. Out of necessity, Italian cooking became a cuisine of preservation. It also follows a natural progression. A loaf of bread is eaten fresh for a day or two. Then it is used for bruschetta, then perhaps panzanella (page 60), and finally any remainder becomes bread crumbs. Hardly a scrap goes unused. ✎ Pantry items are the secret ingredient in creating Tra Vigne's unique style of cooking. At the restaurant we continue to follow the seasonal rhythms of preserving and then use those ingredients in our cooking throughout the year. Our prosciutti and salami hang on the second story of the Cantinetta, protected from abrupt temperature changes by its thick stone walls. We press olive oils from small local groves to serve in saucers with our bakery's breads. We make our own wine vinegar and are beginning to age our own balsamic as well. All the chefs participate in these activities, plus they forage in the vineyards and woods for wild herbs and greens to use in our dishes that day or perhaps to spice a batch of Tra Vigne bar olives. ✎ The process of seeking and creating Italian-inspired ingredients for Tra Vigne had several unforseen consequences. Remembering the intensely flavored oil that surrounded the sun-dried tomatoes stored in my family's cellar, we started experimenting with flavored oils in Tra Vigne's kitchen as a way to add powerful flavors quickly to our dishes. Then we started selling the oils in our Cantinetta. When they became very popular, we started our own label, Consorzio. Our commercial bakery, Pan-O-Rama, began in much the same way. Since the day we opened, we have made bread and pizzas in our wood-fired oven. Guests frequently asked if they could buy a loaf to take home. Eventually, we increased our production and then built our first bakery in Petaluma in 1993. ✎ Whether you experience the same level of success or not, the real joy of investing the time to build a pantry is looking forward to giving these precious flavors away, using them in meals shared with friends, or leaving behind a jar of handmade preserves as a thank you for a visit. A note on the back saying "Please return when empty" assures the cycle will continue. ✎ Making your own is also a way to preserve authentic flavors. My mother made her own chili flakes, drying the chilies, then labeling them as to chili variety and year. Commercially dried chili flakes have a roasted flavor and give Italian sausage a nontraditional chorizo flavor. ✎ Thoughtfully "accessorized" pantries are practical. They allow you to pick up a few fresh ingredients and put a meal together quickly that displays a depth and diversity of flavors impossible to achieve without hours of preparation. It is not necessary to dig a cellar in order to have a pantry. It may be a good idea to install some shelves or a set of inexpensive kitchen cabinets in the garage, as I have at home where I have no cellar. Having a good-size freezer is helpful, too. If nothing else, you can make a batch of a spice mix (pages 192 and 193) to divide up into pretty little jars and give away. But the most important building block of a good pantry is your desire to become more intimately involved with the food you cook and serve. This may mean taking the time when you have it in order to reap the rewards later when you don't. ✎ For instance, on your next hike, take a look around. You may come home with a bag of wild mustard, a bouquet of dried fennel flowers gone to seed, a spray of bay leaves. Remember where those wild grapevines and berry bushes grow and revisit them to see if they have a crop. You may be on your way to some unusual jams. Give your greed free rein at the farmers' market and buy a flat of figs to oven-dry. ❧ You can share the work with family, neighbors, and friends and build community while you preserve summer's tastes to savor in the depths of winter. Nowadays, one person is too often expected to do everything in the kitchen. When I grew up, everyone had a specific job. It's an old trick and one that still works: dividing big tasks into little ones and delegating. ❧ My wife and I share a tomato-canning day every year with three other families. Everyone picks tomatoes first thing in the morning and brings their tomatoes and jars to our house. My job is to sort the tomatoes and peel them. Then I'm kicked out of the kitchen and not allowed back until it's time for me to cook dinner. The only rule is that I can't use tomatoes. Each time we open a jar of those tomatoes, we'll have the memory of that day to savor as well. Having such culinary memory triggers is important to me. They build a shared heritage.

STOCKING THE PANTRY Here are some items to keep on hand. All of these can be purchased in almost any supermarket. Consider these your "basic pantry." Your own additions are what will personalize it, and as you use and combine the elements, you will create your own cooking style. For instance, you can buy a jar of oil-cured olives and then pack them afresh with a varietal olive oil you chose one day at the farmers' market, some orange or lemon zest, a bay leaf you collected on a hike when you got a little lost, and a pinch of coriander seeds you collected from a bolted plant and then separated while talking to your best friend on the telephone. You will soon experience how each dish you prepare will have its own story to tell. And you will never need to say, "But there's nothing in the house to cook!" ❧ KOSHER SALT and GRAY SALT. ❧ WHOLE PEPPERCORNS: This means you *must* have a pepper mill. ❧ EXTRA-VIRGIN and PURE OLIVE OIL: You need pure olive oil for frying and for making mayonnaise. Then you should have several extra-virgin olive oils as well. As you shop and taste, look for a less expensive extra-virgin oil for general cooking—I use an extra-virgin oil regularly because I believe in always starting with the most flavorful ingredients—and two or more high-quality extra-virgin oils for salads and for drizzling on dishes just before serving. Choose zippy early-harvest oils for vegetable preparations and the rounder-tasting late-harvest oils for fish and shellfish. ❧ FRESH GARLIC: Never use that prepeeled or prechopped stuff. ❧ PARMESAN CHEESE in a block. ❧ CHICKEN STOCK or canned low-salt chicken broth. ❧ HIGH-QUALITY DRIED PASTA: I like the bite

and aroma of dried pasta, and the shapes are lots of fun. Fresh pasta is reserved for special preparations. ❧ VINEGAR: Try to keep on hand balsamic (in two grades, if possible, a good commercial one and a pricier traditional one), red wine, sherry, and champagne. ❧ DIJON MUSTARD. ❧ CANNED or HOME-PRESERVED TOMATOES. ❧ COMMERCIALLY DRIED or HOME-DRIED TOMATOES. ❧ HOMEMADE TOMATO SAUCE or good-quality tinned marinara sauce. ❧ Homemade and canned or tinned ROASTED PEPPERS. ❧ DRIED BEANS such as Great Northerns. ❧ One or more signature SPICE BLENDS such as the ones on pages 192 and 193. ❧ Home-dried or purchased RED PEPPER FLAKES. ❧ BRINE-CURED and OIL-CURED OLIVES. ❧ FRESH LEMONS. ❧ ARBORIO RICE. ❧ ARBORIO RICE COATING (page 193). ❧ POLENTA. ❧ FRESH FLAT-LEAF PARSLEY. ❧ UNSALTED BUTTER: Make sure to keep it in the freezer. Without salt it goes bad quickly even under refrigeration. ❧ PROSCIUTTO BITS (page 192) or bacon. ❧ ANCHOVIES. ❧ DRIED OR HOME-PRESERVED MUSHROOMS such as shiitake or porcino. ❧ CRUSTY BREAD: And turn stale bread into bread crumbs. ❧ NUTS: Pine nuts, walnuts, hazelnuts, and almonds. It is a good idea to keep nuts in the freezer to maintain freshness. If you are toasting and skinning them, as you might do with hazelnuts, do more than you need and freeze the rest in a glass jar or rigid plastic container. Items stored for any length of time in a plastic bag begin to taste like the plastic.

Gremolata

This is a delicious little recipe to know. It comes in handy in so many ways: as a soup garnish, to pat on fresh sardines or other fish before roasting, or to sprinkle on vegetables, gratins, even toasted cheese sandwiches. To make a great, really simple pasta, just sauté a little garlic in olive oil until brown and toss with cooked pasta, Gremolata, salt, pepper, and a spoonful of pasta cooking water.

Makes about ¼ cup

1 tablespoon finely chopped toasted pine nuts or hazelnuts
1 teaspoon freshly grated lemon zest
1½ tablespoons fine dried bread crumbs
1½ tablespoons finely chopped fresh flat-leaf parsley
⅛ teaspoon salt
Small pinch freshly ground pepper

Mix together all the ingredients in a small bowl. Refrigerate in an airtight container. Use within 3 days.
CHEF'S NOTE: *Do you know this trick for grating lemon zest on a box grater? Press a piece of parchment paper against the side of the box grater, then grate the lemon. When done, pull off the paper and off will come the zest that is usually frustratingly glued between the holes of the grater.*

Toasted Pumpkin Seeds

These make a delicious snack and a wonderful garnish for all kinds of soups and salads. They would even make an unusual and tasty addition to an herb pesto. If using as a garnish, be sure to toast them until very crispy for good textural contrast. Buy already hulled pumpkin seeds, which are available in many natural-foods stores in bulk. If you like spicy accents, add a teaspoon of Toasted Spice Rub (below) while cooking the seeds.

Makes ½ cup

½ cup hulled pumpkin seeds
1 tablespoon extra-virgin olive oil
Kosher salt

Put the pumpkin seeds and oil in a small skillet over medium heat. Cook, tossing and turning the seeds often, until they pop, puff, and turn brown and crisp. Season to taste with salt and toss well again. Pour into a bowl to cool. Store in an airtight container in a cool, dry place or freeze.

Prosciutto Bits

At Tra Vigne we grind up the shank sections of our homemade prosciutti to make these tasty bits. The hocks are too sinewy to slice for serving as is. Most commercial prosciutti are now sold boned for ease in slicing, however. Buy the prosciutto in a chunk of ½ to 1 pound and save yourself a few minutes by asking the butcher to hand chop it into a fine dice. The meat is so sticky that if he were to grind it, some may stick inside the machine. That would be expensive! Use the crisped bits as you might bacon bits: in eggs, pastas, salads, as an ingredient in poultry stuffing, and in bread and biscuit doughs.

Makes about ½ cup

½ pound prosciutto, finely diced (about 1 generous cup)
1½ teaspoons extra-virgin olive oil

Put the prosciutto and olive oil in a small nonstick skillet over medium heat. Cook slowly over medium to medium-low heat, tossing and stirring occasionally, until the prosciutto is very crispy, 10 to 15 minutes. Remove with a slotted spoon to paper towels to drain. Reserve the fat, if desired.

Store in an airtight container in the refrigerator for up to 1 week or store in the freezer for up to several months. Before using, recrisp, if necessary, in a skillet over medium heat or in a 300°F toaster oven.
CHEF'S NOTES: *In many dishes calling for these bits, you can use an equal amount of very crisp minced bacon as a substitute. I have indicated in each recipe whether bacon would be suitable. The fat left in the pan is wonderful for sautéing potatoes or spinach or frying eggs.*

Toasted Spice Rub

I created a version of this spice mix for what has become a Tra Vigne favorite: spiced chicken. Don't let the chili put you off. I've used mild dried chilies for their spice, not heat, and for their deep red color. The addition of fennel, coriander, and cinnamon gives the mix an exotic twist. I also like to use it on lamb, shrimp, and fish. It is delicious stirred into rice and transforms a pot of beans, too. Keep it close by the stove and add a pinch to soups and even to scrambled eggs or omelets. It makes a great Christmas or house gift packed in a pretty jar. If you are watching your salt intake, leave out the salt. The mixture has plenty of flavor.

Makes about 1 cup

1/4 cup fennel seeds
1 tablespoon coriander seeds
1 tablespoon peppercorns
1 1/2 teaspoons red pepper flakes
1/4 cup (1 ounce) pure California chili powder
2 tablespoons kosher salt
2 tablespoons ground cinnamon

Toast the fennel seeds, coriander seeds, and peppercorns in a small, heavy pan over medium heat. When the fennel turns light brown, work quickly. Turn on the exhaust fan, add the red pepper flakes, and toss, toss, toss, always under the fan. Immediately turn the spice mixture out onto a plate to cool. Put in a blender with the chili powder, salt, and cinnamon and blend until the spices are evenly ground. If you have a small spice mill or a coffee grinder dedicated to grinding spices, grind only the fennel, coriander, pepper, and chili flakes. Pour into a bowl and toss with the remaining ingredients.

CHEF'S NOTES: *Toasting freshens spices, releases their oils, and makes them more fragrant, as well as adding a new dimension of flavor. Keep the spice mix in a glass jar in a cool, dry place or freeze.*

Taste your chili powder and if spicy and hot, cut back the amount. California chilies are almost sweet, not hot.

Fennel Spice

This is my favorite spice mixture. To my mind, there is nothing, well, almost nothing it won't taste good on or in. Try it for spice-encrusted pork ribs,

chops, or tenderloin; veal chops; chicken breasts; duck; beef; liver; or eggplant. Add a teaspoon to lentil soup. Have friends to a dinner featuring the spice, then send them home with a little jar as a present from your house to theirs. If you have a spice mill, you can cut the recipe in half. I've found that a cup is the minimum for grinding in the blender.

Makes about 1 1/4 cups

1 cup fennel seeds
3 tablespoons coriander seeds
2 tablespoons white peppercorns
3 tablespoons kosher salt

Put the fennel seeds, coriander seeds, and peppercorns in a heavy pan over medium heat. Watch carefully, tossing frequently so the seeds toast evenly. When light brown and fragrant, pour the seeds onto a plate to cool. They must be cool before grinding, or they will gum up the blades.

Pour the seeds into a blender and add the salt. Blend to a fine powder, shaking the blender occasionally to redistribute the seeds. Store in a tightly sealed glass jar in a cool, dry place or freeze.

Arborio Rice Coating

The ingredients in this coating are more flexible than you might suspect. For example, you can use just about any rice you prefer with the exception of sticky rice, which does not work well. You could certainly experiment with aromatic rices such as basmati or with brown rice. In my experiments, I have found Arborio works best. You could use garbanzo flour, polenta, or corn flour instead of semolina. I do not much care for the grittiness of uncooked cornmeal, but many people like it very much. If you have a spice mill, you will be able to grind less than 1 cup of rice. You may want to grind even more than a cup, however, and save some of the resulting Arborio rice "flour" to add to "risottos" made out of rice or grains other than Arborio rice. The flour will act as a binding agent to give a risottolike creaminess. In fact, you can use this coating as a general thickener for gravies, soups, and stews. You might also want to divide it up into several batches and flavor them differently, adding red pepper flakes, ground fennel or coriander, or one of the spice mixtures from pages 192 and 193.

Makes about 5 cups

1 cup Arborio rice
1 cup semolina
3 cups all-purpose flour
2 tablespoons table salt (see Chef's Notes)
1 teaspoon freshly ground pepper

Put the rice in a blender and grind until very fine. Shake out into a large bowl and add the semolina, flour, salt, and pepper. Toss until well blended. Store in a sealed container in the freezer to maintain maximum freshness.

CHEF'S NOTE: *This is one place I do use table salt. In general I prefer kosher salt, but kosher salt is too heavy and will not stay distributed throughout the coating.*

Bruschetta *and* Crostini

Call these croutons or toasts. It doesn't matter. What matters is that they be made from good bread. For me, the difference between bruschetta and crostini is the thickness. Crostini are thin, bruschetta are thicker. Both crostini and bruschetta add texture to a dish. Crostini are more elegant and bruschetta are sturdier. Whether thin or thick, do not overbake. They should be crisp on the outside, but still soft within. If they get crisp throughout, they shatter when you eat them instead of holding together. You may leave the bread slices whole for a sandwichlike presentation, or cut them in half, into long narrow "fingers," or other decorative shapes. None of this affects the baking, only thickness does. Although not necessary, a light dusting of Parmesan adds flavor and makes the toasts a terrific snack or accompaniment to soup.

Serves 4

About ½ loaf good, crusty bread such as *ciabatta*
2 tablespoons extra-virgin olive oil
Salt and freshly ground pepper
2 tablespoons freshly grated Parmesan cheese (optional)

Preheat the oven to 375°F. Cut the bread on the diagonal into neat, even slices about ⅓ inch thick for bruschetta and as thinly as possible for crostini. If you have a meat slicer, use it to slice day-old bread into thin, even slices. Otherwise, do your best with a good bread knife. As always, flavor, not looks, is the point, so don't worry if the thickness of your slices vary.

Brush the bread on both sides with the olive oil and season lightly with salt and pepper. Arrange on a baking sheet and bake until crusty and brown on the outside and still soft within, about 15 minutes for bruschetta and about 12 minutes for crostini. Turn once about halfway through cooking, and dust with Parmesan, if using. Serve hot, warm, or at room temperature.

CHEF'S NOTES: *You can vary the flavor of bruschetta and crostini by using flavored olive oils or by rubbing the toasted bread with a clove of raw garlic.*

The toasts may be made ahead and kept warm in a very low oven. In a short time they will dry out and become shatteringly crisp, however. To compensate, undercook them a little.

Piadine Dough

Perhaps you think that making dough is a bother. But once you work with this dough, you will want to do it again. It is one of those textures that begs to be touched, caressed. It feels as smooth and silky as a baby's bottom.

*Makes about 2 pounds dough,
enough for six 8- or 9-inch piadine*

1 envelope active dry yeast
½ cup lukewarm water
About 4 cups all-purpose flour, plus more
    for dusting work surface
1 cup cool water
2 tablespoons extra-virgin olive oil
2 teaspoons salt

Whisk together the yeast, lukewarm water, and ½ cup of the flour in the bowl of a stand mixer. Dust the top lightly with flour, cover the bowl with a tea towel, and leave the sponge to rise until the flour dusting "cracks," showing the yeast is alive and well, about 20 minutes.

Add 3 cups of the flour, the 1 cup cool water, the olive

oil, and the salt. Start kneading at low speed, then increase the speed to medium as the flour is incorporated. Add the remaining ½ cup flour as needed to produce a slightly moist and soft dough. Knead with the dough hook attachment until smooth and silky and the dough adheres to the hook.

Dust the dough lightly with flour and, using a pastry scraper, scrape it out of the bowl onto a lightly floured surface. Knead lightly, folding the dough over on itself. Shape into a ball, flatten slightly, dust lightly with flour, cover with a towel, and leave to rise on a floured surface (or in a bowl) until doubled in bulk, about 1 hour.

Punch the dough down, wrap, and freeze for up to 1 month if not using immediately. Defrost and let rise in a large bowl in the refrigerator.

When ready, continue with chosen recipe.

Pasta Dough

My grandmothers rolled out their pasta by hand. A great pasta maker is distinguished by what their hands know—an instinctual knowledge built by years of intimate contact. With stand mixers, food processors, and pasta machines, we all have the potential to become good home pasta cooks. A proper dough should have a smooth, satiny sheen. If you are not inspired to make pasta from scratch, fresh pasta sheets are becoming more widely available through specialty pasta shops, neighborhood Italian delicatessens, and occasionally even at farmers' markets. This recipe may be doubled.

*Makes about 10 ounces dough,
enough for 3 or 4 servings*

2 extra-large eggs, at room temperature
2 teaspoons extra-virgin olive oil
Pinch salt
Scant 1 cup (about ⅞ cup) all-purpose flour,
    plus more for dusting work surface
½ cup semolina, plus more for dusting pasta

Put the eggs, olive oil, and salt in the bowl of a stand mixer fitted with the paddle attachment or in a food processor. Mix on low until well blended. Add the flour and semolina and continue to mix on low just until mixed

in. If using a food processor, pulse the wet ingredients to blend, then pulse in the dry ingredients just until distributed, not until the mixture forms a ball. Do not overmix or the dough will be tough.

Remove the dough from the bowl and gather it into a ball. On a lightly floured board, knead gently with your palms, folding the dough over onto itself until it forms a smooth mass. Pat into a ball, flatten slightly, wrap in waxed paper or plastic wrap, and refrigerate for 30 minutes or as long as overnight. (The dough may also be frozen at this point for about 1 month. Defrost in the refrigerator.)

If you can, have a helper close at hand when rolling out the dough. Working on a lightly floured surface, and making sure the dough stays lightly dusted with flour at all stages, cut the dough into 3 or 4 equal pieces, depending on the size of your pasta machine. As you roll out the dough, complete each step with all of the pieces before moving onto the next step. This allows the dough to relax between each handling.

Set the rollers on your pasta machine at the widest setting and pass each piece of dough through them. Fold each strip into thirds, turn the dough so an open end faces the rollers, and pass again through the widest setting. Repeat 3 times. Then, run the pieces through successively narrower roller settings, but do not fold the dough between the settings. Run each piece through a single setting, then reset the rollers and begin again with the dough strips.

The dough for ravioli needs to be thin, yet thick enough not to tear when shaping, probably the next to last setting on your pasta machine. Refer to the individual recipes for cutting directions for ravioli. The dough for noodles such as fettuccine may be rolled through the narrowest setting. Let the sheets dry for about 10 minutes before cutting.

To cut the dough for noodles, check your machine for the options it offers, usually a narrow and a wider noodle. Move the hand crank to your choice and pass the dough sheets through the cutters. As you cut each sheet, make a small pile of the noodles and dust lightly with semolina, then toss gently so the noodles are evenly coated. Cover with a tea towel until ready to cook. (The pasta may be made an hour ahead of time or frozen for up to 1 month.) Fresh pasta will cook, in boiling salted water, in a few seconds.

To cut the dough later, wrap the sheets in floured tea towels and enclose in a large plastic bag. They may be refrigerated overnight or frozen for up to 1 month before cutting.

CHEF'S NOTES: *The pasta may, of course, be made the*

old-fashioned way, by hand. Sift the flour and semolina together onto a work surface and make a well in the center. Whisk together the eggs, olive oil, and salt until well blended and pour into the well. Gradually mix the flour into the wet ingredients and knead as directed. You can roll out the dough by hand as well, working on a lightly floured surface. Try to roll it as thinly as possible and in as regular a shape as possible to facilitate cutting. When ready to cut, make sure the sheet is floured or dusted with semolina. Roll it up loosely and cut crosswise with a very sharp knife.

Black Pepper *and* Parmesan Grissini

Bread sticks are coming back into style. They are worth making just because there are so many fun ways to serve them. You can shape them into loops to use as napkin rings, fashion them straight and stack them like cord wood in a napkin holder, or make them extra long and arrange them in a vase with dried grasses and flowers. Cut long strips of dough into inch-long pieces, bake, and use as a homemade substitute for oyster crackers to float in soup. Grissini can be spread with dill mayonnaise and wrapped with a thin slice of smoked salmon, wrapped with ham and cheese to make a kind of inside-out ham sandwich, or broken up to use as croutons in Caesar salad or panzanella (page 60). The opportunities for flavoring the dough are unlimited: Roasted Garlic Paste (page 197), fresh or dried herbs, or roasted chili paste. Or knead in some diced dried figs, then wrap the baked sticks in prosciutto.

Makes about 3 dozen bread sticks

1 recipe focaccia dough (page 41)
Semolina for dusting baking sheets
6 good pinches freshly ground pepper
About 6 tablespoons freshly grated Parmesan cheese
All-purpose flour for dusting work surface

Follow the focaccia recipe as directed through the first rise. Lightly dust 2 or 3 baking sheets with semolina. Divide the dough into 3 pieces. Preheat the oven to 400°F.

Use only enough flour to prevent the dough from sticking to the work surface. You may not need any. It is easiest to work with 1 piece of dough at a time. It will fill a single baking sheet with bread sticks. Get it in the oven, then proceed to the next piece of dough.

Press a good pinch of pepper and a tablespoon of cheese onto the top of each of the 3 pieces of dough. Turn the pieces over and repeat. Roll out 1 piece of dough into as even a rectangle as possible and about ¼ inch thick. Cut into ½-inch-wide strips with a pizza wheel or sharp knife.

Very gently and using both hands, roll each strip under your hands into a long, thin cylinder about the length of a standard baking sheet, 17 inches. Use only enough pressure to get the strip to roll. Do not bear down; instead, gently stretch the dough and even its thickness as much as possible so the bread stick will bake evenly. Pick up each cylinder and arrange on a prepared baking sheet.

Bake until golden and crisp, about 20 minutes. Let cool on the baking sheet or on a rack. Repeat with the remaining dough.

Taste a few bread sticks to see if they are dry enough for your taste. A good bread stick will be dry throughout when snapped in half. If you want to dry them further, lower the heat to 275°F and bake until as dry as you like. Test every 10 to 20 minutes. Baking time and drying time depend on the thickness of the bread sticks. Store in an airtight container.

CHEF'S NOTES: *By adding flavorings after the dough has risen, you can flavor each piece as you like, using cayenne, Fennel Spice (page 193), Toasted Spice Rub (page 192), herbes de Provence, or seeds. If you want the whole batch to have a single flavor, knead it in by hand, if you like, before setting the dough to rise.*

Cantinetta's Cracker Pizzette

Give that pasta machine some exercise! Rolling the dough very thinly and topping with fairly dry ingredients allows the focaccia dough to become crisp and crackery when baked. Pizzette are a favorite Cantinetta item, where they are sold separately as a snack or bread substitute and to accompany salads and soups. Top them with oven-dried tomatoes or try a "tight" pesto made with less than the normal allotment of oil. Or spread with Roasted Garlic Paste (page 197) or roasted garlic oil, some minced anchovies, grated Parmesan, and parsley and serve with Caesar salad. You can experiment with other cheeses as well.

This technique can also be used with Piadine Dough (page 194), but the result is not as tender. A stack of these on a buffet table makes a stunning display. Wrapped well, they stay crisp for several days.

Serves 8 to 10

1 recipe focaccia dough (page 41)
All-purpose flour for dusting work surface
Semolina for dusting baking sheets
About $^{1}/_{3}$ cup extra-virgin olive oil
About $^{1}/_{4}$ cup minced garlic
About $^{1}/_{2}$ cup finely chopped Kalamata olives
About $^{1}/_{2}$ cup freshly grated Parmesan cheese
About 6 ounces ricotta salata cheese
Freshly ground pepper

Follow the focaccia recipe as directed through the first rise. Preheat the oven to 375°F. Dust 2 or more baking sheets with semolina.

Working on a lightly floured surface, cut the dough into 8 to 10 equal pieces. Roll each piece through the widest setting of a pasta machine, then through successively narrower settings until the dough is very thin, setting number #5 out of a possible 6 settings on a pasta machine, the same setting as for ravioli. Put all the dough through each setting before moving to the next setting. This allows the dough to relax between each handling.

Transfer the strips of dough to the prepared baking sheets, cutting them as necessary to fit the sheets. Brush each with olive oil and sprinkle lightly with garlic, olives, and Parmesan. With a vegetable peeler, shave the ricotta salata over each strip. Season with pepper. No salt is required because both cheeses tend to be salty.

Bake until lightly browned and very crisp, about 15 minutes. If using 2 oven racks, rotate the pans top to bottom and front to back halfway through baking. Let cool on the baking sheets or on racks.

Serve warm or at room temperature.

CHEF'S NOTES: *You can make the dough one day, let it rise, punch it down, cover, and refrigerate. Let it come to room temperature the next day, then cut into pieces and continue with the recipe. Instead of pitting and chopping olives, you could use olive paste or tapénade. The amounts of toppings are approximate. If you really love garlic, add more; the same for olives and cheese. Do not load the dough down, or it will not get crisp.*

Roasted Garlic Paste

For me, this is a kitchen staple. If you like, you can draw off part of the oil remaining in the baking dish after roasting the garlic to use separately as a flavored oil.

Makes about 1 cup

1 pound whole garlic heads
$^{1}/_{2}$ cup pure olive oil
Salt and freshly ground pepper

Preheat the oven to 375°F. Peel the outermost layers of skin off the heads of garlic. Cut off the top one-third of the heads to open the cloves. Save the small pieces of garlic for another use (see Chef's Notes). Put the heads, cut sides up, in a small baking dish and pour the olive oil over them. Season with salt and pepper.

Cover tightly, place in the oven, and roast until about three-fourths cooked, about 45 minutes. Uncover and return to the oven until the cloves begin to pop out of their skins and brown, about 15 minutes. Let cool.

When cool enough to handle easily, squeeze the roasted garlic into a small bowl. Press against the skins very well to get out all the sweet roasted garlic you can. Add the oil from the baking dish and mix well until a paste forms. Store, tightly covered, in the refrigerator, for up to 1 week.

CHEF'S NOTES: *It is hard to have too much roasted garlic around. You can roast the little bits from the tips of the garlic heads. Put them in a separate small baking container, such as an individual custard cup. Season with salt and pepper, douse with olive oil, cover, and place in the oven to bake along with the whole garlic heads. Depending on their size, they will be soft and browned in about half the time needed for the whole heads. The little pieces make a good "cook's snack" while preparing dinner, or can be squeezed into tomato sauce, into pasta, and so on.*

Thick Tomato Sauce

This is a sort of vegetable Bolognese sauce. It is the only time I use tomato paste. The paste binds the sauce so it does not separate into liquid and solids, which is important for the eggplant lasagnette (page 112). You don't want to risk a pool of "water" at the bottom of the dish. It's a great tomato sauce for pasta or any other hearty dish needing a tomato sauce. It would be delicious for an eggplant "short stack": alternating slices of grilled eggplant and provolone. You can also use it for fish cooked in parchment or for braising chicken to make a sort of cacciatore. Remember to "overseason" the sauce when using it for the lasagnette, as it provides all the flavor for the eggplant.

Makes about 4 cups

About 5 tablespoons extra-virgin olive oil
2 cups diced red bell pepper (¼-inch dice)
2 tablespoons minced garlic
2 cups diced red onion (¼-inch dice)
Salt and freshly ground pepper
2 tablespoons tomato paste
1 can (28 ounces) whole tomatoes, chopped
1½ cups double-strength chicken stock (page 204), or 3 cups canned low-salt chicken broth boiled until reduced by half
1 bay leaf
2 tablespoons unsalted butter
1 tablespoon finely chopped fresh oregano
1 tablespoon finely chopped fresh flat-leaf parsley
1 tablespoon finely chopped fresh basil

Heat ¼ cup of the olive oil in a heavy saucepan over medium-high heat until hot. Add the bell pepper and sauté until brown, about 7 minutes. Add the remaining 1 tablespoon olive oil, if necessary, and the garlic, and cook briefly until light brown. Add the onion and a pinch of salt (if the pan is dry and the ingredients look as if they might burn, adding salt will release the liquid in the onions), and cook until brown, about 5 minutes. Add the tomato paste and stir to mix well.

Add the tomatoes and their juice, the stock, and bay leaf. Bring to a boil, reduce the heat to low, and simmer the sauce until thick, about 25 minutes. Be sure to stir often to prevent scorching. Add the butter, oregano, parsley, and basil and stir well. Adjust the seasoning with salt and pepper. Use immediately, or let cool, cover, and refrigerate for several days or freeze for up to 1 month.

Quick Tomato Sauce

This book would have been so much easier if Mom were still alive. I could simply have asked how she did her

tomato sauce. As it is, when I taste this sauce I am reminded of her. This is an all-purpose, fresh-tasting sauce (yes, even though made with canned tomatoes) for saucing pasta, spaghetti squash, or gnocchi; for serving with chicken; or for cooking fish fillets. If you can or have a large freezer, make big batches to keep on hand. Do not be afraid to cook a chili in your sauce. Left whole, it adds very little to no discernible spiciness.

Makes about 3½ cups

1 can (28 ounces) whole tomatoes (see Chef's Notes)
3 tablespoons extra-virgin olive oil
1 jalapeño chili (optional)
½ cup finely chopped onion
1 tablespoon minced garlic
1 bay leaf
Salt and freshly ground pepper
¼ cup drained and chopped oil-packed dried tomatoes or Oven-Dried Tomatoes (page 199)
1 tablespoon finely chopped fresh oregano

Open the can of tomatoes and pour off the juice into a bowl. Use the lid to press against the tomatoes to extract as much juice as possible. Then use your hand to squeeze the tomatoes to a pulp. Reserve the juice and pulp separately and set the empty can aside.

Heat the olive oil in a heavy saucepan over medium-high heat until hot. If using the jalapeño, tilt the pan to collect the oil in a little pool against the side and drop the jalapeño into the oil. Cook until light brown, about 2 minutes. Remove the jalapeño and reserve.

Add the onion to the pan and cook, stirring occasionally, until soft, about 2 minutes. Add the garlic and cook briefly until light gold. Add the tomato juice and bring to a boil. Simmer rapidly for several minutes. Add the crushed tomato pulp. Then rinse the remaining pulp out of the can by filling it halfway with water and add that to the pan. Add the bay leaf, the jalapeño, if using, and salt and pepper to taste and return to a boil. Add the dried tomatoes and stir. Lower the heat to medium and simmer, stirring occasionally to prevent scorching, until the mixture thickens and the tomatoes have turned an orange-red versus the pale blue-red they were straight from the can, about 30 minutes. Add the oregano halfway through the cooking.

Discard the bay leaf. Peel, seed, and mash the jalapeño with a spoonful of the sauce and pass at the table so diners can add as much heat as they like to their plates. *Variation for Summer Tomato Sauce:* Substitute 2 pounds vine-ripened tomatoes for the canned tomatoes. Peel the tomatoes, cut in half crosswise, and squeeze out the juice and seeds over a sieve suspended over a bowl. Chop the tomatoes. Proceed as directed, omitting the dried tomatoes and using jalapeño, if desired. You should have about 2¼ cups sauce. The recipe may be increased proportionately.

CHEF'S NOTES: *Many commercial tomato farmers say you can't get commercial-level crops if you grow tomatoes organically. Muir Glen is an exception. A privately held company, it is going to great lengths to produce a healthy product. Canned tomatoes have various things added to them to act as preservatives (usually salt and citric acid) and firming agents such as calcium chloride. The more processed the tomato for canning—that is, chopped versus whole—the more chloride is added. This may explain the slightly chlorine taste of some brands of tomatoes. If you do buy chopped tomatoes, S&W is a great brand. When Muir Glen or S&W are not easily available, I look for a good, low- or no-salt-added brand of canned plum (Roma) tomatoes.*

Tomato Confit *and* Variations

When tomato plants swing into full productivity, turn to this recipe. Even if you don't grow your own, let the smell of farm-fresh tomatoes at farmers' markets inspire you. The long, slow cooking creates intense sweetness. Once you have these on hand, you are only minutes away from bruschetta, pasta, salads. Plan on making as large a batch as you have room for in your oven. Simply increase the recipe proportionately. You can make this recipe with yellow tomatoes, but because they already have low acidity and the cooking drives off even more acid, their flavor will benefit from a shot of balsamic vinegar. You can make several batches and vary the flavor by adding 1½ teaspoons Fennel Spice (page 193), or herbes de Provence, or perhaps some grated orange zest. See the variations for making oven-dried tomatoes.

Makes about 2 cups tomatoes with oil

3 pounds vine-ripened tomatoes such as Early Girl, beefsteak, or plum (Roma) tomatoes
Salt and freshly ground pepper

About 1 teaspoon red pepper flakes (optional)
About 1 cup extra-virgin olive oil
12 garlic cloves, halved or quartered if large
¼ cup finely chopped fresh thyme

Peel the tomatoes, then "fillet" them: Stand them upright and cut off the flesh, but leave the central seed and juice sacs in the middle untouched. It is the same motion as cutting the skin and pith off an orange. Save the juices as you work, including the juices from the cutting board, scraping them into a bowl. Squeeze the juice out of the cores, then use this juice for "Broken" Tomato Vinaigrette (page 52), Bloody Marys, tomato soup, or sauce.

Preheat the oven to 250°F. Arrange the tomatoes, rounded sides up (what was the skin side; this prevents curling during cooking) on large nonreactive rimmed baking sheets. Remove any seeds still clinging to the flesh as you go. Season liberally with salt and pepper. Sprinkle with the red pepper flakes, if desired. Heat several tablespoons of the olive oil in a medium skillet over medium-high heat until hot. Add the garlic and sauté quickly until light gold, about 2 minutes. (This step may be omitted but does add a richer flavor to the garlic and the confit.) Remove from the heat and scatter the garlic and thyme over and around the tomatoes. Add the olive oil from the skillet and enough additional oil so the tomatoes are covered to about half their height. Make sure to oil the tops of the tomatoes so they do not get raisiny.

Bake until the tomatoes have lost half or more of their volume, about 6 hours. The pieces will usually dry unevenly, so check after 4 hours and then every hour to remove pieces that have dried to your taste. Let cool, then pack in a clean jar and refrigerate. Bring to room temperature before using.

Variation for Oven-Dried Tomatoes: The major difference between a tomato confit and oven-dried tomatoes is the cutting technique and the amount of oil. Confits, by definition, swim in oil. To oven-dry cherry tomatoes (they explode with flavor but are tedious to halve, so invite a friend over for a chat while you work): Use 2 pints (about 1½ pounds) cherry tomatoes such as Sweet 100s, halved; salt and freshly ground pepper; ¼ teaspoon red pepper flakes (optional); ½ cup extra-virgin olive oil; 6 garlic cloves; and 2 tablespoons finely chopped fresh thyme. Proceed as directed for confit, arranging the tomatoes cut side up on the rimmed baking sheet, then drizzling the oil over them. They should dry in about 4 hours, but begin tasting after 2 hours. Makes about 1 ½ cups tomatoes with oil.

To oven-dry tomatoes such as Early Girl or plum (Roma): Use the amounts in the confit recipe, but reduce the oil to about ⅔ cup. Cut round tomatoes lengthwise into wedges, and halve or quarter plum tomatoes lengthwise. Proceed as directed for the confit, arranging the tomatoes cut side up on the rimmed baking sheet. The wedges will dry in about 6 hours and the plum tomatoes in about the same time or an hour longer, depending on their size. Makes about 3 cups dried tomatoes with oil.

CHEF'S NOTES: *The tomatoes should be ripe, but still firm. The best way to tell when the tomatoes have dried enough is to taste a piece every hour or so. Remove them when you feel the flavor is intense enough. The next time you make them, you will know how long your oven takes to give you the results you want. Then you can adjust the oven temperature in order to put the tomatoes in at night and get them out in the morning.*

Pesto

I think of pesto as a method of preparation, not as a set of specific ingredients put together in specific proportions. A pesto then becomes a method of dealing with abundance. The final form of a pesto—its viscosity and even the intensity of its flavor—depends on its intended use. If I plan to make a risotto flavored with pesto, I will decrease the oil in the pesto to make a very thick paste. Less oil is necessary because the stock in the risotto will disperse the flavor through the dish. Likewise, if the pesto is destined for a ricotta filling for ravioli, the flavor must be very intense so it will flavor both the ricotta and the pasta. With the addition of coarse bread crumbs, pestos make great "crusts" for cooking poultry and fish. When pestos call for Parmesan, the cheese needs to be very finely grated to yield a smooth texture.

Basil Pesto

This is the traditional Genoese pesto, tweaked a bit so it remains a fresh green. The water-soluble compounds in the herb oxidize, which is what can darken the pesto. Blanching the basil removes most of them (you will notice the blanching water turn brownish). A pinch of vitamin

C acts as another protective agent against oxidation. Buy vitamin C crystals at your pharmacy or grind up a tablet. Pasta with pesto is a good lesson in why Italians so often insist on adding a spoonful of pasta cooking water to pasta sauce. Try it here and you will see how creamy the pesto becomes on the pasta. I use pure olive oil for pesto so the clear flavor of the herb dominates. If you want to freeze pesto, omit the nuts and cheese.

Makes about 1 ½ cups

4 cups packed fresh basil leaves
1 tablespoon minced garlic
Salt and freshly ground pepper
1 cup pure olive oil
2 tablespoons pine nuts, toasted
⅛ teaspoon vitamin C (optional)
½ cup freshly grated Parmesan cheese

Prepare an ice water bath in a large bowl, and bring a large pan of water to a boil. Put the basil in a large sieve and plunge it into the boiling water. Immediately immerse all the basil and stir so that it blanches evenly. Blanch for about 15 seconds. Remove, shake off the excess water, then plunge the basil into the ice water bath and stir again so it cools as fast as possible. Drain well.

Squeeze the water out of the basil with your hands until very dry. Roughly chop the basil and put in a blender. Add the garlic, salt and pepper to taste, olive oil, pine nuts, and the vitamin C, if using. Blend for at least 30 seconds. In this way the green of the basil will thoroughly color the oil. Add the cheese and pulse to combine. The pesto will keep several days in a tightly sealed container in the refrigerator.

Fava Bean Pesto

I particularly like this pesto with thick, hand-cut pastas. It also tastes great spooned on top of "white" risotto (risotto made with onion and chicken broth as the only flavorings), swirled into a white bean soup, or mixed with bread crumbs and spread on a piece of halibut. After I tested this recipe for the book, I took the pesto into Tra Vigne's kitchen for the staff to taste. Later, as I was working on another recipe, one of the chefs, Frank Whitaker, appeared with a piadina spread with the pesto and topped with sautéed rock shrimp, roasted red peppers, and arugula. We devoured it. On the other hand, you don't need to go to any trouble. Just put a bowl of the pesto down with hunks of good fresh bread. Use the lemon zest if the pesto is destined for dipping or for fish and seafood, but not if you plan on using it for pasta. When fava beans are out of season, make this pesto with English peas or lima beans.

Makes about 1 1/4 cups

2 tablespoons plus 1/2 cup pure olive oil
1 tablespoon minced garlic
3/4 cup cooked, peeled fava beans (page 28)
Salt and freshly ground pepper
1/2 teaspoon finely chopped fresh thyme
1/2 teaspoon freshly grated lemon zest (optional)
1/4 cup chicken stock (page 204) or canned low-salt chicken broth (see Chef's Notes)
1/4 cup freshly grated pecorino cheese or Parmesan cheese

Heat the 2 tablespoons olive oil in a small sauté pan over medium-high heat until hot. Add the garlic and sauté briefly until light brown. Be careful not to overcook, or the garlic may burn on its way from the stove to the blender.

Scrape the garlic into the blender and add the fava beans, the remaining 1/2 cup olive oil, salt and pepper to taste, thyme, and the lemon zest, if using. Blend until pureed. Add the stock and blend until smooth. Add the cheese and pulse to combine. The pesto will keep several days in a tightly sealed container in the refrigerator.

CHEF'S NOTES: *You can omit the stock if you like, but homemade stock adds both flavor and body to the pesto. Canned stock works, but results in a thinner puree. Use vegetable stock to make the pesto vegetarian. As noted in the recipe introduction, fresh or frozen English peas or lima beans can be substituted for the fava beans. If you use frozen peas (it's okay; I have and the pesto is delicious), the peas are already cooked. Just defrost them and increase the amount to 1 cup frozen peas.*

Soft Polenta *and* Variations

Worth every single calorie! The ratio of dry to wet ingredients for firm polenta is one to three (see variation). For soft polenta, the amount of wet ingredients increases the ratio to one to five or six. The substitution of semolina for part of the polenta speeds cooking time and gives a creamy result.

Serves 4

1 1/2 cups chicken stock (page 204)
    or canned low-salt chicken broth
1 1/2 cups heavy cream
1/2 teaspoon freshly grated nutmeg
3/4 teaspoon salt
Pinch ground white pepper
5 tablespoons polenta
5 tablespoons semolina
1/4 cup freshly grated Fontina cheese
1/4 cup freshly grated Parmesan cheese

Combine the stock and cream in a heavy saucepan and bring to a simmer. Add the nutmeg, salt, and pepper. Whisk in the polenta and semolina and cook over very low heat, whisking regularly, until the grains are soft, about 8 minutes. Whisk in the cheeses. Serve immediately or reserve.

To encourage polenta to come cleanly out of the pan, put the pan over medium heat. Run a spatula or wooden spoon around the sides of the pan to clean off the polenta. Do not stir, but wait and watch a for few seconds until a large bubble begins to form and push the polenta upward. Pour immediately into a warm dish.

The polenta can be made ahead and reheated: add 1/4 to 1/2 cup water or stock, cover the dish, and reheat in the microwave or over low heat. Whisk well before serving. *Variation for Firm Polenta:* Proceed as directed, but increase the amounts of polenta and semolina each to 1/2 cup, giving a total of 1 cup dry to 3 cups liquid, a ratio of one to three. It will not take longer to cook. Serve immediately or pour onto a parchment-lined baking sheet and spread into an even 1/2-inch-thick layer. Let cool, cover, and refrigerate for several hours or overnight. Cut into thick fingers or triangles and reheat or freeze. To reheat, sprinkle lightly with freshly grated Parmesan cheese and place in a preheated 500°F oven until lightly browned, about 6 minutes. Or fry in butter or olive oil. *Variation for "Pumpkin" Polenta:* Proceed as directed for soft polenta, adding 1 cup Roasted Winter Squash (page 152) at the end of cooking and before the cheese. Omit the Fontina and increase the Parmesan to 1/2 cup. If you want to go to heaven, serve the pumpkin polenta on its own as an appetizer or supper dish drizzled with white truffle oil.

Spiced Candied Nuts

This is a method I learned from my partner Cindy Pawlcyn. Make a large batch so you have enough for yourself as well as some to give away. The nuts are great to eat out of hand, but they also have many other uses. Serve them with a cheese course, or on any fall salad such as pear and Gorgonzola on greens or dried cherries and goat cheese with frisée or spinach. Grind some to a coarse powder and stir them into a ravioli filling such as the roasted winter squash filling on page 156, or stuff a fig with mascarpone and a nut.

Makes 4 cups

4 to 6 cups peanut oil or canola oil for deep-frying
1 teaspoon salt
$1/4$ teaspoon freshly ground pepper
$1/2$ teaspoon ground cinnamon
$1/2$ teaspoon cayenne pepper
4 cups walnut or pecan halves
1 cup powdered sugar, sifted

Bring a large pot of water to a boil. Heat the oil in a deep fryer or deep pot to 350°F to 375°F (see Chef's Notes). Measure the salt, pepper, cinnamon, and cayenne into a small bowl and mix well.

Holding the nuts in a sieve, dip them briefly into the boiling water, about 1 minute for large halves. Immediately transfer to a bowl. You want a little water to remain on the nuts. (Blanching removes some of the tannins and makes the nuts taste very sweet.) While still hot and wet, toss them with the powdered sugar. The sugar will melt and liquefy. Keep stirring and tossing until all the sugar has melted. If hunks of unmelted sugar remain on the nuts, they will not fry properly.

Stir the nuts again just before frying. Using a large slotted spoon and working in small batches, transfer the nuts to the hot oil, allowing the foam to subside before adding the next spoonful. (Otherwise, the oil could foam over and burn you.) Fry until medium brown, about 1 minute for large halves. Be careful not to overcook, as the nuts will continue to cook a little after they are removed from the fryer. Scatter on an unlined baking sheet to cool slightly.

While still warm, transfer the nuts to a bowl and sprinkle evenly with about half the spice mix. Toss well to distribute the spice and then taste a nut. Add more spice mix to taste and toss well after each addition. When cool, pack in a clean, tightly sealed jar.

CHEF'S NOTES: *This method works best with nuts such as walnuts and pecans, which are lobed and fissured to catch and hold the sugar coating. Be sure to use a deep pot with plenty of space between the surface of the oil and the top of the pot. Because the nuts are damp when they go into the oil, the oil foams up and will spill over unless there is plenty of room in the pot.*

glossary

ARBORIO RICE FLOUR: My staff and I worked a long time to find a perfect coating for fried foods. One day we took every flour in the kitchen and mixed them in every combination. Then we ground every grain to make flour out of it, including Arborio rice. It occurred to me to use the rice powder mixed with wheat flour as a coating for fried foods. Rice has a higher sugar content than wheat, so it browns more quickly in the fryer. That way food would not overcook before the coating browned. In addition, the slightly grainy texture of the ground rice makes the coating attractive to the eye as well as the tooth. Even better, it does not get soggy. This allows the cook to make the fried food ahead of time and keep it warm in a low oven. I use Arborio rice to make my rice flour because Tra Vigne is an Italian restaurant. You can use any rice, however, and might try experimenting with brown rice and even black or aromatic rices. You will need to grind at least a cup at a time. Place the rice in a blender and blend until you have tiny granules about the texture of powdered gelatin. One cup rice yields about the same amount of flour.

CALIFORNIA CHILI POWDER: This is not the chili powder found in the spice section of the grocery store. That one is most commonly a blend of powdered chilies, cumin, and oregano. California chili powder is finely ground, dried California chilies with nothing added. The chilies are only mildly hot, and you can find them whole and ground in well-stocked Mexican groceries. Also look for various types of dried chilies at your farmers' market. Tierra Vegetables grows many varieties without pesticides, herbicides, or fumigants. You can order them by mail: 220 Pleasant Ave., Santa Rosa, CA 95403; 707-837-8366.

CAMBOZOLA CHEESE: This is a silky, rich, utterly delicious, triple-cream, Brie-like, blue-veined German cheese. It makes a wonderful party hors d'oeuvre on its own on crostini. I like to scatter it on pizzas and use it for sandwiches. If you have a sandwich press, try this: Butter slices of good, crusty bread, add a generous portion of cheese, and cook in the sandwich press until the bread is browned and the cheese is melted. Open the sandwich and add slices of vine-ripened tomatoes and sprigs of watercress. You will be very happy.

COURT BOUILLON: This is a basic cooking liquid for fish and shellfish, ideal for poaching whole salmon for a buffet centerpiece or for cooking lobster and crabs for a clam-bake. Put the crabs and lobsters to sleep by stroking the tops of their heads just above their mouths. This stimulates a nerve just under the shell that tranquilizes them. Their legs will droop as they snooze and they will slip easily into the stockpot. Combine 7 quarts water; 2 cups kosher salt; 3 lemons, halved; 2 cups distilled white vinegar; $\frac{1}{2}$ cup pickling spice; 2 tablespoons red pepper flakes; and 8 bay leaves in a large nonreactive stockpot and bring to a boil over high heat. Regulate the heat and cook at a moderate simmer for 5 minutes. If not using immediately, cool completely, cover, and refrigerate for several days. Bring to a boil and simmer several minutes before use. Makes about 8 quarts court bouillon.

DOUBLE-STRENGTH BLOND CHICKEN STOCK: Good cooking depends on good ingredients and there is almost nothing more basic than stock. If you choose not to make your own, seek out a high-quality substitute. You may be able to talk a local restaurant into selling you stock, or your butcher shop may make various stocks themselves. If you buy canned broth, look for low-salt versions. Make sure to taste the broth before you cook with it so you know what you are working with. Remember that canned stock lacks the natural body of homemade stock and so sauces made with canned stock will be thinner than those made with homemade. I often like to use a concentrated stock for the extra flavor and body it imparts to dishes which means I boil stock until it has reduced to half its original volume.

My recipe is very simple: 5 pounds chicken bones; 10 cups water; 1 large onion, cut into 1-inch chunks; 2 carrots, cut into 1-inch chunks; 2 celery stalks, cut into 1-inch chunks; 1 bay leaf; 10 peppercorns; 1 small bunch parsley stems. I rinse the bones twice to remove blood and boil the bones in water to cover for 30 minutes. During this time, I skim carefully, then add the rest of the ingredients, continue to simmer, uncovered, very slowly for 4 hours; cool, strain, and defat. If I want a concentrated stock, I boil the stock until it is half its volume. Refrigerate or freeze until needed. *Variation for Brown Chicken Stock:* Preheat the oven to 450°F. After the second rinsing, place the bones in a roasting pan and roast, stirring occasionally, until brown all over. Transfer to the stockpot and simmer with water as directed above. While the bones are simmering for the first 30 minutes, put the vegetables in the same roasting pan and roast until brown all over, stirring occasionally, then add to the stockpot. Immediately put the roasting pan on the stove top over medium heat and add $^1/_2$ cup dry white wine or water. Stir and scrape up all the browned bits from the bottom and sides of the pan and pour into the stock. Proceed as directed above.

Since I am a chef, I have to write a recipe that gives the correct—from my viewpoint—method. Rinsing the bones ahead of time and then skimming the stock well during the first part of its simmering yield dividends in clarity and refinement of flavor. You can dispense with the rinsing and skimming, however. Just put all the ingredients in a pot, bring to a boil, and follow the recipe from there. Save bones in a plastic bag in the freezer. Don't bother to defrost them before you make stock. Save parsley stems and assorted vegetables such as fennel tops, mushroom stems, even scrubbed carrot peelings. The recipe may also be increased proportionately. To save space in the freezer, cook the stock until very, very reduced, then dilute it as needed with boiling water.

FLAVORED OLIVE OIL: My brand, Consorzio, makes several flavored oils, and in 1994, I wrote a small book about making and using flavored oils (*Flavored Oils, 50 Recipes for Cooking with Infused Oils*, published by Chronicle Books). Flavored oils are easily made by briefly pureeing a large amount of fresh herbs with a small amount of oil, filtering the result, and "thinning" with olive oil. Use pure olive oil, not an extra-virgin. Its taste is too distinct and will compete with the herb's flavor. To infuse spices, dried wild mushrooms, and resinous herbs such as rosemary, heat the oil and ingredient together very gently for less than a minute, then filter.

Roasted garlic oil, a wonderful oil with many applications at the stove (I use it to sauté all sorts of vegetables, to add to salad dressings, drizzle on bruschetta, and so on), is the byproduct of making roasted garlic. Or roasted garlic is the byproduct of roasted garlic oil (see page 197 for recipe).

The oils will keep, refrigerated, for about a week or so. I recommend making small batches with the most flavorful herbs and spices you can find. Taste the oil you plan to use to make sure it has a pleasantly neutral flavor. If you haven't made or purchased a flavored oil, simply substitute olive oil and the fresh ingredient—the herb, vegetable, or spice.

FLAVORED VINEGAR: In general, when people refer to flavored vinegar, they are referring to a fairly neutral vinegar such as white wine vinegar or champagne vinegar infused with herbs, spices, or fruit flavors. For me, the category also includes the salad dressings and marinades, such as mango, that I created for my Consorzio brand. They differ from other flavored vinegars in that these are fruit purees mixed with enough vinegar to preserve them, plus some sweetening to provide balance. They then become fat-free salad dressings and marinades or even dessert sauces. The mango, for example, is wonderful over vanilla ice cream mixed with gingersnaps. I wrote a book, *Flavored Vinegars, 50 Recipes for Cooking with Infused Vinegars* (Chronicle Books, 1996), that describes how to make such vinegars at home, as well as recipes for how to use them to infuse creativity into everyday cooking.

FONTINA: This rich, semisoft cow's milk cheese is made in the Piedmont region of Italy. It is similar to Gruyère, but with a buttery flavor and creamier texture. Fontinas produced elsewhere lack the distinguished flavor of the original.

GORGONZOLA: Made in Lombardy, Gorgonzola is a blue-veined, full fat, cow's milk cheese available in two main types: aged and strong tasting, and sweet. The latter, also called Gorgonzola dolce or Gorgonzola dolce latte, has a creamy, soft texture and tastes less salty and less pungent than aged Gorgonzola. For many recipes, including the Blue Cheese Caesar Salad (page 23) and the Rigatoni with Spicy Grilled Tomato Sauce (page 61), I prefer the Gorgonzola dolce, if you can find it. Many specialty cheese shops, Italian delicatessens, and markets with good cheese selections will carry it. As always, taste before deciding how much to add. Some cheeses will be fresher, some older and more pungent. In the case of the latter, you may require less than called for in the ingredient list.

LAMB LOIN: There is nothing mysterious about this cut, except perhaps why it may be difficult to find. It is simply the loin of the animal in a single piece, usually weighing about $^1/_2$ pound. You see it all the time, bone in, as a rack of lamb and sliced into loin lamb chops. While these are delicious, they do take a few minutes longer to cook and limit your serving options. With the loin, the meat cooks evenly and you can cut slices in several ways.

MASCARPONE CHEESE: This sinfully rich fresh cream cheese is the Italian cousin of crème fraîche. It can be made at home by clabbering heavy cream with tartaric acid, but thankfully, it is widely available in specialty groceries and cheese shops.

MOZZARELLA CHEESE: When I was an apprentice in New York City, I went to Little Italy to learn about mozzarella from the cheesemakers there. The cheese is made in the middle of the night. The first night I visited, they would not answer the door. The second night I arrived a little earlier, and they were across the street enjoying a break. They did not want to be bothered with me. On the third night, I arrived even earlier, stopping first across the street for espressos and biscotti, then pounding on the door with my feet. The cheesemakers knew it must be a friend with full hands to knock with his feet. That night and for several nights thereafter, they taught me what truly fresh mozzarella is. Fresh is when you bite into a ball of still-warm cheese and the juice dribbles down your chin. Their cheese was made with cow's milk, and so I learned that the quality of the milk, not the type of animal (buffalo, cow, or goat), and the cheesemaker's skill define great mozzarella. At Tra Vigne, we still hew to those lessons and make our cheese several times a day.

Mozzarella bocconcini are, literally, little balls of mozzarella. They are usually sold in small tubs of water. They are not necessarily of buffalo milk, although they might be. Local cheesemakers, recognizing the demand for high-quality and fresh, really fresh mozzarella, are making mozzarella bocconcini and larger balls of cheese more readily available in specialty cheese shops and Italian delicatessens.

NUTMEG: I call for freshly grated nutmeg, and there really is no reason to buy it ground. The nuts are widely available, keep forever, and are easy to grate. You will be amazed at the heady perfume from a small amount of the freshly grated nut.

OLIVE PASTE: It can be made from either green or black olives, although it is probably more commonly made from black olives. It is simply very finely chopped pitted black olives. Whether it is made from brined olives such as Kalamata or from an intense oil-cured olive will give the paste a different flavor. Black olive paste is the base for tapénade, a typical Provençal spread used on toast as an appetizer. Tapénade is usually flavored with anchovy and capers.

PANCETTA: A cured, unsmoked bacon made from the fat meat of the pig's belly and seasoned with salt, pepper, and spices. It usually comes in a fat roll that is then cut into slices of whatever thickness you need. Cook it as you would bacon.

PARMESAN CHEESE: A cooked-curd, well-aged, hard grating cheese with a strong flavor. Italian Parmesan, Parmigiano Reggiano, has become so famous and beloved that the cheese is widely copied all over the world. None tastes quite like the cheese made in the region around Parma from cows grazing only on fresh grass. The curd is cooked, pressed, and then aged, often for a year or more. To buy the best cheese, look for shops with a high turnover that cut hunks from a large wheel. Look at the rind; if it is the real thing, it will have the words Parmigiano Reggiano etched into the rind. In the winter, when the cows eat dried fodder, a similar cheese, grana, is made by the same method. The flavor is not as refined as that of Parmesan. The same criticism can be made of the Parmesan-style cheeses made in many parts of the world, including the United States. These are often less expensive than Parmesan; taste them and see if you feel the savings are worth the difference in flavor.

Grate your Parmesan fresh for each use. The flavor stays fresher when the cheese is in a block. Also, Parmesan is most often used as a condiment, not as a primary flavor. Use just a little. Invest in one of the slightly curved, rectangular graters used by waiters in restaurants. It makes a very fine dust, which is what you want when dusting a pasta before it goes to the table.

PECORINO CHEESE: Italian hard cheese, made from sheep's milk, has a strong, almost biting flavor. The most renowned is pecorino romano, the quality of which, like Parmesan, is protected by a *consorzio*, the producers. At Tra Vigne, we particularly like pecorino pepato, which is spiced with pepper.

POLENTA: Polenta is a New World food introduced to Europe by explorers who reached the Americas. It fit well into the peasant style of cooking throughout Italy. The word *polenta* is used for both the grain—coarsely ground yellow cornmeal—and the dish made from it.

RED PEPPER FLAKES: Chilies vary in heat from brand to brand. Shop until you find a brand you like, then stick with it. I prefer to use red pepper flakes made from New Mexican chilies, which are medium-hot. You can use the crushed red pepper you find easily in the supermarket, but you may want to cut back on the amount called for in my recipes. You can find New Mexican chilies in well-stocked Mexican groceries. If you cannot find them crushed, buy the dried whole chilies and grind them coarsely. Store in a tightly sealed jar.

RICOTTA SALATA CHEESE: This is a pressed and salted version of fresh ricotta, firm enough to be cut into slices, crumbled, or cubed. It is very moist and has a mild, sweet, lightly salty flavor.

SALT: For everyday cooking I use kosher salt. I like the fact that it is pure salt. Table salt includes other ingredients, such as calcium silicate, dextrose, and potassium iodide. Kosher salt is also inexpensive. If you do not have or cannot find kosher salt, use table salt, but in smaller amounts than called for in my recipes.

My favorite salt, however, is gray salt, also called *selgris* or *fleur de sel,* an unprocessed natural sea salt from Brittany. It has an incredible flavor that has been described as a combination of algae and violets, and it returns salt to the status of precious commodity that it held for so much of its history. I use gray salt not as an ingredient, but as a condiment. For instance, I use it alone, sprinkled on a grilled steak, or to make what to me is the perfect green salad: greens, extra-virgin olive oil, and gray salt.

Gray salt is made by the natural evaporation of sea water. The annual salt harvest occurs in the fall and employs the same tools and methods used by salt makers for centuries. Water from the Bay of Biscay runs into a series of evaporation pools where the sun and wind are allowed to do their work. As the sea water evaporates, salt crystals form. The salt maker rakes the crystals into mounds. Eventually, autumn rains dilute the briny sea water and harvest stops until the following year. The salt remains slightly moist with sea water, has a chunky texture, and is light gray in color, showing its natural origins. It has a lower salt content and a higher flavor content than processed salt, perhaps because it contains all the natural minerals found in sea water. The balance of the salt's trace minerals, including chloride, sodium, sulfur, zinc, magnesium, iron, potassium, manganese, copper, silicon, and iodine, echoes that of the human body. This allows the salt's minerals to be easily assimilated, making a positive nutritional contribution. The gray salt I use is imported by Sea Star, Holly's Cooking Basics, P.O. Box 302, Calistoga, CA 94515; 707-942-9444. It has earned the French equivalent of our organic certification, the highest ranking for purity, *Nature et Progres.*

SEMOLINA: Semolina is produced by milling durum wheat, a hard winter wheat. After the bran is removed and before the grains are ground into flour, large particles of the endosperm are separated out and sold as semolina. It is pale yellow and has a coarse texture. It is used in puddings, as a thickener in soups, and to make pasta. It can be purchased in Italian food markets and in the bulk sections of many natural-foods stores.

VINEGAR-MAKING SUPPLIES: The Cantinetta, our small delicatessen and take-out food shop across the stone courtyard from Tra Vigne, can fit out the new vinegar maker with whatever is needed. We carry a specially designed vinegar-making crock (it comes with a recipe for home-made vinegar) and "active" vinegar we make ourselves. You can write The Cantinetta at Tra Vigne, 1050 Charter Oak Road, St. Helena, CA 94574, or call 707-963-8888. In addition, my *Flavored Vinegar* book has instructions for making your own wine vinegar. Home winemaking shops are another good source for equipment and advice. One such is Napa Fermentation Supplies, P. O. Box 5839, Napa, CA 94581, 707-255-6372. An eight-ounce jar of vinegar mother is $6.95 plus shipping; it is available in either red or white. The mother will arrive with a sheet of instructions. They also sell a small book about vinegar making, *Homemade Vinegar* by Patrick and Carole Watkins.

BENRINER TURNING SLICER: The slicer comes in two models: the horizontal Turning Slicer costs about ninety dollars, and the vertical home version, the Cook's Help, costs under fifty dollars. Both come with three blades, minuscule, tiny, and fine. You will find the slicers in Japantown houseware shops and through the Sur La Table kitchenware catalog (800-243-0852).

complete recipe list

SPRING

Asparagus
Grilled Asparagus with Tangerine Mayonnaise
Asparagus Risotto with Shiitake Mushrooms
Asparagus Pesto with Tiny Potatoes and Pasta
Roasted Asparagus Bundles
Whole Roasted Fish with Asparagus
    and Extra-Virgin Olive Oil

Garlic
Poached Garlic Soup
Piadine with Blue Cheese Caesar Salad
Spaghettini Squared: Pasta with Olive Oil,
    Garlic, and Zucchini
Famous Roast Garlic Crab

Fresh Peas and Shelling Beans
Pan Stew of Scallops, Peas, and Pearl Onions
Pastina Risotto with English Peas,
    Prosciutto Bits, and Carrot Broth
Pasta with Fresh Fava Bean Sauce
Barely Smoked Salmon with Pea
    and Potato Salad

Potatoes
Potato Soup with Warm Clam Salad
The Definitive Mashed Potatoes and Variations
Potato Focaccia
Polpette of Potato with Avocado, Red Onion,
    and Cucumber Salad

SUMMER

Corn
Raw Corn, Arugula, and Pecorino Salad
    with Grilled Chicken Breast
Grilled Corn Salsa
Corn Pasta with Dried Tomatoes
Halibut and Corn Salad
    with "Broken" Tomato Vinaigrette

Tomatoes
Simply Tomatoes
Grilled Avocado and Tomato Salad
    with Basil Pesto
Spiedini of Fresh Mozzarella and Tomatoes
Tomato Carpaccio with Panzanella
Rigatoni with Spicy Grilled Tomato Sauce
Pan Stew of Shellfish and Tomatoes

Bell Peppers
Fusilli Salad with Roasted Pepper Sauce
Rock Shrimp and Spicy Roasted Pepper Pasta
Mom's Meatball-Stuffed Peppers
Stuffed Chicken Thighs
    with Red Pepper-Tomato Sauce
Grilled Flank Steak with Roasted Peppers
    in Tomato Sauce

Summer Squashes
Sautéed Zucchini Batons with Melon "Pasta"
Southern Italian Ratatouille

Southern Italian Ratatouille Four Ways
Crispy Zucchini Salad with Tomato Vinegar
Saltimbocca of Zucchini

AUTUMN

Mushrooms
Fusilli Michelangelo
Grilled Chicken with Grilled Mushroom
    Vinaigrette
Portobello Mushroom Cooked like a Steak
Lamb Shanks with Mushroom Bolognese

Greens
Radicchio Caesar Salad
Autumn Fruit and Frisée Salad
    with Panettone Croutons
Sicilian Harvest Salad
Fettuccine with Mustard Greens
    and Mushrooms
Chicken Piadine with Baby Spinach
Menisha
Chard, White Bean, and Tubbetini Soup

Onions
Schiacciata with Caramelized Onions
Bistecca with Balsamic-Roasted Onions
Crispy Onion Salad
Swordfish with Onion, Raisin,
    and Tomato Agrodolce

Eggplants
Lasagnette of Eggplant and Goat Cheese
Caponata with Polenta Crackers
Fusilli with Roasted Eggplant, Fall Vegetables,
    and Balsamic-Dijon Vinaigrette
Grilled Eggplant Pizza
Roasted Eggplant and Onion Ravioloni
    with Roasted Tomato Sauce

WINTER

Broccoli
Broccoli and Cauliflower with Shell Pasta
Broccoli with Parmesan Fritelle
Very Green Broccoli Soup
Soft Polenta with Pancetta and Broccoli Rabe
Broccoli with Cambozola Sauce

Artichokes
Lemon-Braised Artichokes
Fettuccine with Lemon-Braised Artichokes
Lemon-Braised Artichokes and White Beans
    with Pan-Seared Lamb Loin
Roasted Artichokes, Carrots, and Fennel
    with Pan-Roasted Halibut
Crispy Artichoke and Baby Spinach Salad
    with Creamy Tarragon Dressing

Citrus
Fennel-Spiced Prawns with Citrus Salad
Mixed Green Salad
    with Whole Citrus Vinaigrette

Chicken with Roasted Lemon
    and Rosemary Sauce
Lemon-Baked Sea Bass with Spinach Salad
Roasted Beet, Onion, and Orange Salad

Winter Squashes
Roasted Winter Squash
Roasted Butternut Squash Soup
"Pumpkin" Polenta
    with Medium-Rare Lamb Stew
Roasted Winter Squash Ravioli
Spaghetti Times Two
"Pumpkin" Pastina Served Family Style
    in a Pumpkin

TRA VIGNE CLASSICS

Crispy Herb Gnocchi with Braised Lamb Shanks
    and Wild Mushrooms
Potato Gnocchi
Warm Basil Gnocchi Salad
    with Carpaccio of Tomatoes
Gnocchi della Nonna
Braised Rabbit and Winter Vegetables
Forever Roasted Pork
Monkfish with Roasted Garlic Polenta
    and Tomato Broth
Tra Vigne's Fritto Misto with Tomato Vinegar
Mozzarella Martini with Tomato Consommé

DESSERTS AND COOKIES

Semifreddo
Aiello Family Holiday Cookies
    Bugia
    Pastura
Strawberry, Rhubarb, and Red Banana Crostata
Panettone
Tra Vigne's Chocolate Tiramisù
Tra Vigne's Biscotti

Pantry Recipes
Gremolata
Toasted Pumpkin Seeds
Prosciutto Bits
Toasted Spice Rub
Fennel Spice
Arborio Rice Coating
Bruschetta and Crostini
Piadine Dough
Pasta Dough
Black Pepper and Parmesan Grissini
Cantinetta's Cracker Pizzette
Roasted Garlic Paste
Thick Tomato Sauce
Quick Tomato Sauce
Tomato Confit and Variations
Pesto
Basil Pesto
Fava Bean Pesto
Soft Polenta and Variations
Spiced Candied Nuts

index

table of equivalents

The exact equivalents in the following tables have been rounded for convenience.

U.S.	*Metric*
$1/4$ teaspoon	1.25 milliliters
$1/2$ teaspoon	2.5 milliliters
1 teaspoon	5 milliliters
1 tablespoon (3 teaspoons)	15 milliliters
1 fluid ounce (2 tablespoons)	30 milliliters
$1/4$ cup	60 milliliters
$1/3$ cup	80 milliliters
$1/2$ cup	120 milliliters
1 cup	240 milliliters
1 pint (2 cups)	480 milliliters
1 quart (4 cups, 32 ounces)	960 milliliters
1 gallon (4 quarts)	3.84 liters
1 ounce (by weight)	28 grams
1 pound	454 grams
2.2 pounds	1 kilogram

LENGTH

U.S.	Metric
1/8 inch	3 millimeters
1/4 inch	6 millimeters
1/2 inch	12 millimeters
1 inch	2.5 centimeters

OVEN TEMPERATURE

Fahrenheit	Celsius	Gas
250	120	1/2
275	140	1
300	150	2
325	160	3
350	180	4
375	190	5
400	200	6
425	220	7
450	230	8
475	240	9
500	260	10